Cinema Through Rasa

ऊर्ध्वबाहुः विरोम्यैष न च कश्चित् श‍ृणोति माम्।
धर्मादर्थश्च कामश्च स धर्म किं न सेव्यते॥

ūrdhvabāhuḥ viromyaiṣa na ca kaścit śṛṇoti mām ।
dharmādarthaśca kāmaśca sa dharma kiṁ na sevyate ॥

With both my arms up in the air, I have been crying aloud but nobody listens to me,

It is through *dharma* alone that one can acquire *artha* and *kāma*, why, then, does one not practise it?

– Vedavyāsa, *Mahābhārata*,
Svargārohaṇa Parva, chapter 5, verse 49

Cinema Through Rasa

A Tryst with Masterpieces in the Light of Rasa Siddhānta

Prachand Praveer

Translated from my original Hindi book
"Abhinava Cinema" *by*
Geeta Mirji Narayan

Foreword by
Bharat Gupt
Vishnu Khare

DK
PRINTWORLD
Publishers of Indian Traditions

Cataloging in Publication Data — DK

[Courtesy: D.K. Agencies (P) Ltd. <docinfo@dkagencies.com>]

Pravīra, Pracaṇḍa, author.

[Abhinava sinemā. English]

Cinema through rasa : a tryst with masterpieces in the light of rasa siddhānta / Prachand Praveer ; translated from the original Hindi book "Abhinava cinema" by Geeta Mirji Narayan ; Foreword by Bharat Gupt, Vishnu Khare.

pages cm

Includes bibliographical references.

ISBN 9788124610688 (hardbound)

1. Motion pictures – History. 2. Rasas. I. Narayan, Geeta Mirji, translator. II. Title.

LCC PN1993.5.A1P73 2021 | DDC 791.43 23

ISBN 978-81-246-1068-8 (Hardbound)
978-81-246-1098-5 (Paperback)

First published in India in 2021

Cover concept: Mrinal Chakraborty

Printed and published by:
D.K. Printworld (P) Ltd.
Regd. Office: "Vedaśrī", F-395, Sudarshan Park
ESI Hospital Metro Station, New Delhi – 110015
Phones: (011) 2545-3975; 2546-6019; *Fax*: (011) 2546-5926
E-mail: indology@dkprintworld.com
Website: www.dkprintworld.com

Dedicated to my Teacher

Dr. Sanil V.

whose blessings have enabled me

to contemplate

Beauty and Cinema

Foreword to English Edition

Prachand Praveer has produced an original path-breaking book. He has used his learning of the classical texts, the *Nāṭyaśāstra* of Bharata Muni and its famous commentary, the *Abhinavabhāratī* to connect the ancient thought regarding drama with a modern medium like cinema.

Since the inception of the modern Indian state from the British rule in 1947, a schizophrenia was inserted into the Indian psyche by the first Prime Minister Jawaharlal Nehru through his reformist socialist agenda, that for India modernity was not an inseparable extension of tradition and heritage, but instead a rejection of it. For him alteration in heritage continuity was not essential. Thus, a strike was made on one of the major practices of Indian culture which presumes that cultural change must preserve and embellish tradition.

Indian cinema, for more than half a century, has been looked upon entirely as a creation of modern times. It has also been hailed as a trumpet of socialist reforms meant to preen Indian society of casteism, economic inequalities and religious fanaticism (called communalism in Indian political jargon). Of late, it is aiming to promote gender equality and modern democracy.

While cinema was given the elevated role of being a tool of propagating the ideals of modern (Nehruvian) state, it was hardly ever discussed, if in being so powerfully enticing and entertaining, was it following the principles of performance enshrined in some of the most ancient texts which have nothing to do with modernity? And what is more, does Indian cinema, or in fact world cinema, as and when successful, follow a modern aesthetics of performance or some very ancient theories which we in our socialist fervour, disparaged and rejected. To put it differently, while the body (the medium and its stories) may be very modern, the soul of the art could be most traditional and timeless. Prachand Praveer, in my opinion, has succeeded in showing us precisely this through his book.

Among many things of the past that were summarily discarded from academic discourse, the theory of *rasa* or *rasa-siddhānta* was a major casualty. Most Marxist thought which came to dominate the cultural scene propounded that *rasa* concept was soporific. As the primary aim of *sāhitya* or cinema is to promote the establishment of a Marxist state, *rasa* tends to make the *rasikas* self-centric, inward looking and socially inert. According to Indian tradition, *rasa* prepares *rasikas* to climb to the higher level of spiritual knowledge of *ānanda*. In the Marxist eyes, all this is a Brāhmanical prejudice of capitalism lovers, and hence anathema in the socialist secularist state. Prachand Praveer has boldly restated the foundations of Indian *nāṭya* in eight *rasas* and its analysis by Abhinavagupta. And this, he very clearly states, is rooted in a philosophy (*darśana* – a system of thought for attaining knowledge) which has always reconciled the entertainment efficacy of art (*manorañjana-dharma*) desirable and lovely (*preyas*), with the highest values of life (*śreyas*). In India, art is not a tool for social change or a propaganda nor a political agenda but a delightful aim that leads to highest understanding.

To illustrate the application of eight (*aṣṭa-rasas*), Prachand Praveer has taken the example of Western films and not the Indian ones. Through this he is able to demonstrate the universality of the *rasa-siddhānta*. In this way he also by implications contests the opinion of those literary critics who regard the classical aesthetics of India as dated and outmoded. The films he has picked up are all celebrated ones and perhaps seen by most cinema lovers. Perhaps quite a few of them can be seen on the Internet easily for immediate examination of Praveer's hypothesis.

Explaining why he has taken the *rasa*s in the manner he does, Praveer says:

> For the sake of film-centric-discussions, we will study the *rasa*s manifesting sorrow (Bhayānaka and Vībhatsa), then those telling about joy (Adbhuta and Vīra), then again going back to sorrow (Karuṇa and Raudra) and finally onto the pleasure giving *rasas* (Hāsya and Śṛṅgāra).

During the course of this analysis we see that not only each film is explained how its characters and events result in the emergence of the chosen *sthāyī rasa*, but also a detailed theoretical interpretation of that *rasa* as stated by Bharata Muni and as amplified by Abhinavagupta. This book of Prachand Praveer thus becomes a very worthwhile study of both, some modern European films as explained by *rasa* theory and of the doctrine of *rasa* itself.

It is my earnest desire that while evaluating this work, the experts of the area look upon the arguments put forth by the author. I hope they shall not be preconditioned by the burden of literary fashions that have recently prevented serious textual studies, specially of the classical texts.

This book also reaffirms that theatre and cinema are primarily one, that is, a creative form in which the heard and the seen are presented together as one fused reality. Theatre (*nāṭya*) was desired by Indra, the king of *devatā*s, as a plaything to gratify both the senses of hearing and seeing (*krīḍanīyakam icchāmo yat dṛṣyam ca śrāvyam bhavet*). But Brahmā gave him something special which was not merely a plaything but also the *summum bonum* of all knowledge, the Nāṭyaveda, meant to be partaken by all high and low. By its great expanse, the medium of cinema in the modern world, now transformed into the ever-available digital screen, should be seen as resting on the power of *rasa*, without which nothing makes any meaning (*na hi rasād ṛte kaścid arthaḥ pravartate*). This, in short, is the message of the book.

October 2019 **Bharat Gupt**

Foreword
to Abhinava Cinema (Hindi Edition)

I am surprised by Prachand Praveer's fervent appeal that I write a blurb-esque Foreword to his book (calling it a tome would probably be more appropriate), as I am neither a qualified, technical interpreter of cinema nor a student of the *rasa-siddhānta* of Indian classical aesthetics. The truth is that I personally am of the view that a global, democratic and extremely popular art form like cinema should be kept simple, comprehensible and universal, therefore I have many difficulties in gauging the Sanskritized notions of *rasa* in everyday cinema. Even in literary discourses, thanks to Karl Marx and Dr Nagendra, I have stayed away from *rasa* discourse. When Prachand started publishing excerpts of this book as independent essays, I was disappointed of the whole project. Now when the whole manuscript is in front of me and although I still have a multifaced reservation of his adventure, I am mighty impressed by it. The seriousness with which the author has kept his goals in front of the reader is contagious. This book is by no means superficial or a common read – as books about cinema in Hindi tend to be thought of. Slowly but surely the seriousness of the book grows on you; the only catch here is that one must at least be acquainted with (if not seen) all the films that Prachand Praveer has seen. As the author has himself said that in today's world these films are not at all hard to get, what with the advent of DVDs, torrent, IMDB, MRQE, Palika Bazar, etc.

The book brings along quite a few challenges not only for the author but for the reader too. The reader is presumed to be of age and of such an enlightened mind that the contents will not pose an intellectual hinderance to him. The Sanskrit words and usage will not startle him. The book is filled with ancient and contemporary references and quotations pertaining to our country as well as from all over the world; this, in no way, should be seen as obstacles in our journey, but should be enjoyed as blissful divergents. Any well laid out garden or a well-planned library has arrows or numbered-signs pointing towards the correct direction, which is generally understood by people by just a cursory glance. But this book needs more than just a cursory glance. It often stops and baulks us, and when we look at the various verses and *śloka*s, it makes us wonder whether the author himself knows the meaning of these *śloka*s and can he be trusted? There is no page in this book which does not lead you to argue with yourself about acceptance and rejection of ideas, which does not inspire an intellectual doubt (can the word "war" be used here) within you. You read it while infinitely rejecting or approving these very ideas.

Unfit and corrupt faculty has over the decades, killed postgraduate research work in Hindi in colleges and universities. Publishers too are printing garbage in the name of profound scholarly knowledge and research work, which no self-respecting, Devanāgarī script-knowing swine will even feign to touch with his snout. I am unable to find any Indian language department or even a professor, in the country, who will hold a "peer review" of Prachand Praveer's work. The so-called Hindi faculty do not even understand so much cinema or even so much Sanskrit nor do they understand the *rasa-siddhānta*; and the Sanskrit faculty, who are the mental progeny of the likes of Vidyaniwas Mishra, believe that a tryst with Hindi and English is untouchable, they think that watching cinema is for scoundrels and roadside Romeos. There is no course for cinema study and even if there is one it has been forcefully occupied by dolt and film-illiterate Hindi faculty, who are wallowing in their own and self-created filth as pulp literature has become the syllabi of the MA (Hindi) course. Even in Euro-America, which has a precedent of interdisciplinary research work, it will be difficult to have a "peer review' of this multidisciplinary work because there would be a requirement of at least two specialists on the panel.

The reader should not be deterred by these seemingly heavy and fearful observations. If you have even a passing fancy for cinema you should read this book in one sitting even if you have to mentally fight with the author and his ideas. After a lot of contemplation, I am writing that this book on cinema not only begins to try to benefit the Indian classical critical tradition, but is also the first of its kind in history for world cinema review. The author has taken immense risks in writing this tome. The book may possibly be ridiculed. It is feared that some may find a pseudo-profundity in it. It may not be wrong if I say that not only the author, but his admirers too have a heavy cross to bear. On the other hand, without any exaggeration, we can call Prachand Praveer as the young *avatāra* of Mahavir Prasad Dwivedi or Altaf Hussain Hali in the world of "Film-criticism in Hindi", because despite many disagreements, this book shows an altogether new perspective and has a new vision, creates a new way and is a front-runner.

Of late, in Hindi, we have seen a rise of some very sagacious and remarkable film critics and commentators, who are doing a commendable work. I shall recount their names some other time, they have of course made their mark. A reader like me feels happy, proud and reassured that they have been able to challenge the handful of old film critics with their works. Now, Prachand Praveer, an ambitious, hard-working and indigenous writer has joined them as a companion. He is free from the reactionary and reemerging nationalism which harps on the ethos that "everything was available in Sanskrit and with our ancient sages". He has stood up against the fascists who have stoned theatres, actors, directors and producers and guarded cinema. This book should point towards new studies, but, in itself, be away from the rat race. I must also congratulate the publisher who had the good sense to understand the importance of publishing this book, which common place and thick-headed publishers did not. It is not my habit, but this is such a peerless book that I sincerely recommend that it must be bought individually and publicly and must be respectfully made a part of cinema and Hindi curriculum nationwide.

December 2015 **Vishnu Khare**

Preface

Watching a movie at a cinema hall or a theatre is still considered a taboo in many traditional Indian families. Sometimes the elders of the house condemn movies, calling them trash and a waste of time and money. Their contempt is, of course, not without reasons. Of late we do see unwarranted and unpalatable stuff being shown in the movies. Although other media are also equally responsible and capable of adversely affecting our lives, we squarely lay the blame on cinema. I do believe that such an opposition to cinema has only been because its meaning and innumerable benefits have not had a far-reaching effect. It has by and large been responsible to bring in a frustration and has played on the psyche and desires of the people.

How then should one, even after being surrounded by offending things, reach out to the great works of the world? It is quite ironic that even though great novels by renowned authors are available online without copyright strictures, great music by Bach, Mozart and Beethoven is easily available, great works of art by accomplished artists, i.e. paintings, sculptures, etc. are readily available, our eyes and heart seek ill propagated, vulgar or badly made films and music. It is a matter of concern. One must have discussions and discourses on this aspect because as audience or as viewers, we must be able to choose great and outstanding works of art be it cinema, music or fine art without any external help. The onus is clearly on us and for that, if we must undergo training or learn, so be it. Choice of good works is difficult to exercise without knowledge of its history. Cinema is a fairly recent discovery. Its existence can be traced to around the beginning of the twentieth century. As an art, it is an amalgamation of various forms of arts. It is said that all kinds of art forms can come into play in a movie, all the more reason for a multifaceted person to be acquainted with cinema. Storytelling, singing, dancing, acting, visual effects, music, life sketches, history, travel and technology are some of the arts that are involved in movie making. Once we experience the benevolent light of the sun, we can't be satisfied with the light of a lamp. So, it is of paramount importance that we see excellent movies and, believe me, the sheer number of outstanding films is so large that it will easily take us 10-12 years to see a good number of them.

This book is an effort to bring to the reader the films that are good and bring about a sense of well-being in them. As we all know, drama has always been a part of our rich, multidimensional and glorious culture, India's ancient and classical viewpoint has helped in bringing out the deeper nuances of cinema. This book helps and nudges the reader toward cinema and its achievements. It explores the aesthetic theory bringing forth the ethical, moral and intellectual aspects inducing discussions and learning so that we all are inspired to see great movies and derive seamless pleasure from them. It takes time to see good movies, to understand the subtle points of acting or to decipher the director's viewpoint, etc. If we contemplate from an Indian classical perspective, then one lifetime seems insignificant in the course of eternity. Our culture encompasses the whole world as encapsulated in the phrase *vasudhaiva kuṭumbakam*. The Indian aesthetics brings about a very holistic development in the viewer so that we ourselves, through our intellect, watch excellent films, perceive their greatness and light up our lives through our own enlightenment.

The Indian reader may be familiar with a lot of Hindi movies but may not have come across many films of the West; he must be prepared to watch some silent movies, a few black and white ones or movies with subtitles so as to relish great and excellent films of the bygone era.

Let us discuss some of the movies made by great and renowned directors, in the light of and with the knowledge of the Indian classical aesthetic theory as promulgated by Bharata Muni in his *Nāṭyaśāstra* and as discussed by Abhinavagupta, the tenth-century great Śaiva philosopher in his commentary on the former, the *Abhinavabhāratī*.

Some of the readers may question the choice of great films, but, I have tried to pick films which are world famous as well as critically acclaimed through my limited knowledge. With folded hands, I beg forgiveness for my audacity and hope that they will enjoy and learn just as much.

The book contains some quotes in the original, taken from our holy scriptures; the language has been kept unaltered for a thorough understanding.

October 2015 **Prachand Praveer**

Contents

Acknowledgements

Dr Navjivan Rastogi, a scholar of Abhinavagupta and Kashmir Śaivism, Lucknow University, has been instrumental in showing me the way to study the Indian classical aesthetics. It would not have been possible to write this book without his constructive criticism and blessings.

I am indebted to many of my friends and seniors who have been instrumental in shaping this book; they have boosted my morale with their timely suggestions and inputs. My sincere thanks to Geeta Mirji Narayan, Saurabh Mangal, Saurabh Gupta, Ashish Singh, Pragati Pallavi, Prakriti Priya, Dr Parimal Parag (IISc, Bangalore), Dr Sunthar Visuvalingam, Dr Wagish Shukla (IIT Delhi), Dr Satyapal Sehgal (Panjab University, Chandigarh), Dr Rajeshree Dutta Kumar, Dr Payel Banerjee (Guru Ghasidas University, Chhattisgarh), Pankaj Parag and Peeyush Paani.

Geeta Mirji Narayan, my critic and friend, has not only edited this book but also translated it from the original Hindi. A grateful thanks to her.

November 2020 **Prachand Praveer**

1

Aesthetics of Hindi Cinema

Long Forgotten Directors and Their Outstanding Works

A tried and tested way to study and understand reputed cinema is to watch films made by oft-praised directors. Films are not the work of any one person, they are the sweat and toil of many capable people, but it is prudent to admit that films are shaped by the imagination and vision of the director. This vision can be comprehended in all the films made by that particular director.

Satyajit Ray, Bimal Roy, Guru Dutt and Ritwik Ghatak are some of the names of Indian directors who have made an impact with their cinema on an international level. Their cinema has won acclaim in many international film festivals and is talked about even today. Their names can be taken in the same breath as Yasujiro Ozu, Orson Welles, Carl Dreyer, Alfred Hitchcock, Ingmar Bergman, Akira Kurosawa, Luis Buñuel, etc. Amitabh Bachchan, while accepting an award in 2006, lamented that in spite of having world-renowned film-makers, we still crave for international awards. Let us look at some of the world-acclaimed and oft-lauded films by Indian directors.

Satyajit Ray was influenced by Italian, French and American directors. He decided that his calling was film-making after he watched Vittorio De Sica's (1909-74) *Bicycle Thieves* (1948), at least a hundred times. Guru Dutt in his films brought in the grandiose sets as seen in some of the films of Orson Welles. Vijay Anand in his film *Jewel Thief* (1967) encapsulated the thriller-like adventures seen in Alfred Hitchcock's movies. Films made by William Wyler, Billy Wilder, Frank Capra and Charlie Chaplin have influenced many Hindi films over generations. Charlie Chaplin has been emulated by Raj Kapoor in a number of his films. Even though he copied his mannerisms and actions, he was still able to put across a new perspective in every film of his. He was able to convey that films are so much more than mere acting.

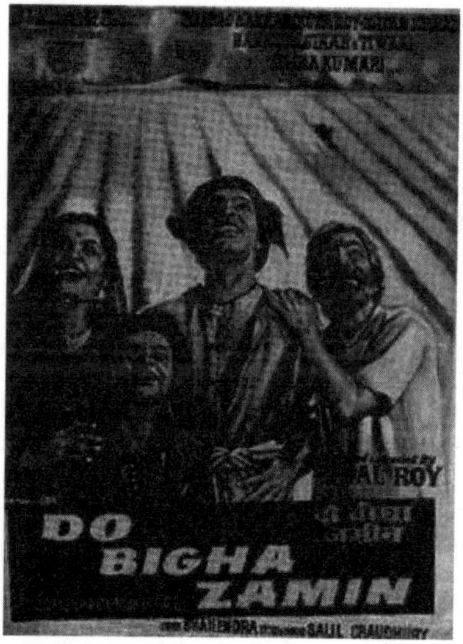

Bimal Roy's *Do Bigha Zameen* (1953)

Bimal Roy (1909-65) made some good commercially viable films like *Do Bigha Zameen* (1953), *Parineeta* (1953), *Madhumati* (1958), *Sujata* (1959) and *Bandini* (1963). Guru Dutt too made a few commercially hit movies before the critically acclaimed *Pyaasa* (1957) and *Kaagaz Ke Phool* (1959). These films were influenced by Western movies.

Apart from the above-mentioned directors, Hindi films had six other directors who made thought-provoking and reputed films. These directors expressed that films were an evolved form of art and not a mere combination of storytelling, dialogues, acting or dancing. Their films were not about film-making alone, but were in accordance to the Indian classical aesthetic theory. Many of these film-makers have been forgotten on the international arena – they were Kamaal Amrohi, Chetan Anand, V. Shantaram, Mehboob

Khan, Satyen Bose and Kedar Sharma. In the decade between 1980-90, three film-makers – Shyam Benegal, Mani Kaul and Kumar Shahani – made excellent art films, but sadly these films did not touch a chord with the audiences.

Films of outstanding directors have been made with a lot of grace and finesse, take for example the seven films made by Andrei Tarkovsky. They are a world treasure today. Alas! Hindi cinema can only count on its fingertips the names of directors who have done such fabulous work. K. Asif (Kareem Asif: 1922-79) and Kamaal Amrohi (Syed Hyder Kamaal Naqvi: 1918-93) are probably the only two who have put their souls into making outstanding films. Their films were not a copy of any films nor were they in any way influenced by films already made.

Kamaal Amrohi in his lifetime made only four films – *Mahal* (1949), *Daera* (1953), *Pakeezah* (1972) and *Razia Sultan* (1983). Of these, the first three were notable. *Mahal* and *Pakeezah* won many accolades, but it was *Daera* which was closest to Amrohi's heart, a fact not known to many. *Daera* brought a touch of bad luck and melancholy in the lives of everyone associated with it. The song writer Kaif Bhopali who wrote gems like *devta tum ho mera sahara* and *chalo dildar chalo*, remained a drunkard to the end and never tasted the fame that his work should have brought. Music director, Jamaal Sen, died in penury despite the film's success. Singer Mubarak Begum faded away into anonymity in spite of having a soul-rendering voice.

Daera is a film with a radical approach, it comes across as an intense poem on screen. The film was made in an era where dialogues were written and used only to influence the audience and to bring in a dramatic effect, for example in the film, the heroine Meena Kumari's husband calls her "his priceless life", to which she responds by saying *jī swāmī*. Meena Kumari's passionless stance at the deathbed of her onscreen husband has to be seen to grasp the delicate nuances of the scene. It may feel absurd in

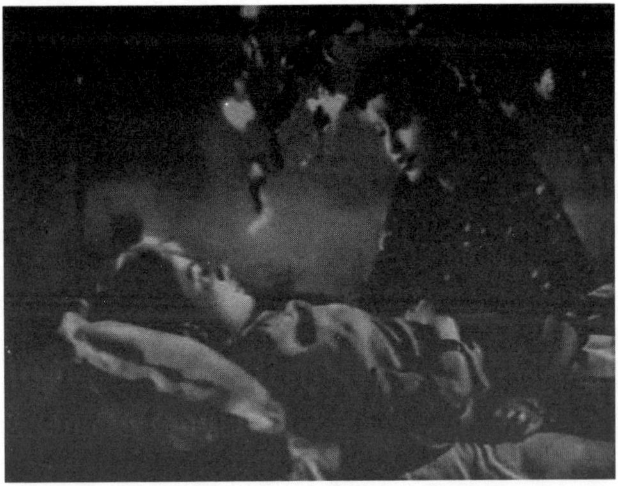

A still from Kamaal Amrohi's *Daera* (1953)

today's age, but in the yesteryears, scenes with such extreme pathos and dramatic dialogues were passé.

The director's vision has to be applauded here, in the whole film, Meena Kumari is shown to be resting under a flower-laden tree which is gently swaying in the breeze. The scene in which the hero Naasir Hussain's vagrant love letter remains at the feet of the heroine reminds us of the scene in Gabriel Garcia Marquez's book, *One Hundred Years of Solitude* where a only trail of blood flows to inform about the murder. The film *Daera* has shown many of the ills plaguing the society at that time, viz. ill treatment of widow, poverty, fasting for the good health of one's husband, love and adulterous relationships, etc. Many films of that age had scenes which prodded the audience to think about one particular aspect of the scene. The climax scene shows Meena Kumari, on her deathbed, hopelessly watching a dance performance on the occasion of the marriage of her beloved for six whole minutes. In the film *Nostalghia* (1983) made by Andrei Tarkovsky, a scene depicts the hero walking with a candle in his hand for nine minutes. It was a hallmark trick in the films of Michelangelo Antonioni, where an empty screen is shown for a long time after all the actors depart. Kamaal Amrohi had certainly predated them all for this particular style, yet this movie of his was not very successful. All this leads us to question ourselves. Are well-made films easy to understand, is the truth so bare? This is where the classical theory of aesthetics comes into play; it takes us by the hand, showing us the intricacies and beauty of cinema along the way.

Chetan Anand (1921-97) was felicitated at the Cannes Film Festival for his film *Neecha Nagar* (1946). Among many of the interesting movies he experimented with, *Heer-Ranjha* (1970), an eternal love story set in rural Punjab, may not cut ice with many Western directors or common man. The film begins with a voice over, reciting a poem of Kaifi Azmi:

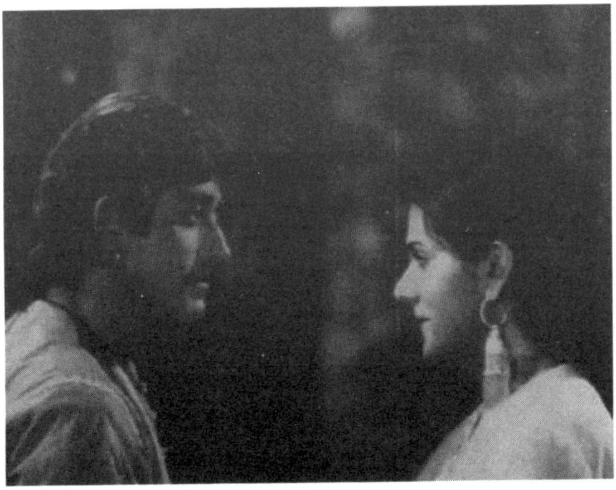

Chetan Anand's *Heer Ranjha* (1970)

Āga merī nā sahī,
Para dhuāṅ merā hai,
Kahānī hīra-rānjhā kī hai,
Para bayāna merā hai.

The fire may not be mine,
But the smoke bears my name
The story is of Heer-Ranjha
But the description is mine

Here the phrase *bayāna merā hai* (my descriptive account) connotates originality, which is very fundamental, it is integral to all art forms. Etymologically, originality points to the newness or freshness and is related to its origin. Such claims of originality can be seen in the poetic dialogues, or in the rural backdrop, the daily life of the common people, the wedding scenes, etc. Camera angles or technical nitty-gritty can't be seen although they are a part of film-making. This kind of attention to detail can only be seen when the audience has the cultural sensitivity toward the subject portrayed.

When we look at the graceful and charming sculptures of the Roman or the Greek empires, we may tend to think that it could be the pinnacle of art as the workmanship is of a very high level, the elegance and beauty of the figurines is unmatched. But when we see the dancing girl statue of Moheṅjo-Daṛo in the Indus Valley Civilization, we are provoked into thinking whether art is only about imitation or the reproduction of our perception. The stone carvings in the temples of Ellorā or the paintings of Ajantā are original in the sense that they do not mimic normal perception. This must bring the audience to wonder whether art is a mere imitation or a careful reproduction. Such an original thinking is required in many facets of our empirical reality.

Satyen Bose (1916-93) was another important director, who with a very radical approach, made films like *Jagriti* (1956), *Chalti ka Naam Gaadi* (1958) and *Raat Aur Din* (1967). His most notable film was *Dosti* (1964). The film is about the friendship between two simple, blind and handicapped boys who have been touched by the ills of society. This is originality at its best. The set and scenes in the film were simple and down to earth but they impacted the audience and critics alike. The film showed the moral values that Indians swear by.

Simplicity, affinity to truth and mutual respect are some of the characteristics that have always ruled Indian drama and cinema.

Hrishikesh Mukherjee, a friend and assistant of Bimal Roy, has portrayed these very values in his predominantly family-oriented films like *Anupama* (1966), *Aashirwad* (1968), *Satyakam* (1969), *Anand* (1971), *Bawarchi* (1972) and *Chupke-Chupke* (1975).

Shantaram Rajaram Vankundre (1909-90) or V. Shantaram, a Maharashtrian by birth, was not only a great director but a connoisseur of art. He firmly believed that films were 80 per cent business and 20 per cent art so that the successful business can always sustain the art. His film *Jhanak Jhanak Payal Baaje* (1955) which had the renowned Kathak dancer, Gopi Krishna as an actor in the lead role, showed India's rich dancing culture and the eminence of the dancer. Another one of his films *Navrang* (1959) was made on the psyche of a poet-singer. His film *Geet Gaya Patharon Ne* (1963) encapsulates the essence of sculpting as prevalent in the stone sculptures and carvings in temples across India, be it the Mīnākṣī Temple at Madurai, the Cennakeśava Temple at Beḷūr, the Dilwāṛā Jain Temple at Mt. Abu, the temples at Ajantā and Ellorā, the Buddhist *stūpas* at Sāñcī, the stone temples at Khajurāho or the epitome of Mughal architecture at the Taj Mahal in Agra. These films depict the originality in art forms and their Indianness without taking away the grandeur of the new art form called cinema. These movies were made just after Independence when the people were in a nation-building mode. It was a gentle reminder that the art forms prevalent in our country show the richness of its heritage, music, dance and sculpture. It was a nudge toward reiterating that without art a human being is nought.

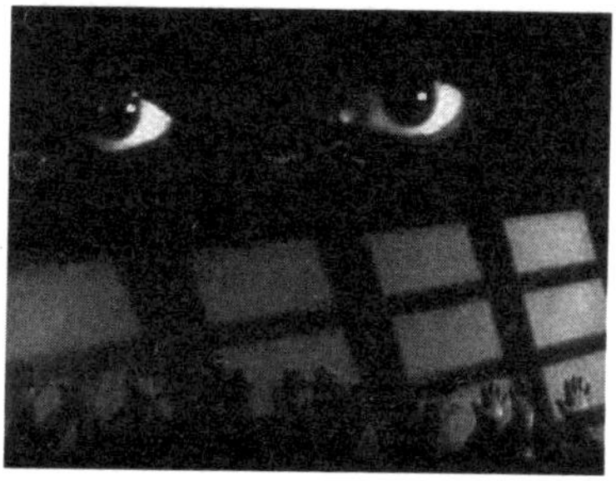

V. Shantaram's *Do Aankhen Barah Hath* (1957)

Two of V. Shantaram's films were scripted by Marāṭhī poet, Padma Shri Gajanan Digambar Madgulkar (1919-77). He is known colloquially by his initials as "Ga Di Mā". The films *Do Aankhen Barah Haath* (1957) and *Navrang* (1959) are to be credited to him. *Do Aankhen Barah Haath*, a true story depicting the open-jail concept, went on to win international fame. In a famous scene of the film, a wide range of emotions are shown: society's attitude to the open-jail concept and a poor old woman's lamentation for her grandson who was taunted by neighbours on account of his father being in jail. V. Shantaram is among the few Indian directors to have made silent films, black and white films and even incredibly beautiful colour films.

Kedar Sharma aka Kidar Nath Sharma (1910-99), another gifted film-maker, was famous for various commercially successful films like *Chitralekha* (1941 and a remake in 1963) and *Bawre Nain* (1950). On the behest of Pt. Jawaharlal Nehru, he made a film exclusively for children – *Jaldeep* (1956), which won fame and awards internationally. In the year 1950, he made a film *Jogan* which depicted the values prevalent in the Indian society, viz. sacrifice, fear of God, freedom from clutches of anger and jealousy, etc. *Jogan* was a film wherein the actors had to depict love in a very virtuous form within the morally accepted norms of the society. The actress was portraying a woman who has renounced worldly love and time and again has to face the pain and hard-hitting barbs of the society. The hero proposes to her repeatedly, whereupon she asks him if he finds the world meaningless! Nargis, the actress

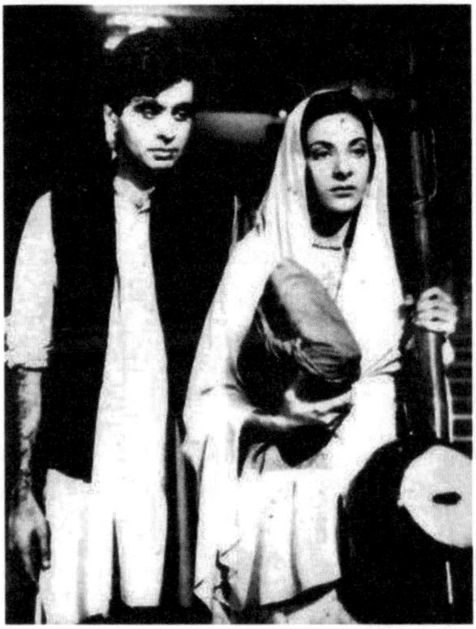

Kedar Sharma's *Jogan* (1950)

who portrayed the *Jogan* (ascetic woman), believed that this was the best role she ever essayed.

Mehboob Khan (1907-64) made *Mother India* in 1957, a film which missed the American Academy award by a single vote. Again, the story showed relevance to the prevalent values in society and a deep understanding of life. Mehboob Khan was uneducated but through his films he taught ethical values to the masses.

We all know that the society has never been free of thievery and dacoity, but no society has ever trampled morality or ethical values. On the similar note, is there any literature or any art form which is independent of moral discourse? Although there is a strong debate about art and literature dealing with morality, it further raises the question about the nature of morality. In a very comprehensive sense, every civilization or even every art form has upheld ethical values. It is therefore, very natural to question ethical values and norms.

La Règle du jeu or *The Rules of the Game* (1939), a French film made by director Jean Renoir (1894–1979) was severely criticized by audiences and critics alike on the very first day it was screened. In fact, one person threatened to burn down the theatre by lighting the newspaper in hand if such a "boring" film was not stopped. About twenty years later the same film was accepted and praised at the Venice Film Festival. Today, it is counted amongst the best films of the world. *Peeping Tom* (1960), a film made by British film-maker Michael Powell (1905-90), was badly received and almost ended the career of its director, but when it was presented to the audience after a few decades it was serenaded. We have seen many instances of films being termed as trash, boring or useless at first, but making a comeback after a few years. It was difficult for Indian audiences to accept thought-provoking films like *Jogan*, *Daera* or *Heer–Ranjha*, but it is necessary to count them along with outstanding films like *Do Bigha Zameen*, *Pyaasa*, *Navrang*, *Madhumati*, *Mughal-E-Azam*, *Sahib Biwi Aur Ghulam*, *Guide* and *Pakeezah*.

Often the movies made by new-age directors, who have made films like *Lunch-Box*, *Taare Zameen Par*, *Peepli Live* and *Ship of Theseus*, are considered as the golden age of Indian cinema. Whether these are excellent or mediocre should be left to the audience to decide. Contemporary film-makers give weightage to good screenplay. Their values lie in new advances in technology or camera angle, speed and thrill. These film-makers do not find it necessary to discuss the old values or new incongruencies as expected through artist's work. I do agree that all old values may not be so useful or worthy, but it can be said that the contemporary directors run away from their moral responsibility of bringing to the audience any useful introspection or integral thought, for them, film-making is mere business, unlike only the 80 per cent as conceived by V. Shantaram.

In the famous novel, *The Name of the Rose* by Italian writer and thinker, Umberto Eco, a character ridiculed and kicked up a storm against "laughter and laughing", likewise, it is difficult to define the parochial approach one has toward art. At the same time, it is not wise to make defeatist, boring films and pass it on as art, also it is blasphemy to cut out entertaining and commercial films from the purview of good cinema.

Although none of the movies is completely detached from the values and tradition of its region, the aesthetics of Hindi films have the same three essential factors which also govern traditional Indian drama, i.e. dance, song and music. We should not have high expectations from people of different cultural backgrounds to appreciate the beauty of Indian cinema as we do. Famous Bengali director Ritwik Ghatak made a heart-wrenching film *Meghe Dhaka Tara* (1960) in which he was able to bring out the pathos at the end of movie through a beautiful song which roughly translates as "Oh, Umā let me embrace you as you leave your father's home, you are the shadow and soul of my wretched life". The song is the permeation of death and bridal farewell. Such nuances cannot be understood without being deeply rooted into the regional culture.

The famous writer and poet Jaishankar Prasad remarked that culture is an original effort for the development of aesthetic apperception (जयशंकर प्रसाद 1939: 20). Films have been assimilated as a part of our culture for the past hundred years. Even radio, television and other means of entertainment have been an important aspect of our culture for quite some time. We need to accept such a dynamic nature of culture. At the same time, we should accept it with sorrow that we have been over-entertained, and this has blunted our aesthetic sensibilities and perception of beauty. In an era of heavy promotion and paid reviews, we have started looking up to films like *Slumdog Millionaire* (2008) by Danny Boyle, *Avatar* (2009) by James Cameron, *Inception* (2010) by Christopher Nolan, which in a debatable way, are technically sound but considered aesthetically average by critics. Similarly, many good Hindi movies are ridiculed at the world level for the use of poor technique and not so profound content. The question now arises, what should we do about contemporary cinema that does not offer a rich content? It then becomes our paramount duty to enhance our understanding and aesthetic sensibility through our intellect. One of the ways is to watch the best of the world cinema. It is not an easy task, as we will have to broaden our outlook, categorize our thinking and revisit history to ascertain that good cinema can help us.

As Søren Kierkegaard said, "Life can only be understood backward; but it must be lived forward". Let us pay a rich tribute to the great artists of world cinema. Let us not travel through life like lost travellers and forget the woes of others. We must in every possible way try to enrich ourselves, this can be done with the concept of beauty and aesthetics. Unknowingly, all of us are seekers of beauty and students of philosophy.

2

Study of World Cinema from an Indian Aesthetic Perspective

The Industrial Revolution brought about many amazing changes in our lives: cars running on fuel instead of horse-pulled ones, air travel bringing two distant places closer and the atomic bomb capable enough to destroy cities in seconds. Films and film-making became a huge business, they brought in a fusion between intellectual debate and art. Along with the society, artists too embraced them and films became a point of debate and discussion. All that which was a part of folklore or was confined to big fat books were now available to the common man at the cost of a few cents. Drama artists or dancers who were considered low in various societies became rich and attained socially envious status. Charlie Chaplin used to charge $10,000 per week, around 100 years ago. He was the most recognized face of the film world then. Films initially were in black and white and were not divided on the basis of language.

In this book, we shall discuss films considered important as per art and film history. We shall also look at the original intent behind these movies. As we know, films are made for an audio-visual pleasure; therefore, no write-up or discussion can do justice to the film except the wholehearted viewing experience of it.

Even so, films must be reviewed, discussed upon and criticized. This not only improves our ability to understand the vision of the director but also helps to enlighten us about the creative intent and sensibility. There are thousands of very beautifully made, appealing films easily available on the Internet. Just as the world of literature is immortal and has a plentiful number of books to read, so also the vast world of cinema has so many films to see that even if one sees one film a day, it will take at least ten years to see the most famous and talked about films, and even then, one would have seen only a portion of world cinema. The precondition here is that one should not shy away from watching silent movies or black and white films or even films made in other languages (with the help of subtitles). For beginners and to initiate a viewer, I recommend Charlie Chaplin's great film *The Kid* (1921) or *City Lights* (1931). Let the magic begin!

Why Films Are Important?

Nineteenth-century German thinker Friedrich Nietzsche and his contemporary theatre director Richard Wagner hypothesized that drama and opera will progress and ultimately culminate into the moving talking images, very similar to that of a film. Before 1929, silent movies were accompanied by music set to different moods and shots of the film, these music pieces were played out by a live band of musicians. Films showed pictures and told stories of faraway lands, different cultures and thus became a big source of entertainment for the common man. The experiment with the movie camera did not stop at entertainment only; many artists, philosophers and journalists used this medium to put forth many experimental views. Painter Salvador Dalí (1904-89), along with Spanish director Luis Buñuel (1900-83) made an astonishing 21-minute film *Un Chien Andalou* (1929), which showed how the eye is cut with a knife. In India too, famous painter Maqbool Fida Hussain (1915–2011) made a 15-minute short film called

Through the Eyes of a Painter (1964), which won the prestigious "Golden Bear" award at the Berlin Film Festival. Nobel Laureate for Literature, Samuel Beckett (1906-86) made a 24-minute film called *Film* (1964), in which comedy actor of the silent era, Buster Keaton had acted. This film was called one of the greatest films of the world by French philosopher Gilles Deleuze (1925-95). Russian film-maker Sergei Parajanov (1924-90) made a film on the life of poet Sayat Nova called *The Colour of Pomegranates* (1969). This film got a deep appreciation from reputed film-makers like Michelangelo Antonioni, Martin Scorsese and Andrei Tarkovsky. These films have been trashed by audiences for lack of entertainment, they have obviously not been understood by them. Many films attract the attention of celebrated intellectuals. Argentinean writer, Jorge Luis Borges (1899–1986), praised film-maker Orson Welles for his film *Citizen Kane*. Film-maker Erich von Stroheim (1885–1957), who made German film *Greed* (1924), and Japanese film-maker Yasujiro Ozu (1903-63) also wholeheartedly appreciated the new techniques and the artistic viewpoint of this film. Nobel laureate, philosopher and writer Jean-Paul Sartre (1905-80), in a famous write-up, dismissed some Italian objections toward the frightening

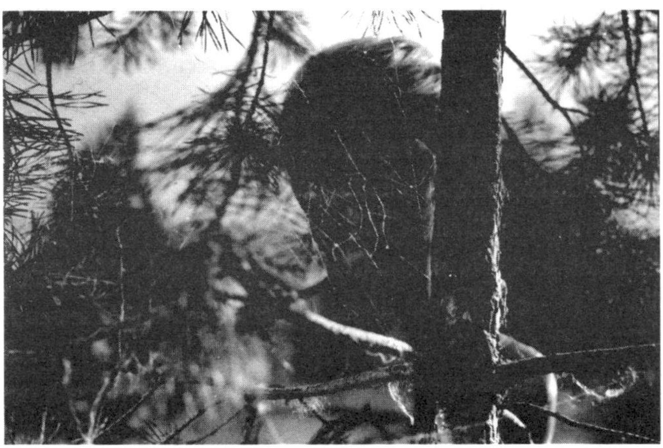

Opening Scene of Tarkovsky's *Ivan's Childhood* (1962)

display of war scenes as depicted in the "Golden Lion" winning film *Ivan's Childhood* (1962) made by Andrei Tarkovsky.

Similarly, such films have, through new experiments, brought about intellectuality in them. Films are a medium through which, in a limited time, one can put forth many ideas in an artistic way. This is practically impossible only through words, pictures, dance and music. Just as every subject face obstacles in the path of its progress and in establishing its superior standards, so do films. These obstacles can only be surmounted by a deep study of difficult to understand cinema. Famous French film director Jean-Luc Godard (b.1930) was a professional film critic when he decided to revolt against the films made during his time and turned into a director with a passion to make new-age and relevant cinema. Today, he is counted as one of the most noteworthy film-makers of the world. Famous American film-maker Quentin Tarantino (b.1963) has named his film company on the name of Godard's film, *Bande à Part* or *Band of Outsiders* (1964).

In the mid-1920s and early 1930s, two important Russian films were made, one by Alexander Dovzenko (1894–1956) called *Earth* (original name *Zemlya* – 1930), and the other by Sergei Eisenstein (1898–1948) called *Battleship Potemkin* (1925). These films are remembered even today for the political awareness they brought in and were a sort of an important artistic message on the changing times and values of that era. The beauty of Satyajit Ray's films *Pather Panchali* (1955), *Aparajito* (1956) and *Apur Sansaar* (1959) and the soulful music of renowned *sitār* player Pt. Ravishankar are absolutely inseparable. Japanese director Akira Kurosawa (1910-98) was so impressed by the works of this Indian maestro that he called Satyajit Ray as the sun and moon of world cinema. Noted film-maker V. Shantaram cast Gopi Krishna, a famous Kathak dancer, in the lead role of his film *Jhanak Jhanak Payal Baaje* (1955). Films are no doubt made with the hard work and perseverance of many artists working together.

Despite numerous financial setbacks, director Orson Welles continued making excellent films all his life, he was rejected by many studios and film companies, but that never deterred him and he never compromised on artistic excellence. But, why do we talk about such films, why not see blockbusters and films which earn crores of rupees in a few days? We must do so because a very few films have the ability to remain in the minds and hearts of people, a very few films transcend distance and time. It is quite important for films to be immortal even after the actors and actresses are no longer with us. It is of utmost importance, therefore, to realize that there is no set rule or tried and tested formula to ascertain if a film is immortal.

Great story writer Munshi Premchand (1880–1936) had a bitter experience in the making of the film *Mazdoor* (1934). After that, in the memory of Hindi literature, he referred to it and he called the director as all powerful and cinema as just a business without any meaning, he turned his back on Hindi cinema. This has never been forgiven or forgotten by connoisseurs of Hindi literature. On the other hand, Urdu poets like Kaifi Azmi and Sahir Ludhianvi literally embraced Hindi cinema and were able to bring to the audience some of the well-known works of Urdu literature. Hindi cinema has been able to boast of only a few rare works which are of an international standard. Nobel laureate, writer Vidyadhar Surajprasad Naipaul has termed Premchand as a minor fabulist. He says that if stories are always about morality then the audience gets bored of it. English language writer Oscar Wilde says:

> There is no such thing as a moral or an immoral book. Books are well written, or badly written. That is all.

Premchand's stories are undoubtedly very beautifully crafted and are humane, but whether common man accepts morality in every which way is seen with a prejudice.

Globalization is not without its dangers, but even with the revolution of the information technology and films being easily available on the Internet, it is strange that in the last 100 years Hindi films which have specialized in showing distorted family dramas, have neither turned fully Western nor have they been truly globalized. Hindi cine viewers do not wonder at the extraordinary situations as to how the hero can suddenly be so good in singing a song or be so perfect in dancing or why do they believe that the actress' beauty is the most important aspect? Characters larger than life or extraordinary circumstances or similarly unbelievable actions do not become a hindrance to viewing pleasure. It can be very well understood with our cultural legacy of myths, drama and literature. It is an altogether different matter that as in the West, Indian films never had that enormous budget to make technically excellent films which would leave a mark on the world. Similarly, despite having such diverse political opinions, political activists have never given up guns to discuss cinema. Sometimes if a daring film-maker strives to make a politically opinionated movie, the film-maker as well as the film both have to face severe protests and censures and the movie never sees the light of the day.

The history of the world of cinema is witness to the fact that film-makers Sergei Eisenstein, Sergei Dovzenko and Sergei Parajanov despite being repeatedly afflicted and tortured by the Russian government made notable, heart-touching, low-budget films. Sergei Parajanov was even accused of rape, taking bribes and homosexuality. He was sentenced for five years and spent four of them in jail. He was ultimately released one year early due to international pressure. All this was possible only because his creations had the power to influence audiences and film-makers alike. The Soviet regime gave him only that much reel so as to make a film in just two takes, but it is definitely the genius of Parajanov who made a wonderful film called *Ashik Kerib* (1988) and left an incredible legacy for the children of the world.

Study of cinema is quite perplexing, a person studying literature will be a litterateur, a student of music – a musician, a student learning science – a scientist, but a person trying to understand the aesthetics and beauty of films cannot be termed as a film-maker nor will he\she be given any recognition in society as an aesthete. Even one's ideological achievements will be negated because the impression that a film has on the audience is certainly different, maybe bigger than what a critic has written in a review. It is a matter of pride that a quest for such knowledge is not for a professional need or to earn bread or even to get an award or fame but purely for the enjoyment such knowledge brings. Such a wish and such a perseverance help a person understand the complicated dimensions of life. It won't be surprising if one learns manners and etiquettes required for a civilized living by watching some of Alfred Hitchcock's thrillers.

Just as philosophy can be understood by the detailed study of its history and chemistry can only be understood by a detailed study of the historic achievements and development in that field, so also, study of films is only effective if films made by its masters are seen and studied. Let us then look at some world-renowned films made by people proficient in film-making.

The question now arises as to who are these masters and what are the qualities to gauge them by?

These masters are those people who have no hesitation or anxiety about the quality of their creation. They are in no way dependent on a critic for a favourable review or on anybody for a suggestion even. Apart from knowing the nuances of their craft, they have a mature and cultivated view of life and are able to express it firmly. For example, an expert singer will be able to catch any false note in a song. He will be his own critic and will be prepared to correct himself through extensive practice and learning. A master film-maker should not only be an able storyteller, but a visionary with inventiveness; he should be able to bring out harmony in music, he should be well versed in legends and folklore; should be able to efficiently manage finances, should have the gall to stand his ground in the face of very severe criticism, should have common business sense and should have a very keen awareness of history.

Film-makers, who make films which transcend time and always remain in the memory of people, are a breed apart. This group of outstanding people are the representatives of their time. If there is evil and wickedness in the world, then art acts as a salve, the wisdom it imparts and the path of truth it shows are able to give sustenance to people who are disheartened, sad or who are weighed down by that evil. Art acts as a soothing and beneficial music and the way to overcome evil with goodness.

Perspicacity into Films as Seen Through the Indian Classical Aesthetics

The Indian philosophical school is divided into two streams. The first stream, consists of the believers in the teachings of the Vedas, and the other comprises of the non-believers. The believers (*āstika*s) are those who believe in:

1. Sāṁkhya–Yoga (philosophy of right knowledge): theoretical as in Sāṁkhya and practical as in Yoga,
2. Nyāya–Vaiśeṣika which promotes the doctrines of intellectual, analytical and logical thinking,
3. Mīmāṁsā–Vedānta, the philosophy based on critical investigations, the Mīmāṁsā–Vedānta are based on the Vedas and try to interpret them, and
4. the doctrines of the Śaiva philosophy.

The non-believers (*nāstika*s), comprise of the Jainas, Buddhists, the materialists, etc. The believers argue in their metaphysical stand, with subtle difference of sentient and insentient, they uphold the maxim that belief in *ātmā* and *Brahman* (Paramaśiva) is the main doctrine of their philosophy. Among the non-believers, the Jainas accept the presence of the *ātmā*. There is also a conflict among the schools about the existence of God and acceptance of the *ātmā*, for example, the Buddhists, Sāṁkhyas, Vaiśeṣikas and Mīmāṁsakas are considered atheists (शर्मा 1995; Hiriyanna 1993). The scope of the book is not to unravel the intricacies of *ātmā–paramātmā* or the metaphysical doctrines of philosophy, but to study the principles of aesthetics to understand cinema.

To understand the ancient Indian perspective and to be inline with the chosen commentary of the *Nāṭyaśāstra* which has been written as per the Kashmir Śaivism, we must understand the classical definition of poetics and art in an internal consistency among other established ideas within the thought system. Great poet, Jaishankar Prasad says that poetics or literature is always trying to open ever new frontiers in the sensibilities of the *ātmā* (soul). The ability to think, the ability to speak after thinking and the unknown life force which brings about a coordination between the two and a balance therein are all the natural actions of the *ātmā*. Poetics is not really concerned with analysis, inference or science. It is only a very dear, a virtuous and a formative fount of knowledge. The Indian tradition looks at poetics in three different ways – verse compilations (taken from the *Ṛgveda* – as it is in the form of verses), prosaic compilations (taken from the *Yajurveda* – as it is in the form of prose) and the musical compilations (taken from the *Sāmaveda* – as it is in the form of songs). The life force accredits every unknown thing in the world; therefore, we can see a new form of it every time. Whatever can be known is speech (*vāṇī*), speech takes this form in order to defend that knowledge. We must try to manifest the perceptions of speech in other possible ways, but due to time–space barriers the pronounced speech is not really available or even understood everywhere, therefore to make it easily accessible it has to be made evident through pictures or sculpture or different styles of expression (जयशंकर प्रसाद 1939: 26-28).

Argentinean writer Jorge Luis Borges has said:

> Poetry always remembers that it was an oral art before it was written. It remembers that it was first a song.

The "Āgamas" are also a sacred text like the Vedas. The Jainas, the Buddhists, the Vaiṣṇavas and the Śaivas all have different Āgama texts. According to the Śaiva Āgamas, *kalā*, a Sanskrit word for art, in the contracted power of action while *vidyā*, a Sanskrit word for knowledge, is the parochial power which knows everything. This accordingly implies that the ultimate state of consciousness is shrunk, by the power of obscuration (*māyā*), and thus is present in everyone as an individual spirit. It is this *māyā* which makes the Infinite appear as finite, and then using various sheaths (partly revealing subjective powers) like art (*kalā*), knowledge (*vidyā*), passionate objective propensity (*rāga*), succession (*kāla*) and causal necessity (*niyati*) manifest an individualized soul. Passionate objective propensity is related to the absolute, while limited succession to eternity and causal efficiency to omnipotence. It is impossible to discuss this aspect of Śaiva philosophy in its totality here. (See Annexure for further details.)

Our classical texts have described fourteen types of knowledge and the sixth-century Sanskrit poet Daṇḍin has enumerated sixty-four art forms. The head poet of the ninth-century Gurjara–Pratihāra empire, Rājaśekhara, in his book *Kāvyamīmāṁsā,* has called poetics as a form of knowledge as against art which he calls as a sub-knowledge. He distinguishes between poetics and art by saying that art is more scientifically inclined and so giving it a very definitive way to address it. Architecture, sculpting and painting are traditionally crafts. The process of revealing oneself in a controlled manner to form new and different selves is called as art (जयशंकर प्रसाद 1939: 28; Deshpande 1989).

Among the sixty-four art forms prevalent during the middle ages in India, Vātsyāyana in his epic work *Kāmasūtra* has enumerated making up one's self, wearing of jewellery, dancing-music, art of entertaining, painting or drawing of pictures, conversing with birds, dexterity in household work, skilfulness in business, house building, water games, solving puzzles, etc. as the various attributes one should have to lead a good life. If a new list is prepared keeping in mind the new age and generation, then many new art forms will get added to it. According to poet Jaishankar Prasad, a person's talent can be used to assess his\her self-worth or a soul searching can be done by three ways: in accordance to one's own nature, or against one's nature or in a totally astonishing way. In these three symbolic regulations itself, the prototype of idealism, realism and individualism are hidden (जयशंकर प्रसाद 1939: 28-29).

According to Śaiva philosophy, there are three bases or foundations of knowledge:

a. perception-based knowledge, which can be directly felt through sensory perception and comprehended,
b. innate, nature-based knowledge which can be comprehended by inference, and
c. self-based knowledge which can be understood with direct cognition of soul.

The first kind of knowledge is one which helps to build up our thoughts and imaginations. The second develops our scientific temperament and behavioural attitudes and the third helps us realize our goal in life by knowing ourselves or soul. Our soul or consciousness perceives three kinds of thoughts: (a) relating to knowledge, (b) relating to actions (*karma*), and (c) relating to emotions or feelings. This knowledge which is emotion based or sentiment based and which is linked with imagination and thoughts is a subject matter of aesthetics and it also bears a relation to how one perceives the social pursuits in his/her life (पाण्डे 2003: 15, 19, 27, 29).

A discussion on films based on the ancient Indian aesthetic principles will show that drama is closest in nature to films. Drama has to be rehearsed and its destiny is the stage. Films though have a different life, unlike on stage, the actors in a film do not have to emote everything all at once, their act can be done in bits and pieces. Films have to be recorded, edited, background music and playback music have to be synchronized, only then they can be shown to the audience. Of course, it is a given that drama and films both are used to convey, within a stipulated time, some message to society. Drama too has the same characteristics, world over at all times. In the Indian context, drama has been called as the best form of poetics. It has been seen that through the ages poetry has primarily remained a form that is heard while drama gives us the audio-visual pleasure of poetry, all this of course is taking us away from our main point of debate and discussion.

The following verses in the epic work *Nāṭyaśāstra*, written by Bharata Muni, explain the utility of drama:

> Drama teaches the glory of duty to those who have forgotten their duty, it guides us on the path to find love, to the ill-tempered and uncouth, it shows how punishment can improve them, to the disciplined it shows how to live in regulation, cowards are taught how to be brave, the brave are shown the virtues of energy and enthusiasm, a person who is unwise is given wisdom and the intelligent are made further wise. The ones who are burdened with sorrow are taught how to be stable in their grief, those who are waylaid are taught discipline and the poor are shown the means to a livelihood.
>
> – *Nāṭyaśāstra* 1.110-16; Ghosh 1950: 15

Drama, in Bharata Muni's words, is an emulation of the work and conduct of the people; it is fulfilling in emotions and highly descriptive in nature. It is bound to the works and life of all people be it good, bad or in-between. Drama brings people together; it gives them the courage, entertains them, brings happiness into their lives and also counsels them whenever required.

The great Sanskrit poet Kālidāsa has expressed his view in the beginning of his play *Mālavikāgnimitra* that drama is such a medium that, on a single platform, fulfils the desires of all the people gathered irrespective of their varied interests.

According to the *Nāṭyaśāstra*, in the Indian tradition, dance, music and playing of musical instruments are an inseparable part of drama which have been unknowingly carried through into films. Due to many differences in the moral and ethical values the Indian traditions seem very queer to the Western eye. This does seem to be one of the reasons why Indian films have not been so popular the world over.

Has one ever wondered why a sad scene makes you cry or why a good drama makes you feel elated and full of *joie de vivre*? The answer lies in philosophy and particularly aesthetics. The extensive and proper study of reality and what governs consciousness, the study of how to gain knowledge and the study of language is not possible without the knowledge of aesthetics. Many Western philosophers believe that it is impossible to know exactly what an audience feels when they see a work of art as such feelings are unknowable.

Cinema has to be understood in the context of poetics, dramatics and aesthetics. Both poetics and dramatics are explained within aesthetics. In the Indian philosophical system, aesthetics and truth do not oppose each other. In a traditional discussion, if truth is scrutinized then we can see that virtue or the right path and pursuit of the worldly pleasing path both are questioned. Our sacred texts, i.e. the Vedas and the Upaniṣads, are the right path chosen to learn the truth (*śreyas*), whereas poetics is akin to the pursuit of the worldly pleasing path (*preyas*). The great poet Jaishankar Prasad has said that poetics is the imaginative experience of the soul, it has nothing to do with any kind of analysis or inference or science. The thinking power of the soul accepts the virtuous path to the truth in its original and elegant form in its exceptional state and in poetics this conviction is the true realization. Hindi poetess Mahadevi Verma has enunciated on poetics and art, thus: "In poetry, the art has reached such an eminence that it can now help knowledge, because truth can be attained through it and beauty helps to achieve it". Traditional literature of the Indian poetics has been divided into eight sects as under (Paranjape and Visuvalingam 2006: 101):[1]

1. Rasa
2. Dhvani
3. Aucitya
4. Rīti
5. Vakrokti
6. Guṇa
7. Doṣa
8. Alaṁkāra

(see Annexure for short descriptions.)

Many Indian philosophers do not prescribe to the above eight traditions of poetic and literary criticism, they feel that the Buddhist and other doctrines have not been given due credit here. Poet Jaishankar Prasad has referred to Rasa, Dhvani and Rīti as the delightful or pleasure-giving sects, whereas the no-soul theory proponents Buddhist art forms have been graded as agonizing ones. Among the above eight schools of poetics, Rasa is considered as the most important. The learned teachers have declared that in poetics *rasa* has been called as the most lively or charming, while the others are parched (जयशंकर प्रसाद 1939: 34; रस्तोगी 2012: 249).

Historically too, it can be said that *rasa* has always been the most discussed and effectually important of all the aesthetic doctrines.

The sentiments, which are felt whenever a drama is seen,

[1] Rajnish Mishra, 2006, "Agamic Assumptions of Indian Literary Theories: An Exposition Based on Abhinavagupta", *Evam*, 4(1/2): 91-129.

have been quantified or listed down, according to the *rasa* theory as against the unknowable feelings described by the German philosopher, Immanuel Kant. Out of these listed sentiments some have been categorized on the basis of the exceptional way they make one realize the feelings shown, they are: anger, laughter, fear, etc. These are above and beyond characters like pride, laziness and worry. The exceptional qualities mentioned above are defined as the *sthāyī bhāvas* which literally means feelings that stay. They are not named so because they are the static feelings which are always prevalent throughout, but they are the most enduring feelings noticed.

Kashmiri Śaiva philosopher, Abhinavagupta opined that every social being is conscious of eight types of distinctive feelings already present in his/her psyche. In the course of watching a drama, a compassionate spectator feels drawn to the emotions being acted out on stage, these emotions (*rasas*) can be recognized from the *sthāyī bhāvas* explained earlier. The spectator loses himself in the feelings which are aroused in him. He feels sated and experiences pleasure which are distinctly different from his day-to-day life experience and personal happiness or sorrow (पारेख 1974: 46-48). The word *rasa* has been used variedly; as in the juice of a fruit or the extract of vital force in the context of the Ayurvedic medicine, etc. (पाण्डे 2003: 95), but while alluding to drama or films we can say that the word *rasa* has been able to bring together a very distinctive, diverse and peculiar meaning to itself. It is an experience of aesthetic emotions and also the subject of these experiences itself (रस्तोगी 2012: 274).

Aristotle while contemplating on tragedies said that the narrative of the plot is the soul of the tragedy. Similarly, to put emphasis on the narrative has become quite a tradition world over. Sanskrit poets have believed that *rasa* is the soul of a drama. Many of them like Kālidāsa in his play *Abhijñānaśākuntalam* and Bhavabhūti in his *Uttararāmacarita* have even twisted and modified the traditional plot of the drama so that *rasa* can be given its due importance. They have written many dramas with this effect. What is important to note is that Sanskrit dramas have a happy ending most of the time, the actor or hero always wins over the anti-hero. The hero is morally an upright person who in the end invokes the blessings of God, to set everything right (द्विवेदी और द्विवेदी 1963: 54).

The Indian tradition of reflection and contemplation lays a lot of emphasis on the realization or the perception of the *rasa*. The traditional metaphysical thought on the other hand gives weightage to a valid means of true knowledge (*pramā*); a true and new knowledge which is perceived and about which there is no ambiguity (शर्मा 1995: 192). Knowledge should be understood as a mental construct, according to the ancient Indian philosophical doctrines. It is therefore necessary to understand it through the rules of grammar and not as the indisputable theorems of mathematics. So also let us not classify films based on their plot (in other words, dry cognitive skeleton of entire presentation), i.e. thrillers, romance, musicals, family drama, love story, war story, etc. Let us, instead, categorize them on the basis of the sentiments or feelings they arouse in us or the *rasa* they invoke in us, the life force as well as the relishment of the presentation.

How old is the theory of aesthetics or the *rasa-siddhānta*? Such a question is very difficult to answer, but we do find descriptions of it in the *Nāṭyaśāstra*. Historians believe that it may have been written by many people in the period between 200 BCE and 200 CE, while scholars are of the view that the present form of *rasa-siddhanta* is a compilation from many texts. The original text may be a few hundred years older, although we do not have any proofs for it. Bharata Muni says that he has taken its concept from the *Atharvaveda* (नगेन्द्र 1969: 12).

Many thinkers put forth their views on the concept of *rasa* after the *Nāṭyaśāstra*. Many thoughts were added, some were deleted and some more were changed by calling them insubstantial. Some of the thinkers who interpreted the *rasa* theory in different ways were; Śaṅkuka, Bhaṭṭanāyaka, Lollaṭa and Bhaṭṭa Tauta (Gnoli 1968; पारेख 1974). The tenth-century Śaiva philosopher Ācārya Abhinavagupta, while extrapolating on the text *Nāṭyaśāstra* also expounded his interpretation of the *rasa-siddhānta* in his text *Abhinavabhāratī*.

Śaiva philosophy, which is related to the Śaiva Āgama texts, is divided into three types: (a) Dvaita or Dualism, (b) Dvaitādvaita, and (c) Advaita or Non-dualism/Monism. The Kashmiri Śaiva philosophy has four branches: (a) Spanda, (b) Pratyabhijñā, (c) Krama, and (d) Kula. (We are not discussing that within this book.).The name of Ācārya Abhinavagupta, a Kashmiri Śaiva philosopher who is very well versed in all these four branches, is taken with great respect in the sphere of the Indian poetics and Indian aesthetics. He was orphaned at an early age due to the death of his mother and his father leading the life of an ascetic. He was raised by his teachers, remained unmarried all his life and devoted his life to learning the Śaiva philosophy. His interests varied from music, to aesthetics, to different philosophies; he wrote altogether forty-one books on these various subjects. According to folklore, Abhinavagupta, along with his 1,200 disciples disappeared into a cave near a village named Bhairav in Gulmarg and never came back. In his disappearance, the Indian philosophical discourse also lost an important link to the Kashmir Śaiva philosophy (Paranjape and Visuvalingam 2006: Foreword).

Let us try and hope to find a resemblance between drama and films as we undertake to study world films through the knowledge of the aesthetic doctrines. Within the perspective of the Indian aesthetic principles let us study all the eight *rasas* (manifestations of emotions) as seen in world cinema chronologically. Films can be rated as the best, good or just watchable using many poetic standards like propriety, virtues of the actors or the faults even. Our study of world films will be limited to films made by expert film-makers and which have won international fame and are incomparable.

Bharata Muni in his *Nāṭyaśāstra* has enumerated eight types of *rasa*. They are:

1. Bhayānaka Rasa (terrible manifestation),
2. Vībhatsa Rasa (odious manifestation),
3. Adbhuta Rasa (marvellous manifestation),
4. Vīra Rasa (heroic manifestation),
5. Karuṇa Rasa (tragic manifestation),
6. Raudra Rasa (furious manifestation),
7. Hāsya Rasa (comic manifestation), and
8. Śṛṅgāra Rasa (erotic manifestation).

In the *Nāṭyaśāstra*, Bharata Muni does not mention the Śānta Rasa as a separate entity and he believes that *rasa* comes into being only because of our perceptions. Abhinavagupta, on the other hand, adds Śānta Rasa to the above eight and has coined the term *navarasa*. Ācārya Abhinavagupta in his text *Abhinavabhāratī*, while discussing the various *rasa*s, has called the *rasa* as manifestations of sentiments and as well as the subject of these manifestations. While doing a detailed study on the *rasa-siddhānta* (concluded principles of aesthetics), we find that many of Abhinavagupta's predecessors were also not of one opinion on some of the concepts of the *rasa-siddhānta*. This was also seen in the case of some western scholars, but this difference of opinion on some philosophical aspects was important for the thought processes that developed during these discussions. It is important to note that right from the origin of *rasa*, to its conception, to its perception and also the differences in it are all matters which have been debated over and over by many philosophers.

To learn and discuss about the vastness and diversity of the *rasa-siddhānta*, many texts have been written post-Abhinavagupta, e.g. the *Daśarūpaka* by Dhanañjaya in the tenth century, the *Nāṭaka-lakṣaṇaratnakośa* by Sāgara Nandī in the eleventh century, the *Śṛṅgāra-Prakāśa* and the *Sarasvatī-Kaṇṭhābharaṇa* by Bhojarāja in the eleventh century, the *Nāṭyadarpaṇa* by Rāmacandra and Guṇacandra in the twelfth century, the *Sāhityadarpaṇa* by Kavirāja Viśvanātha in the fifteenth century, the *Nāṭyacandrikā* by Rūpa Goswāmī in the fifteenth century (नगेन्द्र 1969).

Everything which is beautiful brings a delight to our heart, but everything that is delightful may or may not be beautiful. The Sanskrit derivative of the word *sundara* (loosely translated as beauty) means – "anything which is able to soak the psyche". The word "beautiful" has been used in more than thirty different ways in the Vedas (रस्तोगी 2012: 251). A *śloka* in the *Ṛgveda*, translates to "look at this beautiful creation of God, it neither dies nor ages" (पाण्डे 2003: 54). This suffices to say that the meaning of *sundara* (beauty) is very vast, it integrates even the most mundane of the natural beauty of this world. Many philosophical traditions and many doctrines explain the aesthetic principles in many different ways.

Ācārya Govinda Chandra Pande, while explaining the word "aesthetics", proposes that the pleasure derived from it comes from three sources: (a) from various arts like music, painting and drawing, (b) from poetry, and (c) from natural beauty (पाण्डे 2003: 1). We focus our attention on the aesthetics as drawn from the arts, that too from films. So, without much ado we shall start the study of modern concepts of aesthetic doctrines as in the man-made arts or the making of films. As in drama, films too are the result of the toil and hard work of many people, generally under the leadership of an able director.

Saundarya (loosely translated as aesthetics), according to Abhinavagupta as recorded in his *Abhinavabhāratī,* has been used in the context of the feelings one experiences whenever one comes face to face with a beautiful work of art. According to *Aitareya Brāhmaṇa* 6.27, art is nothing but the learning output of the imitation of divine work (or mental conception). In other words, art is the description or illustration of an artist's psychic conception. A work of art fulfils its meaning if it is understood by the preceptor (रस्तोगी 2012: 273).

The aesthetics of art can be experienced and relished through these three media: (a) *śabda* or word (sound with specific meaning), (b) *rūpa* or form, and (c) *nāda* or resonance (sound without specific meaning) (रस्तोगी 2012: 260).

The word can be in the form of a song or a dialogue, form appearance has its bearing in painting, drawing, wearing different costumes, beautifying the body using make-up, dancing, etc. and musical notes relate to sounds of musical instruments or music per se. It is in the performing arts only that one gets to see a perfect harmony between the word, the form or appearance and the notes. It is in a drama that one sees a permeation of the spoken word in the form of poetry or prose or songs sung by actors. Dramatics brings together dance, music and poetry. Poetics and dramatics are so synced with each other that at some point drama is infused with poetics, while at some other point poetics seems as though drama is yet to be peformed (पाण्डे 2003: 78).

In much a similar way, films too are a beautiful amalgamation of the word, form or appearance and the notes. Film-makers feel that films are not just an extension of drama, but a new way of representing art.

It can be undoubtedly said that *rasa* is related to *nāṭya*. By *nāṭya*, we do not mean the staged drama, but the subject matter of the drama. Abhinavagupta says that dramatics shows us how different sentiments can be portrayed and the complete realization of these sentiments is only through dramatics. Bharata Muni lists the eleven parts of dramatics as follows:

1. *Rasa* is the pleasurable manifestation of emotions felt while watching a drama.
2. *Bhāva* is nature or the character of the feeling.
3. *Abhinaya* is the acting done on stage.

4. *Dharmi* is the nature of transformation which takes place on the stage.
5. *Vṛtti* is the division of the dramatic enactments.
6. *Pravṛtti* is the input of the regional styles in producing drama.
7. *Siddhi* means the success of the play in the eyes of both God and men.
8. *Svara.*
9. *Ātodya.*
10. *Gāna* are all related to the musical aspect of the drama.
11. *Raṅga-mañca* is the theatre house.

Abhinavagupta doesn't count *rasa* as a part of dramatics but calls it the soul (*ātmā*). It can be said with a doubt that films are not only moving dramas, but they are conceptually very near to dramas.

Films, which are a combined effort of many people, are nothing less than poetry and film-making is nothing less than an art. Acting, direction and editing are all art forms. Like dramas, films are a poetic manifestation and an art form. Since *rasa* is the soul of poetics, the study of films on the basis of the *rasa* theory is quite incidental. According to Bharata Muni, dramatics is a pure art form which contains in it many sub-art forms (*Nāṭyaśāstra* 1.117-21; Ghosh 1950: 16). He also says that the *rasa* is the soul of art, though many modern philosophers do not agree on this.

Philosophers will keep on debating on questions about *rasa* being the manifestation in art or the soul of poetics. In a careful study these debates are not only helpful but also complementary. The different divisions of poetics and art, the detailed analysis of the aesthetics and its manifestations, will take us away from our goal. Therefore, we must base our discussions on the limited meanings as consented to by Bharata Muni and Abhinavagupta. The reason for this is that Abhinavagupta's vast explanation gives us all our answers, even though we may not agree to them. Just like how the propositions of Dutch philosopher Baruch Spinoza haven't been dismissed by other philosophers through his line of arguments. Yes, many philosophers have questioned his metaphysical postulates and without trying to find answers have gone on. Abhinavagupta, like Ādi Śaṅkarācārya, has been revered among Indian philosophers. This book is a humble attempt to introduce to the readers his principles. It is possible that some philosophers may not agree with the principles talked about here, so let us leave behind these arguments and counterarguments and get on with our endeavour.

In order to study the beauty of films we must properly interpret the doctrines of poetry, art and aesthetics. The theories of *rasa* are manifested in the aesthetics, poetics and arts, so we must be careful of the questions put to us, for example, the schools of poetics like *rīti* (methods used in drama) and *vakrokti* (language of the drama) cannot on their own explain the aesthetics of any film.

Every drama or film makes us realize the presence of many sentiments, but dramas do have one prominent or supreme *rasa*, it is this chief sentiment which gives the drama a direction. There is a lot of difference of opinion among scholars on this also, some negate the presence of a chief sentiment, while others search out prominent *rasa* even in great poetic epics too. For example, according to Ānandavardhana, the founder of sound (*dhvani*) theory, the *Rāmāyaṇa* has Karuṇa Rasa as the prominent *rasa* while the *Mahābhārata* has Śānta Rasa as the prominent *rasa* (नगेन्द्र 1969: 283-86). We shall study world cinema expecting that the films we mention have a chief sentiment which is manifested and that the *rasa* theory will aid our journey.

We haven't come across any Sanskrit dramas which have Hāsya or Vībhatsa *rasa*s as the chief *rasa* or *aṅgī rasa*. They always, have "Śṛṅgāra" or "Vīra" Rasa as the prominent one. Interestingly Ācārya Viśvanātha, a fourteenth-century scholar, formulates in his book of poetic criticism, *Sāhityadarpaṇa*, that Śṛṅgāra, Vīra or Śānta Rasa should be the chief *rasa* in all dramas.

> शृङ्गार वीर शान्ता नामेकोऽङ्गी रस इष्यते ।
> अङ्गानि सर्वेऽपि रसाः सर्वे नाटकसन्धयः ॥
>
> *śṛṅgāra vīra śāntā nāmeko 'ṅgī rasa iṣyate* ।
> *aṅgāni sarve 'pi rasāḥ sarve nāṭakasandhayaḥ* ॥
>
> – *Sāhityadarpaṇa* 6.317

However, contemporary Indian scholar, Bharat Gupt, argues that there are references of lost Sanskrit drama having Vībhatsa Rasa as *aṅgī rasa*. Probably, Sanskrit drama too had many sorrowful themes but they are not existent now. One such drama is the *Urubhaṅgam* by Bhāsa which has dealt with and depicted death in the drama (Gupt 1994: 210).

Films then can interpret the untouched aspects of life and inspect the scope of new ideas, as cinema is breaking the centuries-old formulas and creating joyous artful medium to explore new vistas.

History has always been taught with a Western perspective; like India was discovered by Vasco-da-Gama, now through this book, let us do the opposite. Let us study and understand world cinema within the scope of the ancient Indian aesthetic theory. We must see the world's great films while giving a cursory look at the numbers of supreme *rasa*s, the prominent *rasa* prevalent, etc. We must benefit by such a study.

3

The Unparalleled World of Frightening Cinema

Films of the Bhayānaka Rasa

Generally, films are studied and classified on the basis of their genre, for example, whether they are thrillers or musicals or science fictions or even love stories. But, film-makers like Jean-Luc Godard, deny calling films as a form of art, they insist that movies are a new kind of expression somewhere in between life and art. Godard says that unlike painting and literature, the cinema both gives to life and takes from it and that he tries to render this concept in his films.

If we look at films from the viewpoint of the ancient Indian aesthetic theory, then the twist and turns in a story or the technical excellence seen in a film or its novelty or even the colours used in the films can only assist in the perception of beauty but does not answer the spirit of arts or many related questions of aesthetics. Therefore, the focus of our study is our own perception, understanding and sensibility. Western philosophers have often accepted the doctrines of aesthetics while keeping in mind the sensibility of the five senses and how our mind perceives these senses. The word "aesthetics" has its origin in the Greek word "aisthesthai", which means to express in a clear way. It also means the pleasure ones feels or one can express after a particular emotion is felt by our senses. The word gradually got changed to "aesthetic" and is now widely used (पाण्डे 2003: 1). Almost all the Indian philosophies adhere to the concept of the mind along with the five senses. Although it is seen that the pleasure derived from our senses is not apart from what our mind perceives, even so the Indian school of thought is of the view that the realization of the *rasa* pertains more to the self than mere enjoyment for our sensory perceptions or titillation.

An enormously popular Hindi thriller, *Mahal* (1949), directed by Kamaal Amrohi, was an example of how fear can be multi-faceted. It had in its cast actor Ashok Kumar and was a film which established the careers of actress Madhubala and playback singer Lata Mangeshkar. The film begins with the commentary in the background, by a middle-aged man, in a loud and harsh voice:

> Thirty years ago, on a rainy, stormy night (*on the screen, scenes of rain and storm flash, showing in snatches a desolate palace*), near Allahabad and about two miles from Naini Railway Station, across the River Yamunā is situated a palatial building named Saṅgam Bhavan. It has been quite derelict and uncared for since long. (*Just then, on the screen is shown the blurred image of a person wearing a raincoat and a hat, entering the palace.*) It is said that on fearful, stormy nights such as this, at mid-night a boat appears from somewhere and drowns in the Yamunā. At the same time a grievous cry can be heard from within the palace. People have been scared and have since termed this palace as haunted, but an old gardener still lives in this palace and he tells the tale of a very tragic love story which happened ages ago in this very palace. ...

This secretive and fearsome narration echoing the Greek myth of Hero and Leander, accompanied by the plaintive voice of a female character singing – *āyegā ānewālā* – is quite enough to scare the wits out of not only the actor Ashok Kumar but the spectator watching the movie as well.

It is important here, to note that before fear actually sets in, the seeds of fear have been sown in the minds of the audience through various sights like a stormy night, a derelict palace, its haunting history, etc. The actor in the movie is scared because of some unforeseeable terrible thing happening, but why is the spectator scared? This is the most important question of aesthetics. It is natural for the actor to feel the fear as he is a part of the scene, but how does the same kind of fear develop in the viewer who is only seeing the film? This is nothing but the manifestation of the feeling of fear or in other words the realization of the Bhayānaka Rasa. This realization is so complete that we seem to be experiencing the same emotion without any distinction.

The heart of every human being is mentally disposed to carry within itself various emotions of which they themselves may not be fully aware of. The mood or state of mind of a spectator can be expressed only by the action that a person does and it is these feelings that let him propensate the action or pursue the action. According to Bharata Muni, it is these mental dispositions which permeate or fulfil the heart, therefore it is called *bhāva* (द्विवेदी 1992: 5; Ghosh 1950). A question can be asked here, as to why such a tendency of the subconscious to behave in this particular manner should be attributed to the heart, instead of the brain? The tenth-century Kashmiri philosopher, Utpaladeva says that the heart here should be equated to our conscious state and not to a mere organ. According to Śaiva epistemology, the mind (*manas*), the intellect (*buddhi*) and the sense of self/ego (*ahaṁkāra*) together form the conscious self (*citta*). It is this *citta* that is conceived in the heart. A glass filled with water only bears the water, there is no interaction between the two. The heart should be understood as the level of consciousness that it not only conceives the pure knowledge (*pramā*) but it also has the capacity of impressing the knower (*pramātā*). When a mental conception or feeling is said to be reaching the heart, or is being felt by the heart, it is to be understood as reflective awareness.

The *bhāvas* (emotions), which always exist in our consciousness in seed-like forms, are called the *sthāyī bhāvas*. The *bhāvas* which come and go and which cause an upheaval are called *vyabhicārī bhāvas* (transitory emotions). They are not stationary and by their character sometimes push the prevalent feelings (*sthāyī bhāvas*) away from the conscious mind (Gupt 1994: 252-54).

A creator is said to be drowned in *rasa* when he is completely overwhelmed by the charms of nature and his own creative experiences. If the meaning-essence of his creation, which is in his heart (reflective awareness of his consciousness), is mediated to the heart of the compassionate and engrossed spectator in a relishable manner, then such a mediation or manifestation is called an aesthetic rapture or wonderment (*camatkāra*). Our conscious mind comprehends these basic feelings like anger, love and hatred. This miraculous comprehension of our feelings (*camatkāra*), accompanied by pleasure, is called *rasa*. The unique enjoyment of the spectator's perception of the meaning of the poem from the heart of the poet is called *rasa*. Hence, the realization of the *rasa* is pleasurable itself and is also the subject of the pleasure too. We can identify *rasa* through the deeply-seated feelings (*sthāyī bhāvas*) (रस्तोगी 2012: 264).

According to Bharata Muni, as recorded in the *Nāṭyaśāstra*, *rasa* are basically of four types:

1. *Śṛṅgāra* (erotic state),
2. *Raudra* (furious state),
3. *Vīra* (heroic state), and
4. *Vībhatsa* (odious state).

Apart from these four main *rasas* there are four more states which arise from these, they are: Hāsya from Śṛṅgāra, Karuṇa from Raudra, Adbhuta from Vīra and Bhayānaka from Vībhatsa. Bharata Muni says that all these manifestations (*rasas*) are born out of each other and are friendly to each other's expression, e.g.

Hāsya is the imitation of Śṛṅgāra, Karuṇa has its roots in Raudra, etc. (द्विवेदी 1992: 110; Ghosh 1950: 107).

In a drama, one dominant state or *rasa* is seen and all other emotions are manifested through this *aṅgī rasa* (chief *rasa*). At one particular time one cannot experience the pleasure of two feelings. Every *rasa* comes with its own dominant states of emotions. Abhinavagupta has connected the four basic *rasa*s with the life goals of a social being. The human-related virtues have been assimilated by drama, for example, to show lust one must arouse pleasure seeking *rati bhāva* along with the erotic (Śṛṅgāra Rasa) or to show *dharma* one must arouse enthusiasm or *utsāha bhāva* along with Vīra Rasa. We shall discuss a lot more about this further into the book, for now, we must know that the dominant state of feeling for Bhayānaka Rasa is *bhaya* (fear) and the *sthāyī bhāva* for Vībhatsa Rasa is *jugupsā* (repulsion/disgust). The social well-being of man and his personal philosophies are interrelated to all the goals he sets for himself.

Abhinavagupta in his epic text *Abhinavabhāratī* has given the Śṛṅgāra Rasa the first place among all the eight *rasa*s. Among the four that a man must live his life by, *kāma* (desire) is the most important. People are naturally attracted to desire. Hāsya Rasa is consequential to Śṛṅgāra Rasa and so comes at the second place, Karuṇa Rasa is the opposite of Hāsya so it comes in third and since Raudra Rasa is interrelated to Karuṇa Rasa it has taken the fourth place. The means of achieving desire, i.e. *artha* is literally embedded in Raudra Rasa. The fifth place is taken by Vīra Rasa as *kāma* and *artha* both arise from *dharma*. The scope of Vīra Rasa is to make people fearless and therefore Bhayānaka Rasa is described after Vīra Rasa. Vībhatsa Rasa takes the seventh place as in characteristics it is quite close to Bhayānaka Rasa. Abhinavagupta has placed Adbhuta Rasa in the eighth place (द्विवेदी 1992: 18-21).

For the sake of film-centric discussions, we will study the *rasa*s manifesting sorrow (Bhayānaka and Vībhatsa), then those telling about joy (Adbhuta and Vīra), then again going back to sorrow (Karuṇa and Raudra) and finally onto the pleasure-giving *rasas* (Hāsya and Śṛṅgāra).

In the *Nāṭyaśāstra*, a list has been written about the reasons why a person feels fear, viz. fearsome voices from background, talk of witches and devils, sounds of owls and jackals, staying in an uninhabited house or in the jungle, seeing someone dear on the deathbed or a near-death experience.

The manifestation or the experience of Bhayānaka Rasa is not possible when someone sees a fearful object or hears the cries of a wild animal, etc. alone, there has to be a heart-wrenching feeling which will send the mind and body into a direction which shows extreme fear, only then can the spectator relish the *rasa*. Ancient literature has given varied meanings to the word *rasa*. It has been used to describe the taste of foods like sour, sweet or salty, to describe desire, power, chemical substances, resin from plants and even poison. *Rasa* as a concept becomes one with all the above complicated meanings. It depends on the expertise of the actor how he is able to arouse the feelings of fright in a viewer. Let us discuss world renowned films made by expert film-makers and get to know how they have affected the common spectator world over.

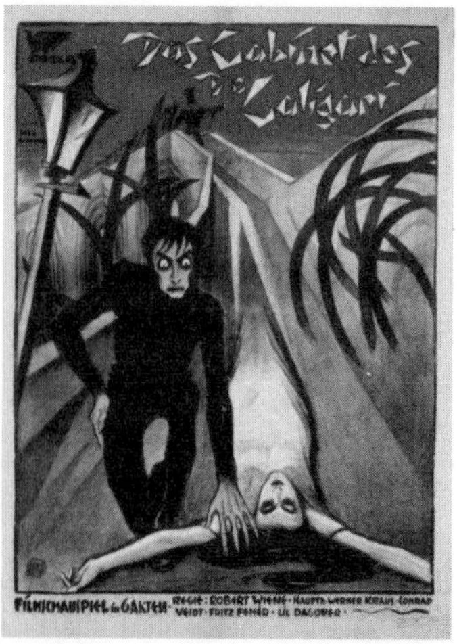

The Cabinet of Dr. Caligari (1920)

One of the milestones in the horror genre and a film which has been serenaded quite openly is *The Cabinet of Dr. Caligari* (1920). This silent and black and white film was made in Germany in collaboration with artists and intellectuals. The film made by director Robert Wiene (1873–1938), tells the story of two friends and the fiancée of one of them. Dr Caligari is a fortune teller and uses a somnambulist to tell the fortune of his clients. The somnambulist sleeps in a coffin belonging to Dr Caligari and at night wanders around killing people. The astonishing thing about this film is the strange backdrop made of criss-cross lines. Drawings of lines denoting cities, fairs, houses and the criss-cross lines showing roads, make-up and dress of the somnambulist, use of the shadows of the various artists all work toward giving a surreal feel to the film. In one scene, the apprentice/somnambulist predicts the death of the hero's friend and as predicted the friend dies a mysterious death the next day. This surely creates a feeling of terror in the audience. This film was responsible for influencing many films to come. A good artist has to face the fight with society and sometimes even ostracism for his/her works. The Nazi Party of Germany banned Robert Wiene's film *Typhoon* (1933), he left Germany soon after and settled in France.

A film which was able to create fear in the audience's mind by using dark scenes and shadows was *Nosferatu* (1922), directed by F.W. Murnau (1888–1931). It is based on the novel *Dracula* (1897), by author Bram Stoker (1847–1912). Many changes were made because the film was made without buying the copyright of the original novel. Even the name Dracula was changed to Nosferatu. After hearing the frightening story of *Dracula* the director decided to extend his imagination even further and dressed up the coach-man and even the horses pulling the coach in pitch black clothes right up to the nails of their feet. The costumes of Nosferatu, the long nails, the big fearsome eyes, walking style and the way he stared, had such a fascinating effect, that famous German director, Werner Herzog (b.1942), along with a reputed actor, Klaus Kinski made a remake of *Nosferatu*, named *Nosferatu: The Vampyre* (1979) as a homage to the original. To set the mood for fear and fright, the coffin in which Nosferatu lived was kept in a dark and dingy basement and the wood of the coffin was decayed and unkempt grass grew on the ground.

Another remake of *Dracula,* featuring American actor Bela Lugosi, was made in 1931. This film with special effects was very successful although the Dracula in it was not so terrible, but the facial expressions and dialogues made up for it.

Noël Carroll, a noted film scholar and philosopher, argues in his book, *The Philosophy of Horror: Or, Paradoxes of the Heart* (1990), that, monsters are the essential element of his conception of horror. As we know that in Indian poetics, where fear typically take a back seat and is never realized as the chief *rasa* deals with the concept differently as we see in the formulation of the *Nāṭyaśāstra.* Much of the conception of horror, depicted in Euro-American cinema, deals with the satanic forces and their tyrannies. It can be contemplated that ancient Indian system deals with the notion of fear, demons and ghost entirely differently, especially Śaiva or Śākta systems where such forces are nothing but different agents of power. To create fear or to frighten the audience, many tried and tested formulae have been used, viz. a headless body, bloodied face, pupils of the eye changing colour, light being streamed into an otherwise empty and uninhabited house, someone shrieking from behind, sharp weapons being bandied about and sometimes objects flying around for no rhyme or reason. The reason for using all these things has been the unconscious agony caused by unfamiliar objects, from which we discern fear and bodily harm. Many expert film-makers have grasped this fear psychosis and have experimented with scenes which create fright.

A film famous for creating fear from only costumes and make-up is *The Phantom of the Opera* (1925). In this film, an unidentified musician in disguise, kidnaps the opera singer and to get her love, keeps her in the dungeon like basement of the opera house. The golden period of horror films is the decade of 1930s; films like *Frankenstein* (1931), *The Old Dark Horse* (1932), *The Invisible Man* (1933) and *Bride of Frankenstein* (1935) are noteworthy. They were directed by an American, James Whale (1889–1957). It is quite strange that when this director, on getting bored of making horror films, switched to other subjects, his career nosedived completely. On account of acute depression, he finally committed suicide in 1957, by drowning in a pool.

Frankenstein and *Bride of Frankenstein* were notable in the ability to create fear, because of the use of frightening sets, costumes and styles of walking and dialogue delivery. Mary Shelley's novel by the same name is the idea behind this movie, in which a scientist, named Frankenstein, tries to create living beings from dead ones. One such experiment takes an ugly turn when the dead body is fitted with a killer's mind and then all hell breaks loose. The hilltop laboratory of the egoistic scientist, huge windmills, costumes of the characters, etc. and excellent marketing strategies put this film at the pinnacle of success. It was no doubt inspired by the fearsome scenes of *The Cabinet of Dr. Caligari* but it certainly went on to inspire many more films in this genre. Many legitimate and non-legitimate sequels were made of this film. When Orson Welles decided to make *Macbeth* (1948), he designed the palace of Macbeth similar to the hilltop laboratory of *Frankenstein*. In all respects, *Bride of Frankenstein* was far better than *Frankenstein*. In fact, the scientist in the film is compelled to make a bride for the monster and the costumes and hairstyling of the bride was praised and continues to be lauded till date.

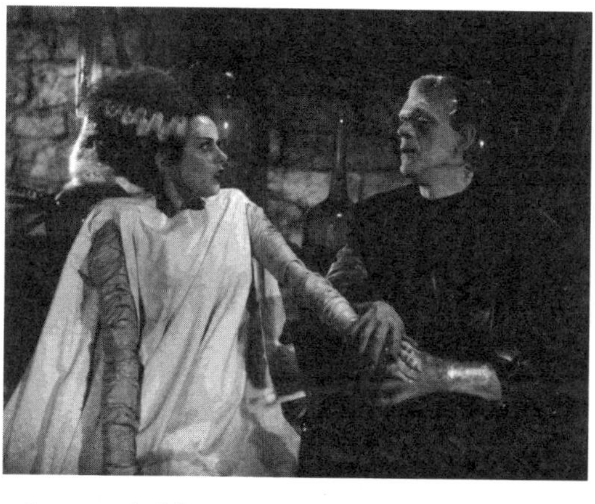

James Whale's *Bride of Frankenstein* (1935)

Many American films made in this decade, like *Dracula* (1931), *Dr. Jekyll and Mr. Hyde* (1931), *The Mummy* (1932), *King Kong* (1933) and *The Black Cat* (1934) were successful, much discussed and were able to scare the wits out of the public.

Director Carl Theodor Dreyer (1889–1968), who made the Franco-German film *Vampyre* (1932), set new rules and standards for films of Bhayānaka Rasa. His films were quite experimentative, for example, the shadow of a man leaving the body (difficult to ascertain whether it is the soul or one's thoughts), seeing his own dead body in a coffin, and a lame watchman seeing his own shadow leave the chair and wander up the stairs and coming back to place. These scenes played tricks on the consciousness of the audience. Many psychologists have tried to explain these films in many different ways.

American director Jacques Tourneur (1904-77), made a film *Cat People* (1942), which was noted for dispelling fear before it even incited it or let it reach the climax. The film is about a tribal woman who believes that in some special circumstances she has the power to turn into a panther. The technique in which the fear factor is steadily increased and then abruptly deflated in a film is called Lewton Bus, after the famous producer Will Lewton. The term derives its identity from a scene in this film where one woman is following the other and is expected to turn into a panther any moment. The camera focuses on the scared and bewildered face of one girl while the sound of a loud hiss is heard, the girl expects a panther, but it is just a bus pulling up – thus the name Lewton Bus. This technique has been used umpteen times since. The idea of eschewing the object of horror as explored in this technique is said to be originated in the literary works of ghost story writers such as in the famous short stories "Green Tea" and "The Familiar" of Sheridan Le Fanu (1814-73) and "Casting the Runes" of M.R. James (1862–1936). Interestingly, Jacques Tourneur adapted the latter story into his British horror movie *Night of the Demon* (1957).

Despite protests from the director and leading actors, a monster was actually shown in the movie which waters down the intended effect of the director.

There are three unforgettable films which use the concept of ghosts, spirits and witchcraft.

- Orson Welles' adaptation of the Shakespearean play *Macbeth* (the film is also named *Macbeth*) show the witches using Voo-Doo to systematically destroy Lady Macbeth. The smoke-filled background is different from the original play, but the three witches portray fear in a very realistic way.
- Japanese director Akira Kurosawa in his adaptation of the same play, in a film called *Throne of Blood* (1957), has been able to depict fear in such a way that it can make a person spend sleepless nights.
- Japanese director Kenji Mizoguchi (1898–1956), in his black and white tragic film *Ugetsu* (1953), has successfully depicted fear during a geisha dance by a cruel dancer, who sings the soulful ghostly song, using just frightening masks and the increasing–decreasing tempo of the musical instruments. Such mastery is unparalleled in world cinema.

Les Diaboliques (1955) is a French film made in the Alfred Hitchcock style, but by French film-maker Henri-Georges Clouzot (1907-70). Clouzot had bought the rights only hours before Hitchcock. In this film, the feeling of guilt after the murder, fear of being caught and mental stress are the main reasons for fear. A scene in the film, where a dead body walks out of the tub, causes a heart attack in one of the actors and is also responsible for the extreme fear caused in the audience.

Famous actor Charles Laughton (1899 –1962) made a solo attempt at directing; his film *The Night of the Hunter* (1955) is known for its storyline, picturization of fearsome night scenes, etc. In the film, a professional killer marries the wife of a man on a

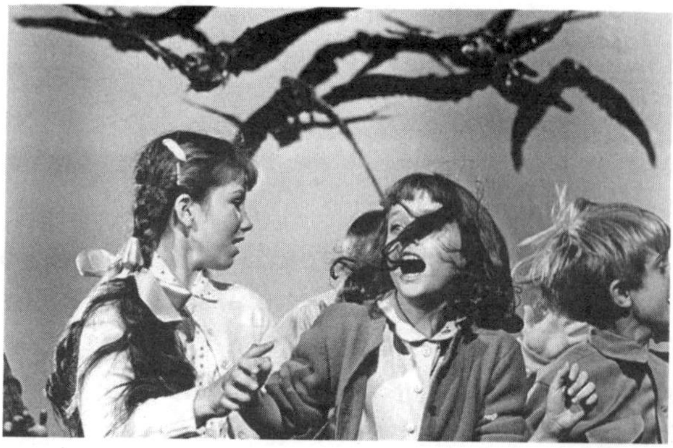

The Birds (1963)

death-row just to get his hands on the wealth of that man. He kills his obstacles one by one. The film, unfortunately did not win the appreciation of the audience or even the critics, but eventually was inspiring to many movies to be made. Charles Laughton ended his directorial career after that.

Alfred Hitchcock (1899–1980) has been the only film-maker in history who has made fear-inducing films without the use of ghosts, spirits or witchcraft. His films are based on murder, mysteries, wrong-doing and psychological behaviour of the human mind. Intriguing plots, the best soundtrack and gentle and polite dialogue delivery have been the forte of Hitchcock's films. *Psycho* (1960) and *The Birds* (1963) are two of his films which stand out in the fright-inducing genre. The scenes of the film *Psycho*: the strange house near the motel, the stuffed bird decorations in the uninhabited office, the melancholic music played in the background during the mysterious murder are scenes no Hitchcock lover would ever forget. This film is also remembered for the fear-invoking bathroom scene, where a woman is murdered and the pupils of her eyes are the centre of attraction so to say. This has to be the most discussed, artistic expression in the history of films. The Hitchcock's film *The Birds* is a magnificent example of how an innocuous-looking flock of birds can terrorise an entire town. In the film, fear is brought on by the attack of birds, for no rhyme or reason and the momentary loss of voice of the actress which is captured by the camera and magnified into intense fear.

Some of the older Hitchcock's films like *Rebecca* (1940), *Strangers on a Train* (1951) and *Dial M for Murder* (1954) have been experimented on for invoking fear, by using romance, commercially appealing scenes and soft-spoken dialogues. The one aspect common to all three films is pseudo fear. In the film *Rebecca*, a simple girl gets married to a rich widower but is tortured by the ex-wife's memories and the servant's rebellious nature. Her husband is also filled with an extreme feeling of guilt. Film *Strangers on a Train* is a story about how two strangers, who meet on a train journey, decide to commit murders to help each other out. They kill a tennis player's wife and then force him to kill his own father. *Dial M for Murder*, a film which has Grace Kelly, the beautiful Princess of Monaco, in a lead role, does not have any mystery about the murderer but the film revolves around how the murder is committed. This keeps the convicted heroine in a state of factitious fear. Ostensible fear remains a fear only until the truth behind it is not divulged.

Fear, borne out of not following laws and orders, has been quite the mainstay of Hitchcock's films. This has a history to it: Hitchcock was locked up in a prison for only five minutes by his father's police friend, as a punishment for being naughty; this left a deep and indelible fear in his mind. It is said that he made films of that nature only to purge himself of that fear. Some of his other films include *Shadow of a Doubt* (1943), *I Confess* (1952), *Rear Window* (1954), *The Wrong Man* (1956), *Marnie* (1964), etc. Whenever we talk about fear, apprehension or murder and mysteries, we invariably take the name of Alfred Hitchcock.

British film-maker, Michael Powell (1905-90) made *Peeping Tom* (1960), whose plot revolves around the thought in the murderer's head that the most frightening of all things is one's own accidental death. To film the greatest horror, he commits many murders. The film was dismissed by critics and Powell's career was finished. Ironically twenty years on, this film is listed among the greats of the world.

Italian director Mario Bava (1914-80) made his debut with *Black Sunday* or *The Mask of Satan*, original name *La maschera del demonio* (1960), that established mediocre archetype of gothic horror movies where a witch returns from her grave after two centuries to take revenge from his brother's descendants. This black and white movie was considered gruesome by the prevalent social standards and therefore was banned in the UK until 1968. This movie establishes a point that gory details become determinants to fear.

Based on Henry James' 1898 novella, British gothic horror black and white movie, *The Innocents* (1961) deals with anxiety of a governess who is trying to save two children from terrible ghosts who are friendly to the young. Although Henry James' narrative deals with confusion and uncertainty about dealing with evil, the movie depicts the ghosts in detail and creates a lasting impression. Building on similar lines of psychological horror in cinema, Robert Wise (1914–2005), made a British movie, *The Haunting* (1963) based on Shirley Jackson's 1959 novel *The Haunting of Hill House*. Robert Wise has earlier directed a horror movie *The Body Snatcher* (1945) based on the short story "The Body Snatcher" by Robert Louis Stevenson, which was the last of three movies where Boris Karloff and Bela Lugosi worked together. *The Haunting* was also shot in black and white, where a ninety-year old house on the hill has a tragic history and is believed to be haunted by the dead. The interiors were specially designed to create claustrophobic effect with unusual pans and tracking shot.

Great film-maker Satyajit Ray made a film based on Nobel Laureate Rabindranath Tagore's novel, *Mohinara*. The film *Teen*

Kanya (1961) tells the story of a witch who is enchanted with jewellery. The objects just at the entrance to her room, like the idol of an owl, skin of dead animals and absolute silence, all cause an agitation in the mind akin to fear.

What if instead of ghosts and spirits, one comes face to face directly with death? In Swedish director Ingmar Bergman's (1919–2007) film, *The Seventh Seal* (1957), the hero, while returning home ten years after the Crusades, meets death on the way. The very fearsome picturization of death, its costume: black clothes and a white face and the way death follows the hero throughout the film leave an absolutely unforgettable image on the viewer's mind. This film has been influenced greatly by Victor Sjostrom's (1879–1960) film *The Phantom Carriage* (1921). The film based on a novel by Nobel Laureate, writer Selma Lagerlof, was very well known for the special effects showing ghosts. Both these Swedish films effectively create the feeling of dread and apprehension, but also cajole the viewer to think and meditate upon the intricacies of life and the cycle of life and death. The hero of the film *The Seventh Seal* played chess with death and bargains for a few days of life from him. But

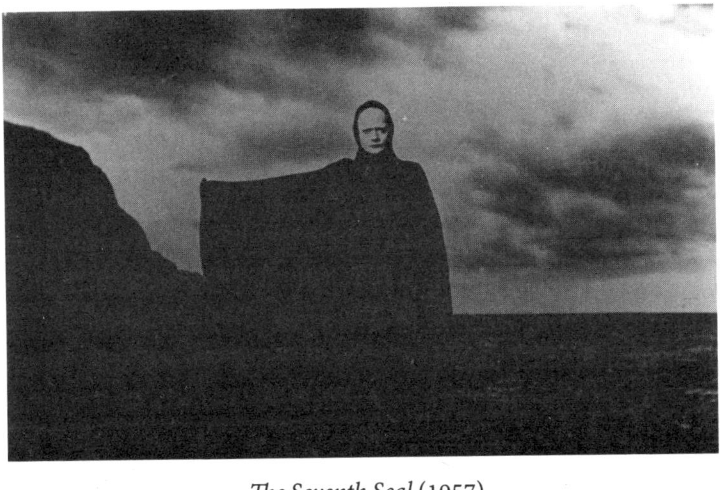

The Seventh Seal (1957)

has death lost to anyone till date? It is quite intriguing to foresee how Ingmar Bergman would have dealt with the mythological story of Sāvitrī and Satyavān. It is said that Ingmar Bergman was a non-believer and would not have made such a film. Despite being an atheist, he has made films which have remained incomparable. One such film is *Hour of the Wolf* (1968), original name *Vargtimmen*, in which one character creates intimidation by pulling out the skin of his face along with the eyes as though they were just spectacles and nothing else.

The apogee of fear is reached when a person gets scared or dreads even the most mundane of things. Let alone headless dead bodies or murder or ghosts and spirits, even the simple task of crossing the road can intimidate a person. This was achieved by Polish director, Roman Polanski (b.1933) in his film *Rosemary's Baby* (1968). A newly-married woman finds herself surrounded by strange neighbours and a crooked husband. She discovers she is pregnant by some devilish forces. She is tormented by loneliness and wonders how she can bring the baby up on her own. The director's vision and the actress' ability went a long way in establishing the true worth of this film. This film was a part of an Apartment Trilogy, made by Roman Polanski. The other two films were *Repulsion* (1965) and *The Tenant* (1976). All the three films dealt with fear-causing circumstances in city apartments. Two other films worth watching by the same director are *Chinatown* (1974) and *The Pianist* (2002).

The Exorcist (1973), made by American director William Friedkin (b.1935), is considered as the most frightening films ever made. The story deals with how a ghost/spirit enters the body of a little girl and the Christian ways to dispel it. The writer of the novel, on which this film is based, claims it is a true incident. The film has won world acclaim and has been very successful commercially too. It boasts of heart-wrenching, fearful scenes wherein the spirit is shown to torture the little girl's body, even rotating her head around.

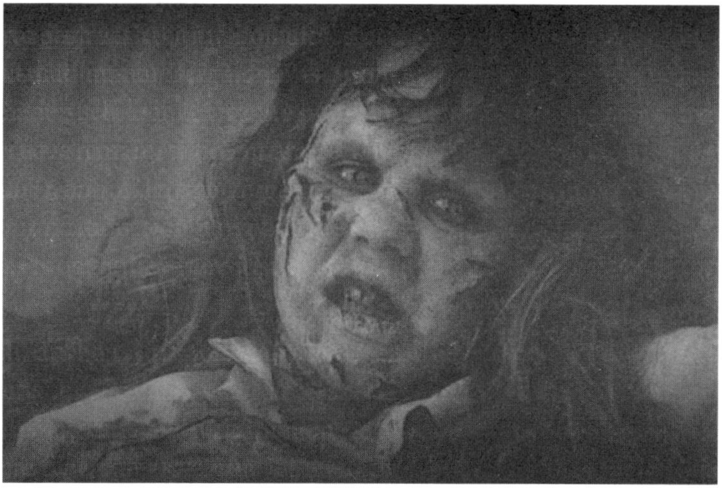

The Exorcist (1973)

Don't Look Now (1973), made by British cinematographer Nicolas Roeg (1928-2018), is a film which shows adumbration. To have a foreboding of imminent danger is extremely fearful and this premonition makes fear very mysterious. In this film, a father is devastated after his daughter's death, of which he had a premonition. Both parents are yet to come to terms with this tragedy, when they meet two elderly ladies, one of who is blind but has a strong sixth sense.

A man, in an uninhabited hotel, is taken over by spirits and is forced to murder his son and wife. This is the plot of *The Shining* (1980), one of the renowned films made by American director, Stanley Kubrick (1928-99). Helplessness against demonic forces are the root cause of fear, and in this movie, it is manifested with no (immediate) nearby help to son and wife.

Japanese and Korean film industries have been producing many fear and dread-inducing horror films, in the last twenty years. The plots of the films are generally the untimely death of young children and they turn into ghosts or spirits. Most of the ghosts shown in these films are blue in colour and are visible in less light or a darkened room. In these films, fear of being killed and the fear of being mutilated have been very impressively integrated. One film which stands out in this genre is Japanese film *Ringu* (1998), it has been serenaded throughout the world and is based on the folklore of Japan. Some of the prevalent techniques used in Indian cinema to create fear like murder, casting a spell on someone or cursing someone have been used in this film.

Let the Right One In (2008) is a Swedish film which revolves around the friendship between a 12-year-old weak boy and a blood-drinking vampire girl of a similar age. The good-hearted vampire teaches the boy how to fight with the injustices done to him. The boy then discovers the true identity of his friend. Technically this film has been greatly applauded. It can be seen as an example where the fearful element no longer remains scary if one makes an ally with the monster or the horror element.

Bharata Muni has alluded the feeling of fear or fright to a *sthāyī bhāva* or an emotion which is prevalent in the human mind. It comes to the fore whenever we see images of ghosts or apparitions, when we see wild animals, when we have to venture into an empty house or go to the forest, when we commit an offence against an office bearer or teacher, when we see the death or torture of our near and dear ones, or when we hear strange contorted laughter or voices, etc.

The *Nāṭyaśāstra* trifurcates Bhayānaka Rasa, viz.:

1. pseudo or fictitious fear,
2. fear born out of wrongdoing, and
3. fear caused by great trouble or hurt or tyranny.

Scenes which use pseudo fear have been done so to prove a particular point. Abhinavagupta says that fear springs out a sense of doom. Pseudo fear brings out the meek or lenient form of fear, whereas fear born out of wrong doing cannot be easily seen in all kinds of people (द्विवेदी 1992: 191-203).

Alfred Hitchcock was famous for films depicting pseudo fear and fear out of wrongdoing. Films which depict fear caused by ghosts/spirits/demons can be very widely seen. It essentially signifies the psyche and being of preceptors.

Expert film-makers do not make films only to intimidate the viewer, but to put across some serious thought. Ingmar Bergman made films to point out the complications in life, while Alfred Hitchcock made films which delved deep into the human psyche. They teach us the nitty-gritty of life; we must remain obliged to them always.

4

Rasa-Siddhānta, Vībhatsa Rasa and World Cinema

Let us go over some crucial points before we start our discussion on Vībhatsa Rasa. Some readers may argue that drama is not about victory of good over evil, nor is it a forerunner of pursuit of knowledge, a triumph of truth or blissful music as proclaimed in the earlier chapter.

It is also true that Bharata Muni does not take the side of good or evil in his treatise *Nāṭyaśāstra* (1.110-16), unlike the ethical discourse in which the righteous or preferred set of actions are contemplated and recommended (Shah 2007: 25; Ghosh 1950: 14). On a similar line, films do not carry the responsibility to teach that good wins against evil. One may have a confused idea that truth and beauty have some inherent correlation. The confusion can be compounded if one thinks that ethical practices are synonymous with objective truth or some absolute truth. The concept of beauty, which we hear of in *satyam, śivam, sundaram,* has not been mentioned in the Vedas or Purāṇas, thus it does not have the approval of classic texts. Probably the mentioned saying has its origins in a Greek sentence, which has been given a modern connotation. Although there is no theoretical protest against the sentence, but it is very important to understand its context to avoid the aforementioned confusion. That is to say, an objective truth or moral ascertainty does not directly build or participate in the active relishment of aesthetic beauty.

According to the *Nāṭyaśāstra*, it is only when human character along with happiness and miseries of the world is depicted on stage, that it should be called a drama. In the first chapter of the *Nāṭyaśāstra*, Lord Brahmā says that drama can be beneficial or detrimental, both to the gods and demons alike. Even so, it is expected that man will gain goodness alone through various kinds of knowledge. This is in no way mandatory, but traditionally, man has confidence over fellow man. Of course, it has been amply seen through the ages and in all countries that someone or the other has learnt evil alone from dramas and films, and have conveniently blamed it on the ill-effects of arts.

One of the main questions often put before aesthetics is the emphasis to be laid on and the effective way to communicate the ethical aspect and good qualities of films and other art forms. The debate on this can go on, but it is not in the purview of our subject, so let us confine our discussion to meritorious and complicated films, because we are being led from darkness toward the light of knowledge by the most intelligent people of this world. While trust or absence of excessive doubt is very important to learning, the truthfulness of knowledge can only be ascertained after the process of learning is done with. Therefore, even though the phrase *satyam, śivam, sundaram* has been brought into our usage from outside, it doesn't oppose the doctrines of Indian philosophy and a certain ambiguity remains in the use of these words. Truth is ageless, but to say that truth is both beautiful and timeless is complicated because of the various connotations it takes on in various situations. Let the reader establish the sanctity of this phrase. It may be possible that our entire discussion can be termed illogical or discordant with philosophy and hence may be dismissed by some perspective. Let us then proceed with an open mind and learn something new, even with the risk of being dismissed entirely.

The Doctrine of the Expression of Rasa in Drama

Let us re-examine the theories of *rasa* and *sthāyī bhāva* as per the *Nāṭyaśāstra* and *Abhinavabhāratī*. The study of Bhayānaka Rasa led us to understand that to feel fear we must have some reasons, for example, an uninhabited place, ghosts and spirits and the fear of impending or approaching death, etc. These inherent reasons by which we enjoy the manifestation of *rasa* are called *vibhāva*. These *vibhāva*s are also called as signifiers or determinants. They are of two types – (a) *ālambana* (supporting reasons), they bring the viewer nearer to the meaning, and (b) *uddīpana* (inciting reasons), they increase the effect of the expression.

It is these *vibhāva*s which help in the expression of all the emotions in the viewer. The meaning which emerges when *vibhāva*s are characterized into words, bodily actions and mental or psychological acting, they are credited into becoming feelings (*bhāva*s). With the aid of various forms of acting, they are able to arouse the *rasa*, hence they are called as *bhāva*s (द्विवेदी 1992: 237-49).

In a drama, the actors depict these intrinsic sentiments through wordplay and bodily actions; these are called as *anubhāva*s (effects or consequents) of the drama. Primarily, the bodily actions which help depict the inner feelings or sentiments are called *anubhāva*s. The consequents are shown through facial expressions or body expressions, although they deal with the feelings pertaining to the mind. *Anubhāva* (effect of the manifestation) of the *rasa* does not happen after the sentiments are felt or are registered in the mind, they happen along with the feelings felt, i.e. the sentiment and the action/effect of the sentiment go hand in hand. Abhinavagupta explains that *anubhāva* and *bhāva* are born together and also terminate together. But, because these are made perceivable through the acting done on stage, they are called as *anubhāva*

(द्विवेदी 1992: 251-53). For example, to demonstrate the effects of Bhayānaka Rasa, the actors in a drama are shown to scream, shout or fall down unconscious, etc. All this is *anubhāva*.

Acting has been recognized to have four forms; communication using gestures and actions, using dialogues, communication by wearing different costumes and lastly communication made more potent by evoking the quality of inner involvement, i.e. using physio-psychological acting. Of these, only bodily actions or using grand dialogues do not bring about the desired effect in the heart and mind of the spectator, even the physio-psychological acting is also necessary to bring the *anubhāva* into effect.

The *bhāva*s are of three types:

1. *Sthāyī bhāva*s (dominant sentiments) are of eight types.
2. *Vyabhicārī bhāva*s (transitory sentiments) are of thirty-three types.
3. *Sāttvika bhāva*s (involuntary physio-psychological sentiments) are of eight types.

There is an important *śloka* explaining these feelings: If the meaning of the drama or film touches the heart of the spectator and is able to overwhelm him, then it can be said without a doubt that the manifestation of the *rasa* is complete, that he is feeling so is because his being is pervaded by *rasa*, just as dry wood ignites the minute it is lighted (द्विवेदी 1992: 254). Here, it is imperative to understand that those meanings, which are not able to affect the heart, are also not able to realize the *rasa* at all.

The *vyabhicārī bhāva*s (transitory feelings) are of thirty-three types and this has been gleaned from the ancient Indian dramas, because the *Nāṭyaśāstra* does not describe all the manifestations and feelings item-wise. These are as follows:

1. *nirveda* (self-disparagement),
2. *glāni* (remorse),

3. *śaṅkā* (doubt),
4. *asūya* (jealousy),
5. *mada* (arrogance),
6. *śrama* (hard work),
7. *ālasya* (lethargy),
8. *dainya* (abject humility),
9. *cintā* (retrospection),
10. *moha* (delusion),
11. *smr̥ti* (remembrance),
12. *dhr̥ti* (calmness),
13. *vrīḍā* (shyness),
14. *capalatā* (inconsistency),
15. *harṣa* (delight),
16. *āvega* (impulsiveness),
17. *jaḍatā* (stupor),
18. *garva* (pride),
19. *viṣāda* (despair),
20. *utsukatā* (curiosity),
21. *nidrā* (sleep),
22. *apasmāra* (forgetfulness),
23. *supta* (sleepiness),
24. *vibodha* (awakening),
25. *amarṣa* (impatience),
26. *avahitya* (dissimulation),
27. *ugratā* (ferocity),
28. *mati* (determination),
29. *vyāḍi* (illness),

30. *unmāda* (madness),

31. *maraṇa* (death),

32. *trāsa* (fright), and

33. *vitarka* (wrong argument) (द्विवेदी 1992: 269-311; Ghosh 1950: 125-43).

This serialized description is a sort of a useful list for actors and poets who want to bring forth a creative expression that can lead to the realization of *rasa* in the viewer. The number of *rasa*, the number of *vyabhicārī bhāva*s or even the number of *anubhāva*s is not our criterion, neither is it of importance in our study because the learned often brush-off the importance of such counting and go ahead.

The *sāttvika bhāva*s are the involuntary physio-psychological sentiments which arise out of our sensitive heart and mind; they are the physical expressions of the concentrated feelings of our mind, for example, tears and horripilation. Therefore, the feelings, which are born in the involved mind but are manifested physically, are called *sāttvika bhāva*s. In a way, *sāttvika bhāva*s can be called as *anubhāva*s, but in a true sense they are not so because *anubhāva*s are the consequents of the feelings born in the mind but expressed through actions, gestures and dialogues or song or dance. They are voluntary expressions of feelings. According to Bharata Muni, *sāttvika bhāva*s are of eight types:

1. *stambha* (paralysis),

2. *sveda* (sweating),

3. *romāñca* (horripilation),

4. *svarabheda* (feebleness or change in voice),

5. *vepathu* (trembling),

6. *vaivarṇya* (change of colour of face),

7. *aśru* (shedding tears), and

8. *pralaya* (loss of senses or fainting).

These are expressed without any effort, along with the *anubhāvas* (द्विवेदी और द्विवेदी 1963: 183-84).

According to the *Nāṭyaśāstra*, the amalgamation of *vibhāvas*, *anubhāvas* and *vyabhicārī bhāvas* help the complete manifestation of *rasa*. They help the drama to be successful. In a drama, the *vibhāvas* (determinant causes) are interpreted with the understanding of the *anubhāvas* (consequences) and *vyabhicārī bhāvas* (transitory feelings); the *vibhāvas* trigger the external manifestation and let the *sthāyī bhāvas* present in the consciousness of the spectator be consummated as the *rasa*. *Rasa* is said to be relished outside of an individual's personal life. *Rasa* and *bhāvas* (sentiments) are related to each other like a seed is to a tree. The tree grows from the seed and it is from the seed itself that another tree grows (द्विवेदी 1992: 101-07). Initially these sentiments are inherent in the creator/poet/author's mind and are conveyed through the drama into the heart of the spectator. How this feeling gets manifested into the heart of the viewer is a question which is apt for the aesthetic enquiry.

A more perplexing question arises, and that is, how can such sentiments overwhelm a large number of people at the same time and in a similar way? The theory of aesthetics (*rasa-siddhānta*) has the perfect answer to this.

According to Bharata Muni, whenever an apt determinant gets associated with an apt consequent, the *sthāyī bhāvas* (dominant sentiments) get expressed as the *rasa*. Bharata Muni says that some people having similar mental attributes, similar physical features and having great capabilities and attitudes such as grace, knowledge, virtue and skill become exceptional like kings, while others, who are probably less capable, remain subservient. Similarly, the determinants, the consequents and the transient sentiments are completely reliant on the *sthāyī bhāvas*. As a king is noble among men and a *guru* is higher than his students, so also, the *sthāyī bhāva* is the most exceptional among all sentiments (द्विवेदी 1992: 257). Abhinavagupta agrees with Bharata Muni who says that it is the *sthāyī bhāva* which ultimately forms the *rasa*. But, Abhinavagupta negates the other philosophers who had previously postulated that *sthāyī bhāva* gets degenerated into *rasa*, by saying that *rasa* can be recognized by the *sthāyī bhāva* it is associated with. The *rasa* and the attendant *sthāyī bhāva* are as follows:

Rasa	*Bhāva*
• Bhayānaka	*Bhaya* (fear)
• Vībhatsa	*Jugupsa* (hideousness)
• Adbhuta	*Vismaya* (wonderment)
• Vīra	*Utsāha* (heroism)
• Karuṇa	*Śoka* (pathos)
• Raudra	*Krodha* (anger)
• Hāsya	*Hāsa* (comedy)
• Śṛṅgāra	*Rati* (eroticism)

Apart from these, in poetic criticism, traditionally three more *rasa*s are discussed, they are: *śānta rasa* (peace) which according to Abhinavagupta is the fundamental *rasa*, *vātsalya rasa* (parental affection) and *bhakti rasa* (devotion). In some texts, there is a mention of *sākhya rasa* (friendship) too (नगेन्द्र 1969: 237-46). Instead of delving deep into the *rasa-siddhānta*, for our study of films, let us limit our exercise to the above-mentioned eight *rasas* only.

Abhinavagupta avers that *rasa* is not actually manifested in the sense of causal genesis but it is only implied or perceived by a spectator. *Rasa* is not formed anywhere, it is not present anywhere that it can be procured. It is simply an impromptu perception of sentiments which have formed in our heart and mind and which are accepted without any obstacle (रस्तोगी 2012: 273; द्विवेदी 1992: 58-61).

Abhinavagupta comments that the famous *rasa sūtra* or *rasa* formula is not the production of *rasa*, by which *rasa* is expressed or manifested, thus this formula should be understood as the process of '*rasa* identification' (द्विवेदी 1992: 74-77).

The non-worldly nature of *rasa* should be distinguished from the causality and epistemological discourse. Abhinavagupta argues that the determinant is not the cause and *rasa* is not the effect of this said causation in the aesthic apperception. If there is an absence of causation the effect should continue to exist, but in the case of *rasa*, the determinants continue to be essential for the *rasa* manifestation. Similarly, proposition of knower–known relationship for *rasa* does not hold as the object to be known must be present before and after the establishment of knowledge, which is not the case here (द्विवेदी 1992: 78-80).

His exposition of the theory of *rasa* says that the determinants are easily accepted by everyone due to generalization of the sentiments (*sādhāraṇīkaraṇa*). Here the term generalization means that all viewers are affected in the same manner and at the same time. For example, in a drama when the protagonist enters the stage in the garb of Lord Rāma, the entire audience sees him as the Lord Himself rather than an actor. This is generalization per se. The emotions depicted in a scene are able to reach out to the audience depending on how well it is generalized.

Like in a drama, the realization of the *rasa* in a painting, dance or music depends on different sources. The philosophers of the *rasa* theory enumerate that a knowledge of notes (*svaras*), tune (*laya*), and beats (*tālas*) act as the enhancing determinants for enjoying the music, the supporting determinants help reflect the oscillations of the consciousness and the mental dispositions are the sentiments which lead to the relishing of the *rasa* in music (पाण्डे 2003: 79-80).

Bharata Muni says that the embodiment of Bhayānaka Rasa becomes evident whenever there is a display of the following transient and psychological sentiments: sweating, horripilation, trembling of voice, death, change of colour of face, paralysis or fear. Similarly, Vībhatsa Rasa becomes evident through the following sentiments: forgetfulness or loss of memory, illness, madness, despair, loss of senses, death, fear, etc. (द्विवेदी 1992: 196-98).

Hideous (Jugupsā) Sentiment and Vībhatsa Rasa

Let us now discuss the hideous sentiment through which Vībhatsa Rasa is recognized. Leading contemporary Indian philosopher, Arindam Chakrabarti (2002), has mentioned Saadat Hasan Manto's short story "Jelly" in his article on Vībhatsa Rasa. Let us study the story, "Jelly":

> At six o'clock one morning, near a petrol pump, a man who was selling ice on a hand-cart was stabbed with a knife and killed. His dead body lay on the street till seven o'clock and the ice on the cart was melting and dripping slowly onto his body. At quarter past seven, the police came and took away the dead body. The cart and the ice were left behind. A horse cart drove past and the child sitting in it saw the shining clots of blood and his mouth watered. He pulled at the sleeve of his mother's dress and pointing to the coagulated blood exclaimed, "Look mummy! Jelly".

This scene shows the hideous picture of a dead body and a vague sort of repulsion toward it. The child referring to the blood clots as "jelly" shows a tendency towards cannibalism. According to Abhinavagupta, a hideous scene in a drama gives an extraordinary feeling of having relished a deep emotion wherein the immortality, ephemeral and dissipatory nature of the human being, is brought to the fore. According to Bharata Muni, the hideous or repulsive sentiment which is the *sthāyī bhāva* of Vībhatsa Rasa can be determined or is manifested when we see, hear and discuss, smell, taste, touch and speak about unacceptable, obnoxious, undesirable, malignant, virulent things (द्विवेदी 1992: 197).

According to Bharata Muni, Vībhatsa Rasa is of two types:

1. *Distasteful* (Udvegī) *or manifestation of the* rasa *due to anxiety:* the determinants for this are human body waste

such as urine, faeces, vomit, worms from body and dribbling of saliva. These give rise to extreme hatred and disgust. The heart gets jolted when such repulsive things are seen.

2. Kṣobhaja Vībhatsa *or the manifestation of the* rasa *due to the extreme agitation caused to the heart and mind*: The determinants for this are seeing blood, intestines being pulled out or pictures of dead bodies, etc. (द्विवेदी 1992: 204).

It is quite natural to ask here whether Vībhatsa Rasa can actually be relished. Why did the ancient Indian aesthetic philosophers brand it as a different *rasa*? How can something which causes such intense disgust and repulsion qualify as a thing of beauty?

Through this theory, we are not studying the beauty of nature. We are not bothered about why the early morning sunrise feels so blissful? Why clouds and rivers enchant our heart thus? Many philosophers have wondered and thought about relishing human art rather than nature's beauty. It is certainly a faulted human tendency, where many men and women, instead of helping an accident victim get medical help, stand around clicking pictures or making videos of suffering as though seeking aspects of beauty there too. This is nothing but a faulty thought process or dereliction of duty.

A creator/poet/author has to try very hard to bring the intended feelings into the heart of the spectator/reader/listener. In some cases, the actor has to use the determinants of the Vībhatsa Rasa to convey his message. To show that war can be horrible, murder can be nefarious, madness can be disgusting, dramatists and film-makers use Vībhatsa Rasa. There is a world of difference between *vībhatsa* and common street fight. When the zenith of violence is able to show the effects of extreme disgust on the body then it is truly repulsive. Therefore, the rape scene in the B.R. Chopra directed *Insaaf ka Tarazu* (remake of American film *Lipstick* – 1976) and the repulsive antics of the hero in famous American director,

Stanley Kubrick's (1928-99) film, *A Clockwork Orange* (1971) do not come under the purview of disgust. Many Hollywood films have shown repulsive scenes like killing and mutilating bodies to be as easy as eating ice-cream. Some famous examples of slasher movies are: *Cannibal Holocaust* (1980), *The Thing* (1982) and *Saw* (2004). Similarly, much discussed film, *The Exorcist* (1973) shows a scene, wherein a small girl who is in the grip of an evil spirit, vomits a green liquid on the priest. This is to create a fear of spirits in the heart of the priest and is not a repulsive scene showing Vībhatsa Rasa. As we know, not a single drama or film can depict the emergence of one particular *rasa*, so we shall study films made by experts whose aim is not to shake or jolt the viewer and manifest the sentiment of repulsion, but much much more.

Unsavoury Disgust (Udvegī Vībhatsa)

While on the topic of distasteful and unpalatable films, it is imperative to discuss two outstanding, but difficult to understand, extremely gifted but impalpable film directors. They have been keenly associated with literature and have made arduous films which have withstood the test of time. They are: Italian director, thinker, poet, journalist – Pier Paolo Pasolini (1922-75) and American director, David Lynch (b.1946).

Pier Paolo Pasolini was quite notorious for his revolutionary Marxist political views. His prominent films are: *The Gospel According to St. Matthew* (1964), *Edipo Re* (1967), *Teorema* (1968), *Boccaccio's Decameron* (1971), *Chaucer's Canterbury Tales* (1972), *Il Fiore Delle Mille e Una Notte* or *The Flower of 1001 Nights* (1974) and *Salo o le 120 Giornate di Sodoma* or *The 120 Days of Sodom* (1975). If anyone watches, *Teorema* or *The 120 Days of Sodom* before watching his films *The Gospel According to St. Matthew* and *The Flower of 1001 Nights*, they will for sure name Pasolini mad, neurotic or unrighteous. *The 120 Days of Sodom* was based on Marquis de Sade's infamous love novel. Just days before the

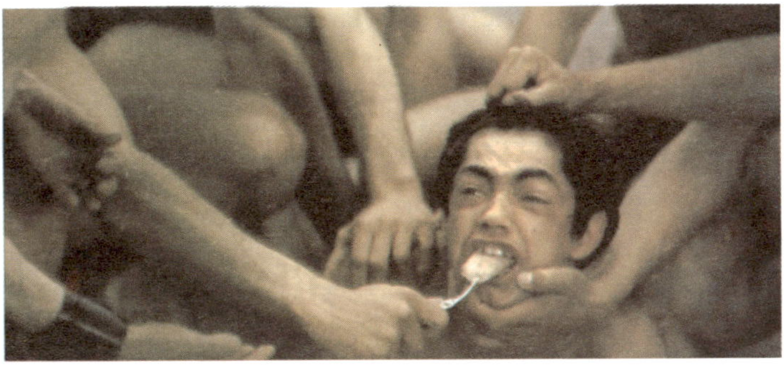

Pasolini's *The 120 Days of Sodom* (1975)

release of this film, Pasolini was murdered quite brutally and repulsively by being crushed many times by his own car. The reason for the murder remains unknown. Marquis de Sade was a politician and spent the last thirty-two years of his life in a mental asylum. The word "sadism" (sadomasochism) is credited to him, it means the perverse sexual pleasure one gets when he/she sees someone afflicted by physical pain.

Pasolini's last film astounds critics and viewers alike. Even today many countries have banned *The 120 Days of Sodom*. Many critics have termed it as one of the most exceptional films of the world. Pasolini has based this film in twentieth-century fascist Italy, instead of eighteenth-century France. In the film, many youth are taken prisoners by powerful bureaucrats, defence authorities, judges and security officials of the priests and are kept in a large palace. The youth are then subjected to distasteful sexual abuse by the powerful and reputed authorities with the help of some prostitutes. One disgusting scene shows that the imprisoned youth are being fed human excreta, to make this look real Pasolini used black chocolate. To show the mental perverseness of the fascists, the tongues of the youth were cut and the eyes gauged out before they were hanged to death, this last scene of the film is the most repulsive. This is not a pornographic film because nobody can derive any kind of sexual pleasure from watching it. Western film enthusiasts and critics have tried in vain to classify it as a "horror" film. This is an artistically important film which invokes pure disgust and repulsion in the viewer. This film is also a mockery on fascist ideology and industrially made foodstuff like biscuits and noodles. It is also a matter of concern that if such films are not seen then how its message can reach people. It is opportune to remember a quote by Franz Kafka in this context:

> I think we ought to read only those kind of books that wound or stab us. If the book we're reading doesn't wake us up with a blow to the head, what are we reading for? So that it will make us happy, as you write? Good Lord, we would be happy precisely if we had no books, and the kind of books that make us happy are the kind we could write ourselves if we had to. But we need books that affect us like a disaster, that grieve us deeply, like the death of someone we loved more than ourselves, like being banished into forests far from everyone, like a suicide. A book must be the axe for the frozen sea within us. That is my belief.

This debatable film by Pasolini, aims to do just that.

David Lynch was greatly influenced by writer Franz Kafka, Russian writer Nikolai Gogol and the Indian Upaniṣads. He is well known for films like: *Eraserhead* (1977), *The Elephant Man* (1980), *Blue Velvet* (1986), *Twin Peaks: Fire Walk with Me* (1992), *Lost Highway* (1997), *Mulholland Drive* (2001) and *Inland Empire* (2006).

The repulsive sentiment has been very well captured in the film *Eraserhead*. In a scene of this futuristic film it is shown that when the protagonist is eating chicken with his family, the cooked chicken gets up and starts walking and while walking it starts bleeding. The hero's girlfriend doesn't want to take the responsibility of their newborn child and leaves them and goes away. The form and appearance of the newborn child is quite disgusting and distasteful; it has a snake-like face, his body swathed in bandages, a thin neck, death-like expression on the face, etc. Psychologist Sigmund Freud's theories are the mainstay of the story of this film. In the end, Henry,

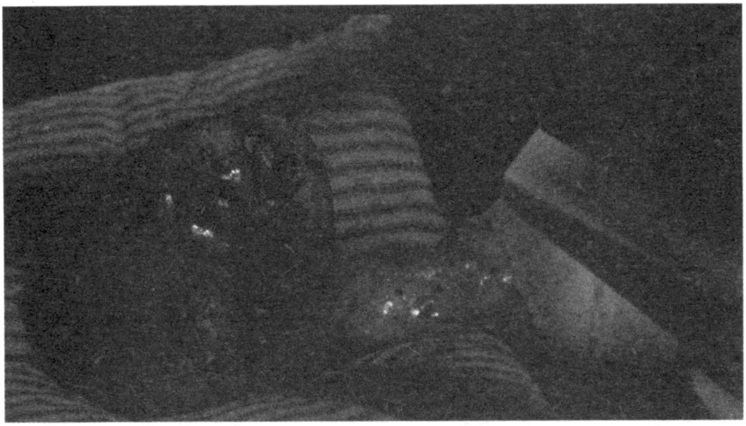

David Lynch's *Eraserhead* (1977)

the protagonist, cuts off all the bandages from his child's body, it is quite loathsome to find out that the internal organs of the child are actually held together by the bandages. When the child starts screaming, the father stabs the child with the scissors in his hand and then instead of the expected red blood, a different fluid starts flowing out.

In much the same way in the film *The Elephant Man*, the hero is shown to have some physical deformity and the film *Blue Velvet* starts with the meeting of two cut-off ears, travelling into the secretive underworld. These films try to awaken the repulsive feelings through the grotesque scenes. Instead of dialogues, David Lynch would rather måke a film which has a bizarre storyline, handicapped bodies, etc.

Come and See (1985) is a Belarussian film which depicts the horrors of the Second World War. Through the life story of a youth the hideous sentiment has been captured in the film. The story is about Nazi crimes against Jews, the young boy, who is ready to fight the Nazis, comes face to face with the murder of his mother and twin sisters. He also sees the dreadful scenes of death, when along with some Russian soldiers he goes in search of food. People being

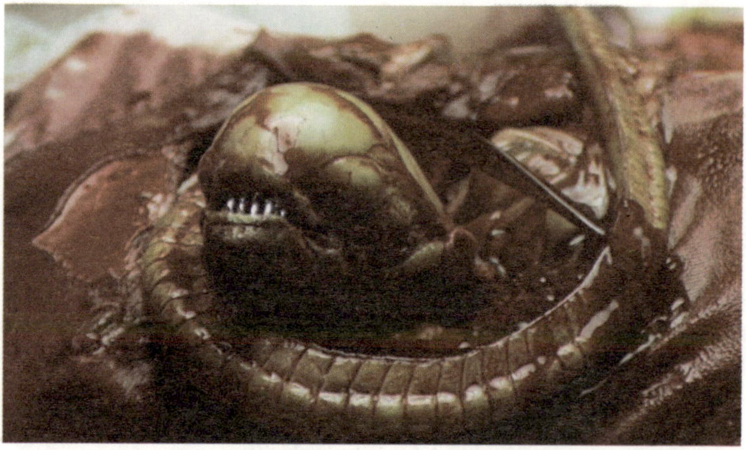

Ridley Scott's *Alien* (1979)

killed, animals being slaughtered, Jews being burnt alive are some of the ghastly scenes the boy witnesses. The film was a commercial success and has been enumerated as a great film world over. It has depicted the repulsive and disgusting scenes with a great aplomb. The director Elem Klinov (1933–2003) has not made any other film after this; he said that whatever he had to say and do, he did it in this film.

Manifestation due to Extreme Agitation (Kṣobhaja Vībhatsa)

American director Ridley Scott (b.1937) has made two films which show the extreme form of hideousness; the films *Alien* (1979) and *Hannibal* (2001) have been able to disconcert the mind with their disgusting scenes. The film, *Alien* is about how an alien mistakenly gets into the spaceship and traveling to the earth. The scene where the alien comes out of the stomach of an astronaut is the epitome of disgust. The hideousness shown in this scene has become unforgettable. If one reads the history of this film, it can be known that a lot of zoological study had been done on the form and appearance of the alien to film it most realistically, it was the hard work of a lot of technicians and the vision of the director and not just the story, which made this film such a huge success. Director Ridley Scott changed the character of Dr Hannibal, when he made the second part of the famous film *The Silence of the Lambs* (1991). The end of the film shows an extremely unpalatable scene, wherein a devilish character acts as Dr Hannibal and cuts open one man's skull, cuts a piece of his brain and fries it and serves it to him. The background music used for the scene, the filmography and the actress' helplessness is worth watching to understand the feeling of repulsion and disgust which are manifested in the film.

Danish director Lars von Trier (b.1956) is also known for making unsavoury and disgust-filled films. Two of them, *The Element of Crime* (1984) and *Dancer in the Dark* (2000), are much discussed and remembered films. One of his films *Antichrist* (2009) deals with the feeling of guilt a couple faces after the death of their only child. To deal with their depression, they retreat to a cabin in a forest. The wife, in a fit of madness, makes a hole in her unconscious husband's foot and ties a stone to it. She is shown to cut-off her delicate body parts to assuage the feeling of guilt, in the end she is afflicted by her husband. The film has been named *Antichrist* as it is a challenge to the religious values of Christianity. The film tries to show that the world has been created by the devil instead of God and that the nature is a temple of the devil. In this very attempt the film crosses the genre from horror to the hideous. Abhinavagupta says that the philosophy behind the determinants for the realization of the hideous sentiments is the root cause for the manifestation of fear and horror.

Pure Disgust

Bharata Muni considers Kṣobhaja Vībhatsa as the pure form of disgust, because these are the feelings that bring about hatred toward this world. Abhinavagupta's teacher, Bhaṭṭa Tauta, considers "Pure Disgust" separate from the other two forms of Vībhatsa Rasa because he avers that contemplation on disgust can help one attain the goal of *mokṣa* (liberation) (द्विवेदी 1992: 204-05). Bhaṭṭa

Tauta says that Udvegī Vībhatsa and Kṣobhaja Vībhatsa are impure forms because they have been realized through impure determinant causes. The thought that "time" and "death" are our greatest destroyers and that we are being eaten by our own food, will make us develop, a feeling of disgust toward our own bodies and wishes, these are the purest form of disgustive thoughts. They motivate a man to achieve the last goal of life, i.e. *mokṣa*. Abhinavagupta in his dissertation says that this kind of "Pure Disgust" is difficult to achieve.

Celebrated Japanese director Kon Ichikawa (1915–2008) made an award-winning and much discussed film, *The Burmese Harp* (1956). The film is a story of a regiment of Japanese soldiers, fighting in the Second World War in Burma. One gentle-hearted soldier, who also played the harp, gets separated from his mates and on seeing widespread death all around him, decides to become an ascetic. The defeated Japanese soldiers, on their way home, decide to look for their lost musician companion. The film was successful in depicting the influence of "Pure Disgust" or the thoughts of "time" and "death" on life.

Waltz with Bashir (2008), an animated film, made by Israeli

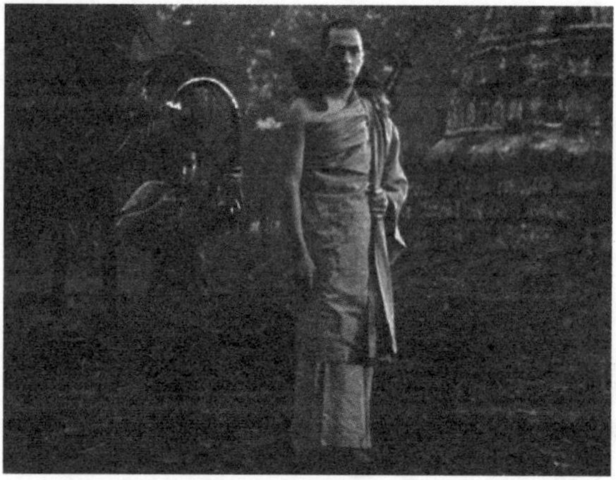

The Burmese Harp (1956)

director Ari Folman (b.1962), depicts the mental condition of a soldier fighting a war. After seeing death and dead bodies on an everyday basis, the soldier conditions his mind into thinking that he is watching a film. His thoughts let him do his duty unfalteringly. One day, however, he sees the hideous scene of many wounded horses moaning before death claimed them; it is then that the cloak of indifference falls away and he gets completely depressed. Although the entire movie is not about pure disgust, but certain powerful scenes bring the spectator's (perception) relishment close to pure disgust amidst otherwise sorrowful depiction.

In our interpretation, it is important to remember that happiness and miseries of the world and appreciation of art are two different things. Such a thought itself is the concept of beauty endowed with bliss, while Buddhists are against this concept as they think that form and appearance are physical and contemplative (जयशंकर प्रसाद 1939: 62; पाण्डे 2003). The concept wherein beauty brings bliss, and there is no unhappiness or sorrow is aesthetic relishing. The concepts which put forth that beauty can bring unhappiness have been refuted, and it is also outside the purview of this book. Here it is necessary to explain that the word "beauty" has been used to expound that "happiness savoured due to art" is different from worldly happiness. "Happiness savoured due to art" is the happiness one derives from creation. In Sanskrit literature, *vībhatsa* is generally seen in the description of a cremation ground. Some traditional philosophers of aesthetics state that the killing of an enemy by the protagonist is never hideous, only because the spectator believes that it is a natural justice done to society. But, aesthetics is not the study of common meanings and their entertaining effects; it is the study of philosophy and reality.

5

Astonishment and Miracle

Remarkable Films of the Adbhuta Rasa

Reading and understanding ancient philosophical theories is quite an uphill task. On the one hand, there are so many viewpoints and unique traditions and on the other, they all have such varied differences in opinions that in the rundown it is difficult to understand which word means what. What is referred to as the mind, consciousness, inner psyche, intellect and ego in the Sāṁkhya–Yoga may mean something else in the Nyāya–Vaiśeṣika system. Among the branches of the Buddhist school – the Mādhyamikas and the Yogācāras itself, the meaning of the word intellect (*buddhi*) is defined variedly. The word, *Īśvara* too is perceived differently in the ancient Vaiśeṣika and the widespread, ancient Sāṁkhya system (शर्मा 1995: 6, 155). It is indeed a matter to be thought about, as to why some people are adept at blowing the trumpets of their own cultures or are trying to belittle the cultures of others by asking them, "who are you?". It becomes imperative to question them about the meanings of the words that they so carelessly use. The philosophers of the world face a tedious task; they want to interpret the meaning of all things and thought processes in this limitless universe with the help of a limited number of words. This is precisely why a word has so many connotative meanings. Caution must, therefore, be used to understand the correct connotation. It is the reason that a commentary is typically subscribed to a thought system for an internal consistency with the rest of established ideas.

To understand the manifestation of Adbhuta Rasa one must understand the *Vismaya* (amazement) *bhāva*. Viśvanātha Kavirāja, an Odiya scholar of the fifteenth century, has called magic/miracle (*camatkāra*) as the synonym of astonishment: *camatkāraścittavistāra rūpo vismayāparyāyaḥ*: The miracle that the heart and soul feel when any awe-inspiring sentiment is seen beyond the perimeter of mundaneness is called amazement. It has been widely accepted that Sanskrit dramas mostly end with Adbhuta Rasa (द्विवेदी और द्विवेदी 1963).

Let us retrospect about two films before we go into the study of Adbhuta Rasa and world cinema. In 2011, director Martin Scorsese (b.1942) made a film, *Hugo*, in which he talked about the director of a 1902 film *Le Voyage dans la Lune* (*A Trip to the Moon*). Sixty-seven years before man stepped on the lunar surface, this eighteen-minute film which was influenced by Jules Verne's novel, showed that some human beings went to the moon and their lunar tourism was even opposed by the inhabitants of the moon. This imaginatively creative film, made on special sets, was in colour in some parts.

A twelve-minute, American film *The Great Train Robbery* (1903), depicted some people robbing a train and then some others following the thieves, catching them and killing them. In one scene in the film, a body is shown to be thrown out of a moving train. This was the first time that a dummy was used in movie making. Due to the radical use of technology and a great plot this film went on to become a great hit.

Both these films have astonished viewers. It is quite obvious that in today's age of technological advancement nobody will look at these old films. It is also true that to be dazzled or amazed one has to undergo a miracle. The film *Hugo* with its 3D effect was successful in doing just that.

According to the *Nāṭyaśāstra* for Adbhuta Rasa to originate, the following *vibhāvas* which are able to cause astonishment are mentioned: opulent palaces, grand entry into palaces, seeing any supernatural scenes or witnessing any magic. Abhinavagupta says that any sentence, artwork or action, which contains a very keen meaning, should be considered as the *vibhāvas* which help manifest Adbhuta Rasa.

Adbhuta Rasa is recognized as two types: (a) supernatural (*alaukika*), and (b) manifested through pleasure (*ānandajanya*) (द्विवेदी 1992: 205). In Alaukika Adbhuta Rasa one can perceive a supernatural occurring, while Ānandajanya Adbhuta Rasa talks about that kind of pleasure which one never expects to happen or which happens rarely.

Alaukika (Supernatural) Adbhuta Rasa

The history of films shows that many of the big-budgeted and commercially successful films are usually counted under this genre. *Pirates of the Caribbean*, *Spider Man*, *Harry Potter*, *Batman: The Dark Knight*, *Star Wars*, *Superman*, *James Bond Movie Series*, *X-Men*, *Lord of the Rings Trilogy*, *Matrix Trilogy*, *Transformer*, etc. are all films which depict Alaukika Adbhuta Rasa.

Many directors have tried to show the astonishing sentiment (*vismaya bhāva*) by using grandiose and huge sets. Many such projects have been quite successful. The most leading director of the silent era, D.W. Griffith (1875–1948), made the most expensive film of that time *Intolerance* (1916), in answer to the bitter criticism he faced after his extremely successful and racist film *The Birth of a Nation* (1915). This film showing extensive war scenes and the grand sets of the royal court of Babylon was made brilliantly. But the film company had to close down as the film was a flop. The grand royal court of Babylon sets, which were made for the film, had to be destroyed even though they had become quite an attraction for the local people. This film had employed 3000 extras and is even today considered an artistic achievement.

Unforgettable films like *The Wiery Death* or *Destiny* (1921), *Dr. Mabuse, the Gambler* (1922), *M* (1931) and *The Testament of Dr. Mabuse* (1933) were directed by German director, Fritz Lang. He also made the most expensive silent film of the world, at that time, *Metropolis* (1927). To recreate a feeling of amazement (*vismaya bhāva*) in the movie, Fritz Lang had used very opulent sets, huge factories, thousands of extra actors to represent crowds, a mad scientist – wearing a black glove in only one hand (one can see the effect of this in the film *Dr. Strangelove*, made by Stanley Kubrick in 1964) and even a female robot. Many difficulties were faced even while shooting this movie, for example, 500 small children were required to shoot for fifteen days in cold water, which in itself was a tremendous task. During the socialistic revolutions of the world, the director tried to pass on this message that the heart serves as a connection between the hand and the brain.

Frau im Mond or *Woman in the Moon* (1929) was an important

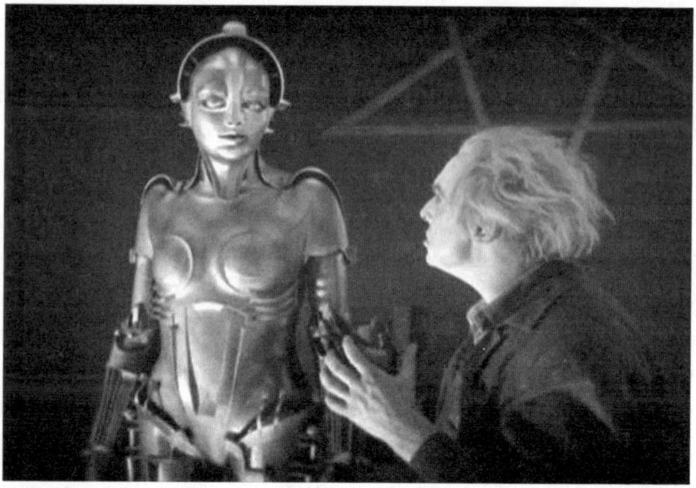

Fritz Lang's *Metropolis* (1927)

silent era sci-fi film, made after *Metropolis*, in which a space voyage in a rocket has been shown for the first time. The effect this film has left on future generations is so profound that even today all rocket or spacecraft launches are done using the "countdown to zero" system that was shown in this film. The rocket and space scientists of that time were the advisors in this project. The plot of the film revolves around how some enthusiastic people are trapped by conspirators, who want to travel to the moon to bring back the gold that is present on the far side of the moon.

It is quite astonishing to note that Fritz Lang's film *Dr. Mabuse, the Gambler* is a sort of a forecaster for the rise of the Nazi Party in Germany. This film depicts how Dr. Mabuse uses his voice, keen scrutinizing eyes, hypnotic abilities and with the help of a few trusted people, he is able to commit big crimes. It just shows how an artists' keen sense of observation can sometimes warn people of approaching dangers.

American director Victor Fleming (1875–1948) is famous for two of America's most magnificent films: *The Wizard of Oz* (1939) and *Gone with the Wind* (1939). Both the films are fine examples of Adbhuta Rasa. The film *The Wizard of Oz* is a musical fantasy film about Dorothy, a kid who meets unusual characters in a fantasy land. This magical film did not make much profits until the television broadcasts started in 1956 and it went on to be called as one of the most famous films of America. *Gone with the Wind* is an epic historical romance, which, even when adjusted for monetary inflation remains the most commercially successful film ever. The film shows an amazingly heartrendering scene wherein a homestead catches fire and is gutted.

One extraordinary director, who made an amazing film at the end of his remarkable career, is Cecil B. DeMille (1881–1959). His last film was the astounding *The Ten Commandments* (1956), which is remembered for its majestical sets, art and fantastic earnings at the box office. The film dramatizes the Biblical story of Moses and

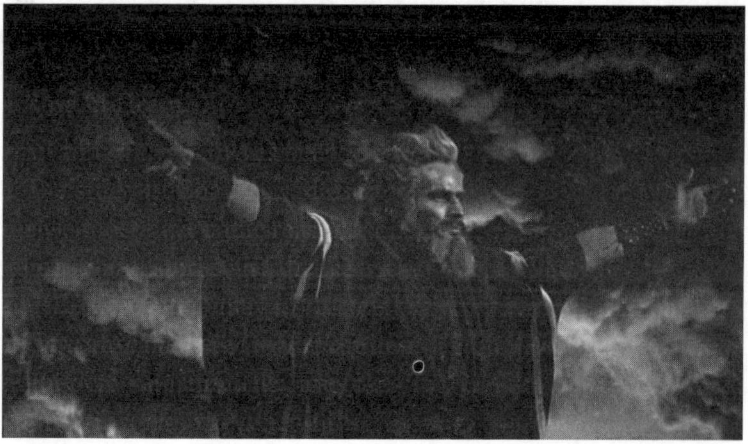

The Ten Commandments (1956)

the country of Egypt. The film showcases an in-depth study of the history of Egypt, use of new technology, the clothes worn almost 3,000 years ago, etc. It is also an experiment on how the pyramids were constructed, how the ancient Egyptian women used a metallic sheet as looking glass (glass mirrors were used only after the eleventh century and silver-coated mirrors only in 1834). One of the most miraculous scenes of the film was the parting of the Red Sea by Moses to allow the people to flee their enemies. The filming of this scene remains etched in the history of movie making.

American director William Wyler (1902-81) was known for his romantic and period drama films. His film *Ben-Hur* (1959), made on the life of a Jewish merchant Judah Ben-Hur, was the largest grossing film of that year and it won eleven Academy awards. The film is famous for the marvellous and dangerous chariot race between Ben-Hur and his one-time friend. It is a unique example of Adbhuta Rasa.

British film director David Lean (1908-91), who is famous for period drama films like *Great Expectations* (1946), *Oliver Twist* (1948) and *Brief Encounter* (1945), has made two beautiful and splendid films – *Lawrence of Arabia* (1962) and *Dr. Zhivago* (1965).

These films, apart from being opulent, were also a landmark in the artistic sense. The films took us through different countries and different situations, for example, in *Lawrence of Arabia*, it was shown that a dynamic man traverses a long desert, starts a guerrilla war against the Turks and in *Dr. Zhivago*, it was shown that after many years of separation, two lovers meet and the vast icy wilderness of Siberia give the film a magical, magnificent quality which has to be seen to be believed.

The maker of famous drama film *All About Eve* (1950), American director Joseph L. Mankiewicz (1909-93), is also known for the very expensive and grandiose film *Cleopatra* (1963). This six-hour long film was cut and recut to fit into a three-hour slot. This film incurred a loss of forty-four million dollars notwithstanding the fact that it was the highest grossing film of that year. Veteran actress, Elizabeth Taylor created a record for the maximum number of costumes she changed, i.e. sixty-five, when she played the lead role of Cleopatra in the film.

Julie Andrews (b.1935) played the lead role in the magical-fantasy-filled film, produced by cartoonist and film producer Walt Disney (1901-66) called *Mary Poppins* (1964). This film has time and again been associated with Adbhuta Rasa. Mary Poppins is a children's nanny who by her magical powers goes on different adventures with her wards. The film is based on the novel by the same name. Great music, superb editing and effective sets have made this film a much discussed and high-earning film in the world. Critics have rated this film as the greatest achievement of the father of Mickey Mouse, Walt Disney.

To make a big budget film, one needs a lot of money as well as courage to take huge risks. Japanese director Akira Kurosawa (1910-98) was contemplating the making of an ambitious and big-budget film called *Red Beard* or *Akahige* (1965); he wanted this film to be his most distinguished film, a sort of a divisive point from among all his films. Nobel laureate, Gabriel Marquez was a huge fan of this film. This great film was the swan song for the invincible duo of Akira Kurosawa and actor Toshiro Mifune. The two had had the good fortune of working with each other in sixteen films. Akira Kurosawa was not able to sustain the loss and this exceptionally talented director even tried to commit suicide. The maker of *Star Wars*, George Lucas (b.1944) (who has accepted the impact of Kurosawa's film *The Hidden Fortress* on his famous film) and that monetary help from the maker of *Godfather*, Francis Ford Coppola has helped him to make films in his old age. Kurosawa's last epic and also his finest film, *Ran* (1985), was made with the help of a French producer. Kurosawa had conceived the story and had already made the detailed storyboard of this film about ten years earlier. The film is about an old king who wants to divide his three castles among his three sons and retire. The scenes using the first two castles were shot on actual location, but for the third castle, which was to witness intense fighting and burning of the castle, Kurosawa decided to build a castle set which was as grandiose as the other two real castles. It is because of the intense hard work and big budget that such an exceptional film like *Ran* was able to compete with his other great films.

Let us now talk about two outstanding directors, who have been overwhelmed by Adbhuta Rasa. The opulence and magnificence of this *rasa* is incomplete without the mention of these two directors.

One is James Cameron (b.1954) and the other is Steven Spielberg (b.1946).

James Cameron made films like *Aliens* (1986), *Titanic* (1997) and *Avatar* (2009) on very big budgets and magnificent sets. *Titanic* was the most expensively made and highest grossing film of its time. To recreate the opulence of the real ship, Cameron used similar-looking carpets, crockery, furniture, etc. on the grand set of the film, he used the newest technology to create the effect of fright and despondency for the film. The portrayal of such a special equilibrium is akin to Adbhuta Rasa. Cameron has used either a risky plot or a love story for all his films.

Steven Spielberg has developed a special style to incorporate magnificence and amazement (Adbhuta Rasa) into all his films, which could be easily recognized. He directed amazing films like *E.T. – The Extra Terrestrial* (1982), *Jurassic Park* (1993), *The Indiana Jones Series* (1984, 1989 and 2008) and *The Adventures of Tintin* (2011). His films always showed scenes of astonishment like accidentally finding lost things or a speeding car being saved from dangers and obstacles, etc. He was able to entertain viewers with the amazing shots of the alien in the film *E.T. – The Extra Terrestrial.* He used life-sized models and computer-generated images to create a sense of miracle and wonder when he made *Jurassic Park*, a film on the lost dinosaurs, who inhabited the earth millions of years ago. We are indeed indebted to Spielberg, as he brought the discovery of scientists and historians to the general public in the form of entertainment, through an extremely artistic medium.

British director Ridley Scott (b.1937) made a heavenly or supernatural, American film *Blade Runner* (1982). To show the supernatural Adbhuta Rasa and the exceptional technology being used, the director of the "Star Wars Series", George Lucas, stopped the shooting of the film after three episodes till such time that the technological advancements were to his liking. Therefore, all the subsequent episodes of *Star Wars* are in tune with the advancements made in technology and the first three appear quite jaded. The film *Blade Runner* did not depend on the technical advancements at all. In this film, to build a residential colony on other planets, the help of biotechnologists is sought. But the life of these biotechnologists is only three years and they revolt against this. The film's story-line, cinematography and some philosophical problems all come together to create a sense of astonishment or manifestation of Adbhuta Rasa.

Yeelen or *Brightness* (1987) is an African–Malinese film based on magic and miracles. Director Souleymane Cissé (b.1940) tells the story of a thirteenth-century magician and his son, wherein the scallywag of a father, who is a magician, to kill his son carries a pure and miraculous log of wood on his shoulder on a long journey. The good natured, magician son, helps people through his magic. The "Jury Award" was given to this film in the Cannes Film Festival, for portraying nationalism, a historical view, duty toward fellow human beings and beautiful sentiments of wonderment. Nigerian writer Chinua Achebe says that African history must always be written by Africans alone, a European's version will never be able to do justice to their motherland. In the above-mentioned film, the director, through the medium of magic wants to show that European view and perception about African culture and customs is very biased and prejudiced.

Hayao Miyazaki (b.1941), a Japanese director-producer, who is famous for his animated films and as co-founder of Studio Ghibli, has made several animated films like *My Neighbour Totoro* or *Tonari no Totoro* (1988), *Princess Mononoke* or *Mononoke-hime* (1997), *Spirited Away* (2001)and *The Wind Rises* (2013). The film *My Neighbour Totoro* tells the story of a professor who starts to live in a village with his two daughters after the Second World War. The daughters befriend a forest dweller named Totoro. Similarly, in the film *Spirited Away*, a small girl accidentally enters the world of spirits and ghosts and rescues her father and mother and brings them back to the world of human beings.

Guillermo del Toro (b.1964), a Mexican director, made a Spanish–Mexican film, *Pan's Labyrinth* or *El Laberinto del Fauno* (2006), which was based on myths and magic. The film made on many Christian values was much discussed for its imaginative sets, make-up and different emotionality. It won critical acclaim from the world over. This film was influenced by many gothic stories, but the use of beautiful colours and excellent photography makes the film outstanding.

All the above-mentioned films have mesmerized and amazed

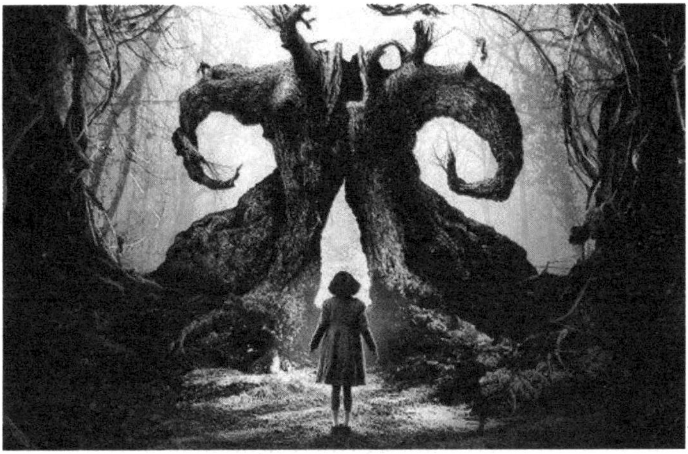

Pan's Labyrinth (2006)

people with the use of grandiosity and new technology. They are all prime examples of Alaukika Adbhuta Rasa.

Ānandaja (Pleasurable) Adbhuta Rasa

Just as there is a vast difference between hatred and disgust, so also there is a good deal of difference between surprise and amazement. The following example can explain it better – any conduct or behaviour that is totally unexpected is said to be a surprise, like the re-entry of a character, in a drama or film, who has been proclaimed dead. But when something totally different happens from what one has conceptualized, then, it is called amazement. This is generally taken in a pleasurable sense. When a poor man suddenly gets to see the inside of a palace, he is pleasantly amazed. When someone, who has never seen the beautiful forts of Rajasthan or the marvellous Sun Temple at Koṇārk or the majestic Kailāsa Temple at Ellorā or even the magnificent Cennakeśava Temple at Beḷūr, witnesses these marvels will feel astonished. It will leave him wondering and unexpectedly happy.

This kind of unexpected happiness is due to our five senses which trigger our mind into expressing this pleasure. The following are some examples of this kind of pleasure;

The film *Zerkalo* or *The Mirror* (1975), made by Andrei Tarkovsky (1932-86), gives the viewer an immense visual pleasure. The film is a loose flow of visually oneiric images. Noted film-maker Akira Kurosawa's film *Dreams* (1990) deals with magic realism. The film is inspired by the dreams which Kurosawa himself saw; it does not have a single narration but is episodic in nature. The description of two such episodes will give the reader an insight into the miraculous sentiments evoked through the film. In Japanese folklore, it is said that when the sun shines while raining, the foxes celebrate their marriages and perform a dance to signify it. A small boy unwittingly witnesses this celebration, and on his return home, is asked by his mother to commit suicide to atone for his mistake. The boy decides to seek forgiveness from the foxes and so goes in search of them. While on his mission, in the midst of a valley, he sees magnificent rainbows which completely mesmerize him. In the second episode, the ritual dance of the Doll Festival

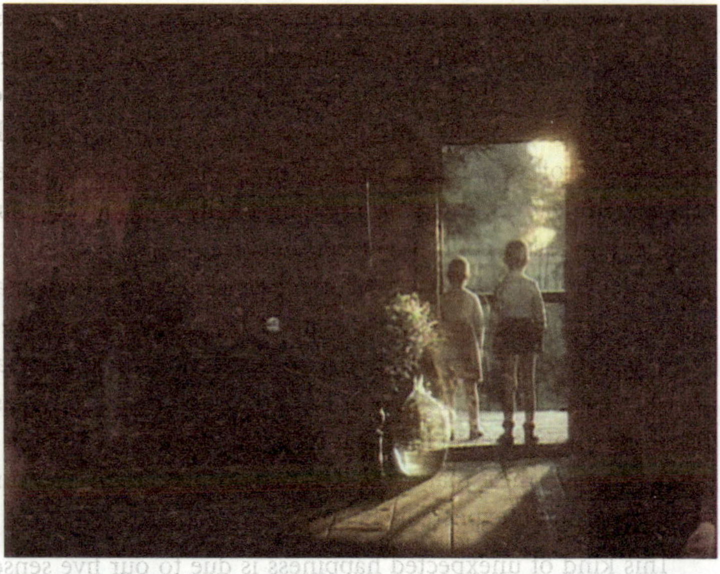

Tarkovsky's *Zerkalo* or *The Mirror* (1975)

or "Hinamatsuri" in traditional peach orchards is a symbolic representation of everlasting hope. The visuals and the story of the film, both are able to evoke the emotions of wonder and amazement in the spectator. Similarly, *The Lord of the Rings* trilogy (2001, 2002, 2003), made by American director Peter Jackson (b.1961), is known for its amazing scenes. The film *2001: A Space Odyssey* (1968), made by Stanley Kubrick, is unforgettable due to its magnificent scenes of outer space and spacecrafts. A Polish–Swedish film, *The Mill and the Cross* (2011), focuses on a dozen of the 500 characters depicted in Bruegel's painting of 1564. Each and every frame of the film feels as though someone has captured a brilliantly coloured, beautiful painting in a photograph.

Whosoever has seen director Vijay Bhatt's *Baiju Bawra* (1952), in which the famous acting pair of Meena Kumari and Bharat Bhushan were cast and the film *Tansen* (1943), in which the immortal singer-actor Kundan Lal Saigal sang can understand and believe the magic of music. Music can light a fire on plain water; it can light up an extinguished lamp and has the power to unwrap a closed bud to set the captured bee, free. Miloš Forman-directed film, *Amadeus* (1984), based on the great musician Mozart's life, is a keen example of Adbhuta Rasa. This film revolves around the last and the best composition of the critically ill, Mozart called "Requiem". A very few people are aware of the fact that Mozart and the almost deaf Beethoven, composed their music and wrote them in musical connotations without any editing before being played to an audience.

Babette's Feast (1987) is an Oscar Award-winning film, based on Danish writer Karen Blixen's (pseudonym – Isak Dinesen) story of the same name. The film is about a magnificent feast and the effect it has on the invitees. The exclusive meal, cooked by Babette, became so famous that some restaurants included her recipes in their menu. This film is a tribute to a great writer, even the Nobel Literature Committee has agreed that not bestowing the

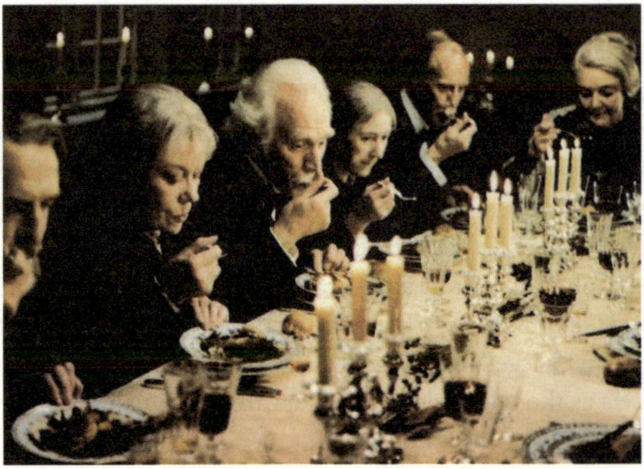

Babette's Feast (1987)

Nobel to Isak Dinesen was a huge mistake.

German director Tom Tykwer's (b.1965) film *Perfume: The Story of a Murderer* (2006) is based on the novel written by Patrick Suskind, *Perfume* (1985). The film is an amazing story of an orphan who is a superhuman olfactory genius; he can identify a person's natural odour even in a crowd. The boy uses this talent to make various kinds of perfumes. In his quest to make the most exclusive perfume which will get him everlasting love he starts to kill young and beautiful women in order to capture their natural scent. He succeeds in the end but is devoured by the crowd who want that perfect scent too.

Famous director Arthur Penn (1922–2010), who made films like *Bonnie and Clyde* (1967) and *The Chase* (1966), has at the start of his career, made a film on the life of a blind, deaf and dumb genius Helen Keller called *The Miracle Worker* (1962). This wonder-filled film shows how Helen Keller was taught everything using the sense of touch. Even though her teacher and parents had almost given up, she surprised them by uttering the name of her teacher by touching water. This miraculous scene was also adapted in the Hindi film

Black (2005), which was inspired by *The Miracle Worker*.

By seeing or reading about the above-mentioned films, we can surmise that many of these films can be categorized as the films of the heroic genre (Vīra Rasa). Sometimes, to call these films purely of the astonishment genre (Adbhuta Rasa) alone would be an exaggeration. Many of these films urge us to think and teach us new things. The association between Adbhuta Rasa and Vīra Rasa is somewhat like the relation between Vībhatsa Rasa and Bhayānaka Rasa. Some films of Vībhatsa Rasa have to deal with the frightening aspect of Bhayānaka Rasa, while some others don't. This is true for Adbhuta and Vīra Rasa too. But our aim is not to find and name the various *rasas*, only to experience and relish them.

Be it cinema or any other form of art, it is magical. A good poem, a melodious song, a pleasing musical composition or a comely picture – all are magical wonders. Anybody who can experience this magical wonder can never age. This is not a ridicule on old age, because traditionally old age is associated with the renunciation of pleasures and seeking of pure knowledge.

Voltaire (1694–1778) said that illusion is the beginnng of all pleasures. Art is a struggle which takes the refuge of many illusions and with the confusions present in the mind of men, leads them to the truth. To differentiate between the perception of entertainment and beauty, famous German philosopher, Immanuel Kant, gives an example; he says that if you are invited to a dinner party and there you find that good music is being played in the background then, it is only to help you pass the time and nothing else. It is only for entertainment and not a realization of beauty. Kant has differentiated between knowledge of beauty and knowledge. He says that knowledge needs to be assessed on the basis of truth and untruth, while the knowledge of beauty depends solely on imagination (पाण्डे 2003: 28).

It is imperative that instead of only colouring our imagination vividly, we must let the *rasas* pervade our hearts and minds. This will be the true achievement and meaning of art. The ability of superior art is to enable the heart to realize the emotions and *rasas* and let the mind realize the truth. Truth is complicated and difficult to comprehend; therefore, art has to use endless options so that it can continue to astonish people time after time.

6

World Renowned and Unforgettable Films of the Vīra Rasa

A friend, while discussing about this book, films and aesthetics, very enthusiastically suggested that I must include two films in which Hindi film actor Mithun Chakraborty has played the lead roles: *Jeene ki Arzoo* (1981) and *Pyari Behna* (1985). I was even berated for not having seen such wonderful remakes of the South Indian films, the former a remake of the Kannada film, *Hunnimeya Rathriyalli* (1980) and the latter a remake of the Malayalam film *Mullum Malarum* (1978). It is important here not to take my friend's fervour amiss. German philosopher, Immanuel Kant, says that in the conception of beauty, a person does not say that a thing is beautiful for himself alone but includes the whole world in his statement. Everyone at one point or the other thinks that what they find beautiful others will too, it is difficult for them to understand that it is not so. He has given a few theories on this aspect; which an interested reader must make an effort to read and understand, after all, knowledge comes from trying.

Kant says that if time is pleasurably spent, then it is entertainment. If he signifies entertainment as pleasurable and desirable, then beauty is said to be a complex amalgamation of imagination and comprehension. Following Kant-like thinking, many will dismiss commercially successful films as "only for entertainment". But the question which arises here is, whether people see films only to pass their time? If so, then a major aspect of films business, which has to do with the madness and wildness of people's behaviour cannot be ignored. For example, the Malayalam film *Harikrishnans* (1998) in which the lead role was played by super stars Mammootty, Mohanlal and Juhi Chawla, had to have two separately shot and filmed endings so that the emotional expectations of the fans of both the lead actors could be met. In one film, the actress marries Mamooty and in the other she marries Mohanlal. This was done to avert the madness with which fans worshipped their own individual idols (*Indian Express*, 12 September 1998). We have heard of instances from South India where heroes and heroines are worshipped and temples are dedicated to them.

Perhaps this kind of craziness is neither realization of beauty nor is it entertainment; it is in fact only a reflection of one's ego and attachment. More often than not the hidden desires to exhibit oneself in the name of heroism is displayed when they show this kind of rash behaviour about films. Such a petty meaning given to valour is attributed to the wrong connotation of heroism. Let us look at the classical meaning of heroism.

Bharata Muni, in his *Nāṭyaśāstra*, has identified three types of Vīra Rasa (द्विवेदी 1992: 203):

1. Dāna Vīra (one who gives *dāna*),
2. Dharma Vīra (one who adheres to *dharma*), and
3. Yuddha Vīra (one who fights the enemy).

This theory in the *Nāṭyaśāstra* may have been a contribution of many scholars, but we do see cohesion in all their views. Without much ado, all the *bhāva*s, along with their favourable *vibhāva*s and *anubhāva*s are duly listed. In the *Nāṭyaśāstra*, the congenial *vyabhicārī bhāva*s and the *sāttvika bhāva*s which will help realize the *utsāha bhāva* are enumerated as below:

- intelligence – *mati* (the perceptive ability of a wise human being),
- virtue – *dhṛti* (pleasure got from earning money, fame, gaining knowledge and purity),
- enthusiasm – *utsāha,*
- ferocity or rudeness – *ugratā,*
- impulsiveness – *āvega,*
- cheerfulness – *harṣa,*
- jealousy – *asūyā,*
- passion – *amarṣa* (arising on being insulted by an important person, mixed with anger and hatred),
- anger – *krodha,*
- *svarbhaṅga* (change in voice),
- *vaivarṇya* (change of colour of face),
- arrogance – *mada,*
- pride – *garva* (the obnoxious behaviour shown to others because of money power, beauty, social standing and fame: it may include not greeting others or talking with an indifference or insulting others), and
- argument – *vitarka.*

These *vibhāvas* do enumerate the qualities of a valorous person, but they certainly do not belong to a saintly person.

Among the eleven main Upaniṣads, *Taittirīya Upaniṣad,* which is a part of the *Yajurveda*, says that nobility in a person can be recognized by his good thoughts, ability to offer good counsel to others, be immersed in his own work and ethics, is of a gentle nature and adheres to his *dharma*. It further elucidates that a noble person can be valorous and a valorous person can be noble, but it is not necessary that both these qualities be present in the same person at the same time. Therefore, we must understand heroism or valour in reference to enthusiasm alone (शर्मा 2015: 103).

According to Abhinavagupta, Vīra Rasa can be identified by good character and enthusiasm as the *sthāyī bhāva*. It originates from the following *vibhāvas*:

- *naya* (prudence),
- *vinaya* (control on body and mind),
- *bala* (show of strength with use of elephants, horses, chariots and large army),
- *parākrama* (defeat of enemy in war),
- *śakti* (ability to go to war),
- *pratāpa* (the fame got by winning over enemies), and
- *prabhāva* (earning fame, money and prestige for the family through one's position).

The diligence with which a person feels enthusiastic without being oppressed or awestruck or even attached to anything is in the real sense enthusiasm (द्विवेदी 1992: 187-90).

Dāna Vīra Rasa

Some texts translate *dāna* as giving of gifts (Ghosh 1950: 117). Normally, the giving and receiving of gifts which is an age-old practice in many cultures is not allowed for religious persons. Many people believe that the giver is thought to be bigger than the receiver and so it is best to be detached from this kind of a game. In original Sanskrit, *dānavīratā*, is the first form of Vīra Rasa. This is the special meaning of *vīratā*, i.e. whatever one can give, one should give. The meaning of *dāna* is not giving to beggars or equating it to charity. *Dāna* is the highest form of giving, it means to give as a duty, things which are inseparable to oneself, to someone else who needs it more, forever. In the course of one's life, a person sometimes does get that kind of an opportunity, wherein he can give selflessly and this is the true symbol of a heroic person. Such

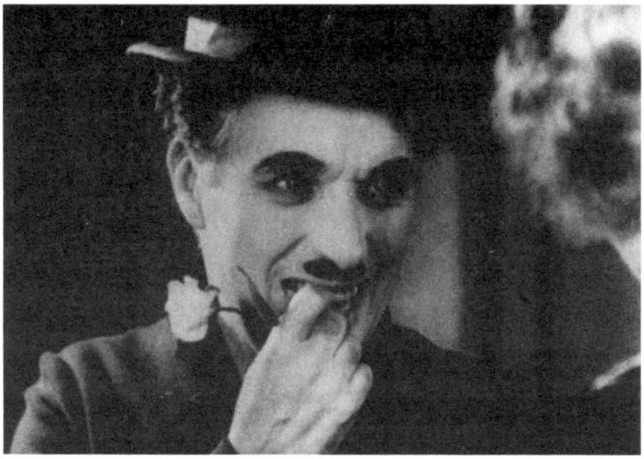

Charlie Chaplin's *City Lights* (1931)

valour shows the true character of a person rather than just physical strength. Sir Charles Spencer Chaplin or Charlie Chaplin, the great actor-director-producer, was a prime example of someone who understood the true meaning of this kind of heroic act of giving, as he grew up in abject poverty and was denied even elementary school education.

In 1929, with the coming of the movie talkies, everyone believed that it was the end of the silent movie era, except Charlie Chaplin, who made the most beautiful and his most expensive silent film, *City Lights* (1931). The opening shot of this film even mocks the talkies. *City Lights* is the story of a homeless tramp who in spite of endless troubles has a positive attitude toward life. A blind, beautiful and poor flower-seller mistakes the humane tramp for a rich man and Charlie Chaplin, in the role of the tramp, tries, in all possible ways to help the poor girl. He gives away various gifts to help her even though he has to face difficulties, at one time being jailed too. The last scene of the film, where the tramp meets the girl (after her vision is restored by a surgery paid for by the tramp) is one of the most touching in the history of cinema. It seems as though the whole world is crying for the poor but enthusiastic tramp. It seems as though all the lights of the city have come on and are applauding the valour and kindness of the tramp. People do realize that happiness is hidden in kindness and heroism.

This film has often been categorized as a love story by many Western thinkers. However, love and kindness have only accentuated the heroic deeds in the film, although the authority on which the affection is based is not true. Many of Chaplin's films are based on the heroic sentiment (Vīra Rasa). *The Kid* (1921) is one such film where Chaplin, as the actor in the lead role, takes care of a four-year old orphan, despite poverty, police atrocities and other difficulties. We must, through such a study, change the limited understanding of the word *vīra*, so that we can understand life better.

The Gift of the Magi and *The Last Leaf* are two famous stories of O. Henry which have been adapted into films worldwide. *The Gift of the Magi* is the story of a couple who are deeply in love and to show their love, buy gifts for each other during Christmas, at times selling their cherished possessions. These acts do not symbolize Vīra Rasa, rather show love. *The Last Leaf*, on the other hand, shows *dānavīratā* aptly. The old artist sacrifices his life to paint a leaf just to give eternal hope to young, ill-patient in the hospital. Hindi films, *Raincoat* (2004) is based on *The Gift of the Magi* and *Lootera* (2013) is based on *The Last Leaf*.

The director of the much talked about film, *The City of Lost Children* (1995), Jean-Pierre Jeunet (b.1953), made a French film *Amelie* (2001), about a lonely, introverted girl Amelie, who lived a fulfilling and zestful life by just helping people in need. In *Amelie*, the protagonist finds a very old compass box in her apartment and decides to search for the owner and gift him the lost compass box. When the owner, now an old man, receives an unexpected gift of something long forgotten, he gets into an introspection of his own life and decides to meet his long-lost daughter and grandchild to make amends. Amelie's valour and heroism lies in her kindness and the happiness she gives to people all around her.

A contender for the Oscar for Foreign Films, Iranian film *Children of Heaven* (1997), made by director Majid Majidi, tells the story of poverty-stricken siblings Ali and Zahra. When Zahra's shoes are stolen, Ali lends her his shoes and they swap them in the afternoon. To avoid being a burden on his poor father, Ali decides to take part in a race and come third as the prizes are a pair of shoes. The film does not show giving as a societal responsibility but as an act of kindness and love between the siblings. It is *dānavīratā* and the actor goes about it with an unmatched ardour.

Dharma Vīra Rasa

Karma (action) is the work done by a being using his knowledge for fulfilling his desires and by using his efforts. In *karma*, the effort put in is according to *dharma*, the knowledge used is in accordance with the *artha*, the desire to do the work is according to the *kāma* and the pleasure or displeasure got from the result of the work done can be classified as *mokṣa* or *mukti* (गोस्वामी 2011: 254-62). According to *Manusmṛti* 2.12, the work, done or action taken when *śruti, smṛti, sadācāra* and one's preference are satisfied or are brought together, is fit to be called as *dharma* (शर्मा 2015). Here *śruti* should be allied to the Vedas and Upaniṣads and *smṛti* should be allied to the Purāṇas and epics like the *Rāmāyaṇa* and *Mahābhārata* and *sadācāra* should be taken as the righteous behaviour of prestigious men who are in honourable positions in the society. At the end is the work which is liked by oneself and which pleases the soul. All this is the basis for *dharma*. Modern philosopher Ācārya Goswami Shyam Manohar-Ji, elucidates that *dharma* can never be against *nīti, nīti* cannot be against *vyavahāra, vyavāhara* can never be without *karma, karma* can never be caused without any *prabhāva* and *prabhāva* can never be realized without being aided by the *svabhāva* of a being (गोस्वामी 2011: 317-18). (See Annexure for further details.)

The widespread meaning of *dharma* can be gathered from the above example, also if misunderstood, it can lead to many different thoughts leading on to various new doctrines. The actors of films can go on to state that they are not well-read or that they cannot think on their own but that they only believe that their moral ethics permit them to speak up against wrongdoers or injustice and that is what they will do. Many of our films are made on this very principle that the hero will have to face extreme situations and fight the villain as it is his moral duty. Here, it is not mandatory to keep in mind the purity and sanctity of the feelings and conscience. The flip side of this is that some people would say that the law enforcement agencies alone should tackle miscreants or villains and not actors, etc. Yes, as citizens we have the right to criticize these law enforcers or even revolt against their inaction but we do not have the right to take the law into our hands. Have we forgotten the path of non-violence taught by Mahatma Gandhi?

The golden age of Hollywood saw many such films being made which were based on the actor's enthusiasm and righteous way of living. Famous American director Frank Capra (1897–1991) was immensely dissatisfied after making the five Oscar award-winning film, *It Happened One Night* (1934). This film was remade twice in Hindi: *Chori-Chori* (1956), in which Raj Kapoor played the lead role and *Dil Hai Ki Manta Nahin* (1991), made by director Mahesh Bhatt. Frank Capra made three very meaningful films: *Mr. Smith Goes to Washington* (1939), *Meet John Doe* (1941) and *It's a Wonderful Life* (1946). In the first film, he describes the helpful nature of the actor who stands up against the corrupt ministers of the parliament all alone. In the third, he tells the story of a person who sets up a bank to help society instead of his own happiness. In a dialogue, he says that if one has friends, one never loses in life. Frank Capra's popularity kept on declining as he went on to make more and more value-based films. We shall have to call it the short-term misfortune of cinema and the long-term good fortune of mankind.

Sergeant York (1941) is the true story of an innocent, American village soldier, Alvin York, who is a morally upright person and an unfailing marksman. He is enrolled in the army, much against his wishes during the First World War. He remains true to his principle of non-violence and hates killing people, but on one occasion, he is able to arrest 132 German soldiers singlehandedly. The actor's heroism does not end here; it does in fact come to the fore because of his steadfast belief in his principles, when he refuses to accept any commercial accolades for his bravery. He remains satisfied with a small plot of land and a house. This great film is a gift to cine-lovers from the director Howard Hawks (1896–1977), who also gave us films like *Scarface* (1932), *Bringing up Baby* (1938), *His Girl Friday* (1940) and *Red River* (1948). This is all about intelligence and determination. Sergeant York was not even ready to agree for a film on his life, until he realized he desperately needed funds to build a school in his village. We, on a daily basis, come across so many people who are given respect and are adorned with medals and accolades, but are not loathe to advertising harmful products and ideas just for monetary gains. Is their inner conscience dead?

The concept of the actor is highly ingrained in Vīra Rasa. Normally in any story, we want to see that the actor is excited and is victorious in the end, French director Jean Renoir (1894–1979), has been able to capture these very emotions in his film *La Grande Illusion* or *The Grand Illusion* (1937). This film is a story on the enthusiasm and philosophical aspects of actors of different countries at the outbreak of the world war, how they understand their country, prison, life and freedom. The great director Orson Welles has called it as one of the best films of the world. In his own films, the actor's impatience, anger and pride are shown with aplomb. His films *Citizen Kane* (1941) and *The Magnificent Ambersons* (1942) are prime examples of this. The beauty in these films is not just in the story, but in the creative imagination and use of new techniques. Even then, many of these films show the

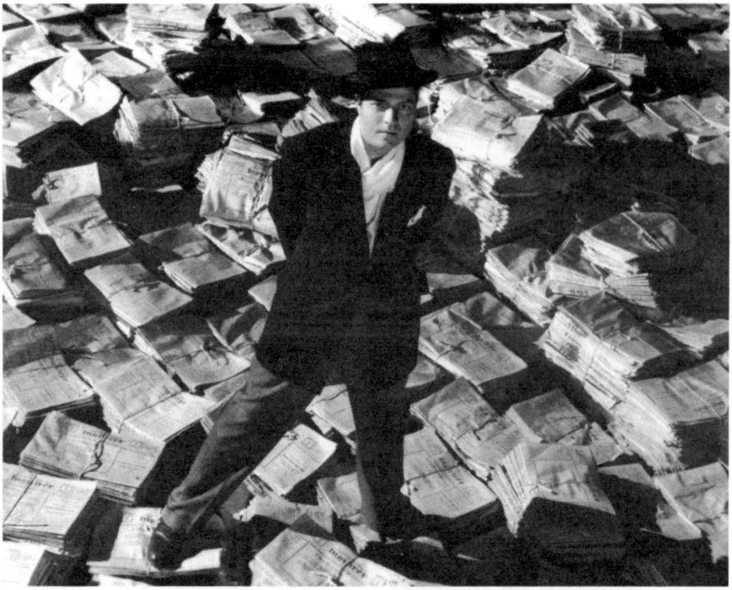

Orson Welles's *Citizen Kane* (1941)

negative side of bravery, i.e. pride, violence and ill-intention, which is the failure of *vīratā*. Wise men say that Bhayānaka Rasa, Vībhatsa Rasa, Krodha Rasa and Karuṇa Rasa are the *rasas* which feature negative thoughts, while the rest of the eight *rasas*, i.e. Hāsya Rasa, Śṛṅgāra Rasa, Vīra Rasa and Adbhuta Rasa are all positive thought-inducing *rasas*. On seeing these films, it seems that a reinterpretation or a relook is necessary. An astonishing fact is that the trailer of *Citizen Kane* did not have even one scene of the film in it. The story of this all-time-great film is of a very rich owner of a newspaper conglomerate, whose life remains loveless and empty because of his shallow approach toward his moral values. The film *The Magnificent Ambersons* was based on the 1918 Pulitzer Prize-winning novel of the same name. In it too, the actor sacrifices his love for his principles. Orson Welles faced tremendous work pressures during the making of these films; directing and editing rights were taken away and he had a fall-out with the producer too. Such bad luck followed his entire career of film-making.

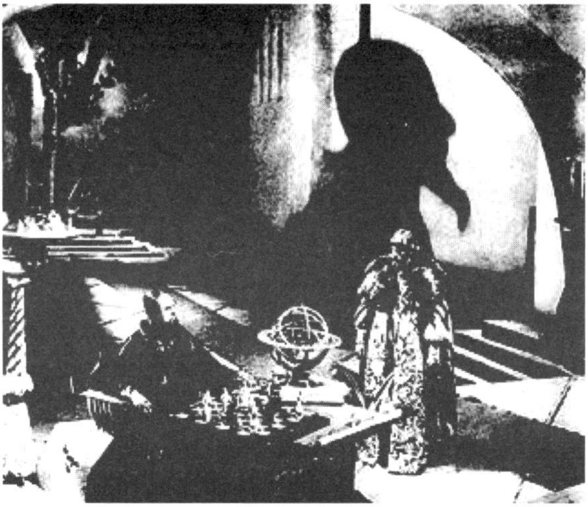

Ivan the Terrible (1958)

Many a times, the characters who represent valour or courage are kings or high-ranking ministers. As they are associated with such posts, people have great expectations from them. Their valour is often debated and discussed and their decisions are weighed by time and morality for eons to come. Russian director Sergei Eisenstein (1898–1948), made his last film called *Ivan the Terrible* in two parts, the first one made in 1944 was very well received, but the second, released in 1958 was seen as a conspiracy against the Russian government and the reels of the film were confiscated. It was finally released only ten years after the director's death. There was a third part too, but the film was confiscated and destroyed. The film was the life story of the Russian Tsar, Ivan, who had managed to consolidate the entire Russian empire. Charlie Chaplin had called this a historically epic film. With its unmatched music, great photography and use of new camera angles and technique, this film was able to depict the great patriotic king's anger, intelligence, impatience and ferocity. Some portions of the second part are in colour. This is an achievement of a film expert. In the film, many a time, Tsar Ivan, is shown to have done away with the suggestions of his war ministers, by saying that the Tsar is the one who takes decisions and others are just his servants. Pseudo anger is also a part of the sentiments of Vīra Rasa.

The film which started "Italian Neorealism" is Roberto Rossellini's (1906-77) film *Rome, Open City* (1945). This film is the story of a priest who was brutally murdered when he tried to save a group of revolutionaries who were revolting against some fiendish foreigners during Second World War at the time when Rome was an open city. The effect of Italian Neorealism can be seen in the films of Bimal Roy and Satyajit Ray. There are two unforgettable films which show immense character determination and undying belief in justice; they are *Twelve Angry Men* (1957) and *To Kill a Mocking Bird* (1962). In the film *Twelve Angry Men*; twelve jury members have been asked to give their opinions on the fate of an alleged murderer, one of the jury members starts to convince the others against the verdict on the basis of lack of crucial evidence. He ultimately succeeds and averts an innocent young man being sent to the gallows. The film *To Kill a Mocking Bird* is based on the best-selling novel of the same name. Set in a period when racism was at its peak, a white man, who is also a widower and is bringing up his children singlehandedly, fights a case for a poor Negro, which he wins. The hero fights for justice and truth and establishes the real meaning of courage and bravery. Every country and every age need valorous men like them.

Italian director Gillo Pontecorvo (1919–2006) made a famous film, *La Battagliadi Algeri* or *The Battle of Algiers* (1966), in which he showed, how, through guerrilla warfare, the French occupation of Algeria was being targeted. This film was banned in France for five years. It was shot in the newsreel documentary style, using amateur actors, shot on locale; the director had to explain this to audiences in America before the screening of the film. In fact, many film critics have criticized the inhuman killing by the revolutionaries in this film. All we can say is that the director did not have a global Gandhi-istic humanitarian vision on this matter. This film has been viewed by insurgent groups, separatist groups and revolutionaries as an important commentary on urban guerrilla warfare. This film, associated with Dharma Vīra Rasa, shows the complexity of the *rasa-siddhānta.* It is an apt example where even though audiences and critics do not show similarity with the thoughts of the director, they are free to voice their own praises of art.

Various films on sports, like *The Pride of the Yankees* (1942), *Breaking Away* (1979) and *Chariots of Fire* (1981), have shown Vīra Rasa in a new light. Anybody can be brave; this has been proved time and again by the films based on the horrors of war.

Some women-centric films which depict courage and valour are *The Passion of Joan of Arc* (1928), *Jezebel* (1937), *All About Eve* (1950), etc.

Danish director, Carl Dreyer's (1889–1968) film *The Passion of Joan of Arc* is a medieval age, historical film about Joan of Arc, who is captured by clergymen and burnt to death for her unshakeable faith in God and patriotism toward her country. The actress, who portrayed Joan of Arc, did not act in any other film after this because of the numerous ordeals she had to undergo while filming. This film is a heritage in film history because of the exceptional acting and intensely emotional scenes. Many of the edited versions of this film were released amidst huge uproar. The original reel of the film was lost and was finally found in a mental institution in Oslo, Norway. This great work of art is remembered for its superb acting, many close-up scenes and fine editing.

The film *Jezebel*, directed by American director William Wyler (1902-81), is a must see for those who wish to see the portrayal of pride, jealousy, determination, change in voice (*svarabhaṅga*) and change in colour of face (*vaivaraṇya*) in the acting of a female lead. The film is the story of a very beautiful but egoistic girl, portrayed by Bette Davis, who doesn't think twice about hurting her lover notwithstanding the societal rules and rituals.

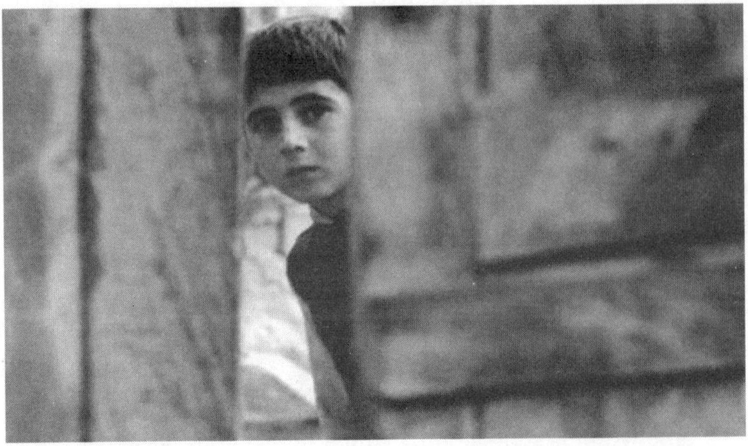

Abbas Kiarostami's *Where Is the Friend's Home* (1987)

All About Eve is a film remembered for the unmatched acting of four actresses, directed by Joseph Mankiewicz (1909-93). The story is about how Anne Baxter, manages to insinuate herself into the life and roles of an ageing but famous actress, Bette Davis. She manages to climb the ladders of success by hoodwinking her friends and acquaintances and because of her extreme ambitions.

Where Is the Friend's Home (1987) is a film by Iranian director Abbas Kiarostami (1940–2016) which portrays the story of a school boy Ahmed, who mistakenly brings home his friend's notebook. He knows that if his friend does not do the homework, he will be expelled the next day and so goes in search of his friend's home to the neighbouring village. His search is in vain and he ultimately does the homework for his friend himself. The expression on young Ahmed's face, on his failure to find his friend's home, is so beautifully captured on camera that we have to believe that if the director's vision is good, one can find beauty anywhere.

Yuddha Vīra Rasa

Let us discuss those films which understand enthusiasm in their normalized meaning, i.e. a fight with an enemy. Violence is not bravery, neither is war-related violence. The desire for victory should be over and above the reason for anger. In this context, it is of importance that there must exist an enemy for bravery also to exist. In many instances, it is a personal enemy, in some others, the various obstacles in the way of work are thought to be enemies. Many a time the enemy pertains to the whole society and it is propagated that way too. During training, the army men are taught that whatever you target at is your enemy. A soldier's work is not to identify the enemy but to annihilate them. A courageous person with a high morality will see his enemy's character first. The nobler the brave, the nobler his enemy. There is an old saying in *Sanskrit Subhāṣita* which explains this fact aptly:

> गुणी गुणं वेत्ति न वेत्ति निर्गुणो, बली बलं वेत्ति न वेत्ति निर्बल: ।
> पिको वसन्तस्य गुणं न वायस: करीच सिंहस्य बलं न मूषक: ॥
>
> *guṇī guṇaṁ vetti na vetti nirguṇo, balī balaṁ vetti na vetti nirbalaḥ* ।
> *piko vasantasya guṇaṁ na vāyasaḥ karī ca siṁhasya balaṁ na mūṣakaḥ* ॥
>
> It is said that a person with virtue always recognizes another with virtue, while a virtueless cannot. A strong person easily recognizes another's strength, while a weakling cannot, just as the onset of spring is easily recognized by the cuckoo and not the crow and the lion's might is understood by an elephant and not the mouse.

The following lines from Tulsīdāsa's *Rāmacaritamānasa* (Laṅkākāṇḍa) also underline the same:

> प्रीति बिरोध समान सन करिअ नीति असि आहि ।
> जौं मृगपति बध मेड़ुकन्हि भल कि कहइ कोउ ताहि ॥२३(ग) ॥
>
> *prīti birodha samāna sana karia nīti asi āhi* ।
> *jauṅ mṛgapati badha meḍukanhi bhola ki kahai kou tāhi* ॥
>
> As per a good policy, affection and adversity should be held with equals. If a lion kills a frog, nobody will consider that as good.

Taking this into account, it becomes imperative to inflate the size of the enemy or obstacle or accident in a movie with super heroes or super actors, etc. In the film, *Superman* (1978), it is shown that the very essence of time is being changed just to show the supernatural powers of the hero. In the Spiderman series (2002, 2004, 2007, 2012 and 2014), the enemy or the anti-hero is shown to be extremely powerful, who pushes the supernatural power of the hero to its limits. The Batman series, made by Christopher Nolan (b.1970), *Batman Begins* (2005), *The Dark Knight* (2008) and *The Dark Knight Rises* (2012), all have villains who are not from the other world but who are as intelligent and resourceful as the super hero.

Hindi poetess Subhadra Kumari Chauhan has summed up the characteristics of a valorous person, albeit in the Indian context, in her poem "वीरों का कैसा हो वसंत"

> गलबाँहें हों या हो कृपाण
> चल चितवन हो या धनुष बाण
> हो रसविलास या दलितत्राण
> अब यही समस्या है दुरंत – वीरों का कैसा हो वसंत

> *galabāheṅ hoṅ yā ho kr̥pāṇa*
> *cala citavana ho yā dhanuṣa bāṇa*
> *ho rasavilāsa yā dalitatrāṇa*
> *aba yahī samasyā hai duraṅta – vīroṅ kā kaisā ho vasaṅta*

In Sanskrit dramas too, there is a detailed description of the various types of heroes, which explains that there are no set rules for choosing a courageous person. In the Indian panorama, whenever we think of a brave person, the names of Shivaji Maharaj, Maharana Pratap, Guru Gobind Singh, etc. come immediately to the mind. They had various types of arms and armaments at their disposal and strong, well-bred horses to carry them across. After the Industrial Revolution, these images cannot be justified. In a film plot, we never see a hero hellbent on destruction using an atom bomb; such actions are generally reserved for the villains. The brave and courageous have always been depicted carrying some or the other firearm in the movies.

Many Western films have been lauded as films of Vīra Rasa. Western movies is the term used for those movies which were set in the nineteenth century America, which depicted the Western areas where the local residents used to fight each other, travel on horseback and carry firearms to intimidate people. This formula in film-making was very successful and is still being used. It was first used and given a respectful genre of its own by the American director of Irish origin, John Ford (1894–1973), in his film *Stage Coach* (1939). Renowned film-makers like Orson Welles, Akira Kurosawa, Satyajit Ray, Federico Fellini, Ingmar Bergman, Martin Scorsese, Jean-Luc Godard, Alfred Hitchcock and Clint Eastwood bow down to John Ford and have accepted the influence of his films over theirs. The films made by John Ford *The Informer* (1935), *The Grapes of Wrath* (1940), *How Green Was My Valley* (1941), *My Darling Clementine* (1946), *Fort Apache* (1948), *She Wore a Yellow Ribbon* (1949), *The Searchers* (1956) and *The Man Who Shot Liberty Valance* (1962) have earned an enviable place in world film history dues to its great cinematography, photography and direction. To show the sentiment of courage in an actor he showed in them a sense of determination, pride, anger, etc. Many times, the actors he chose were asked to show charity, compassion but with arrogance and an indomitable bodily strength. The courageous heroes he cast were shown to be down to earth, often crossing hot deserts, climbing up high mountains, fielding a barrage of gunshots and defending poor and weak people.

American films such as Fritz Lang's *Western Union* (1941) and *Rancho Notorious* (1952), George Steven's *Shane* (1953) and Howard Hawks' *Rio Bravo* (1959) are perfect examples of typical stylized Westerns involving town sheriffs and good-natured brave men riding horses fighting with law evaders or the wicked with their guns.

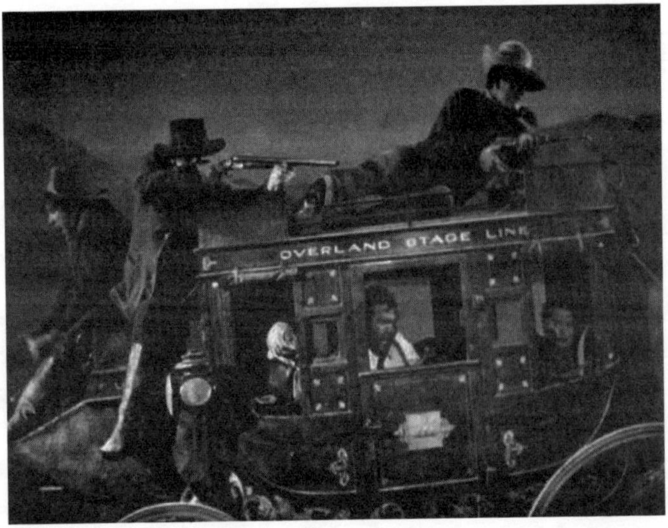

John Ford's *Stage Coach* (1939)

Typical visual elements depicted are vast farmland, houses made of wood, men engaged in physical labour such as wood cutting.

Austrian born, American director Fred Zinnemann (1907-97), made many films based on Vīra Rasa. His film *High Noon* (1952) is based on real time zone where the hero, on the day of his wedding, takes on a group of thugs, single-handedly, as a part of his duty as the town Marshall. The film's duration is eighty-five minutes, which is the exact time the hero takes to catch the goons. In another of his films, *A Man for All Seasons* (1966), a minister's commitment toward his thoughts and duties is very beautifully shown. Zinneman's film *The Day of the Jackal* (1973) is famous for the bravery and courage it portrays of the bureaucrats who are duty-bound to foil the assassination attempt on the President of France.

In Hindi cinema, the "Angry Young Man" image of Amitabh Bachchan, was the advent of films where the hero was all powerful, highly intelligent, strong, a good marksman and trustworthy. The very famous film *Sholay* (1975) was deeply influenced by many Western films like *The Magnificent Seven* (1960), which was based on Akira Kurosawa's film *Seven Samurai* (1954), Italian director Sergio Leone's (1929-89) film *For a Few Dollars More* (1965), *The Good, the Bad and the Ugly* (1966) based on Kurosawa's *Yojimbo* (1961), *Once Upon a Time in the West* (1968), *The Wild Bunch* (1969), a film by Sam Peckinpah (1925-84), *The Butch Cassidy and the Sundance Kid* (1969), a true story of two bank robberies. All these above-mentioned great films must be seen by viewers who desire to see them as they are freely available on the Internet nowadays.

American director Sam Peckinpah made films depicting Vīra Rasa and Vībhatsa Rasa all his life. *Cross of Iron* (1977) is an Anglo-German film which is based on the events during the Second World War. In this film, bravery, duty and awards are very well discussed and depicted. In all the Western films discussed above, bravery and valour were portrayed by revengeful acts, perpetrating violence for revenge, marksmanship, beautiful women trying to attract the hero, etc. Renowned Hindi poetess, Subhadra Kumari Chauhan, describes the standards of valour as depicted in her poem वीरो का कैसा हो वसंत. It should be remembered that such a generalization is for merely relishing the *rasa*, a common spectator may commit the mistake of emulating this and the answer to it is that a compassionate viewer will relish the sentiments and identify with them completely.

Renowned Japanese director Akira Kurosawa was highly influenced by John Ford and made some remarkable films like *Seven Samurai* (1954), *The Hidden Fortress* (1958), *Yojimbo* (1961), *High and Low* (1963) and *Dersu Uzala* (1975). These films had many untouched and everlasting dimensions depicting the enthusiastic sentiment or the *utsāha bhāva*.

Before discussing on these films, let us ponder over the difference between bravery and cowardice. Normally, a person is said to be a coward if he fears to do any work which is treacherous and may be life threatening and so he/she will make excuses not to do the work. Cowardice may also be defined as the human tendency to avoid the work which is interrupted by some fear, for example, we cannot expect bravery from a weak or debilitated or an old person. If there is a sure failure in the work given, then declining that assignment cannot be called as cowardice; for example, if someone asks us to jump into a valley from a mountain without any safety harness or asks us to jump from an airplane without a parachute, then refusal to do such acts cannot be termed cowardice. Such stunts are usually performed by professionals or people who have enough practice. Such refusals are not cowardice but intelligence. In the film, *The Wages of Fear* (1953), made by French director Henri-Georges Clouzot (1907-77), during a debate on bravery and cowardice, a character says the young people take risks because they have no previous experience, while people above forty understand the correct meaning of bravery. This film is unique in that it won both the Golden Bear (Berlin Film Festival) and the Palme d'Or (Cannes Film Festival) awards.

On the Waterfront (1954) is a film directed by an American, Elia Kazan (1909–2003), about the mafia and labourers working in the port. Marlon Brando plays the lead role and is shown to be filled with intense anger due to the injustice he has to face. In the end, he gives vent to his anger by resistance and opposition. This film turned around the way acting and direction were followed and done in America. The film ends when the actor's conscience awakens and he is victorious over his enemy due to his indomitable enthusiasm. The Hindi remake of this film is named *Ghulam* (1997) and the lead role is played by Aamir Khan.

In all of Japanese director Akira Kurosawa's films, bravery has always been shown in contrast with cowardice. In the great film *Seven Samurai*, the actors were first moulded into the characteristics of simple villagers, and then the samurai warriors got the weak villagers to ready themselves for self-defence. This was in itself a great achievement. The film begins with this dialogue:

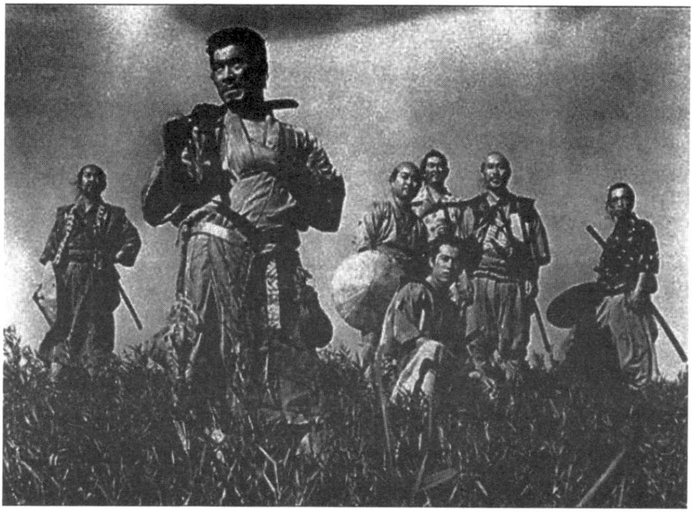

Akira Kurosawa's *Seven Samurai* (1954)

> In a small village in the valley, lie the graves of four samurai warriors. When Japan was burdened with over ambitious samurai warriors, these seven warriors fought for the safety of the poor farmers and not for their ambitions. Three of them did not die in the war and they left the village never to look back again. They fought bravely and sacrificed themselves for the sake of the villagers, this is remembered with great respect and awe. They were the samurai.

The film *Star Wars, Episode IV: A New Hope* (1977), made by American director George Lucas (b.1944), was hugely influenced by Akira Kurosawa's film *The Hidden Fortress*. The plot of the film is about how an army commander is trying to save the life of the princess of his kingdom, by hiding in a secret and hidden fortress. They are promised safe journey by two poor, greedy and cowardly peasants. This black and white film will remain unmatched and forever in the hearts of the people due to its story, beautiful princess' versatility and love for justice, famous swordsman in the commander and his bravery and the picturesque secret fortress and gold hidden under water. This film brings a feeling of shame that, till date, the Hindi film industry has not been able to make even one film based on the famous novels *Chandrakanta* or *Chandrakanta Santati* or even a thriller like *Bhoothnath* or a romance like *Kadambari*.

Toshiro Mifune, a famous Japanese hero, has played the role of a samurai in the film *Yojimbo;* he defeats the thugs in an inter-gang war, by using his intelligence and courage. The climax shows the hero killing all the villains. In this film, the goons are shown to be dim-witted and cowardly. The film *High and Low* is a police drama, wherein the son of a rich man's driver is kidnapped by mistake. The kidnappers demand the same ransom for the driver's son too. Since the driver has only one son, the rich man appeases his wife and pays up the ransom. The police ultimately catch the kidnappers. This film is an example of how films of the mystery-thriller genre, swing between the excitement and fear sentiment and how the films of Yuddha Vīra Rasa do not show victory in wars alone but victory over the enemy too.

The films of Akira Kurosawa were not known only for their dialogues, but they were embellished by brilliant acting, real and moral values depicted and use of fine body movements. The scenes of these films are etched in memory. Kurosawa was a very meticulous director; he himself edited the scenes of his films and took great pains to get a shot ready. Not only Akira Kurosawa, but other expert film-makers like Alfred Hitchcock, Orson Welles, Ingmar Bergman and Andrei Tarkovsky imagine and work out every aspect of the scene before they actually start shooting. These aspects are given more importance than the narrative itself, and more often than not, outdo the acting, background music, etc. These films, therefore, are seen again and again, just to get a delightful experience.

Clint Eastwood, who played the role of a police inspector, fighting against crime, in the film series – *Dirty Harry* (1971, 1973, 1976, 1983, 1986) – won immense popularity from the film

Dollar Trilogy made by Sergei Leone also. As a director, Eastwood made two movies – *Unforgiven* (1992) and *Million Dollar Baby* (2004) – which have won Oscar awards. *Unforgiven* is the story of an ageing outlaw who agrees to kill thugs for money, his journey is a marvellous mixture of many valorous deeds, understanding his own duties and the atrocity of the killers.

It is not at all necessary that the character of a hero be strong and exemplary. *Film Noir* is a genre of films which were quite popular in the decade between the 1940s and the 1950s, and they had heroes who were agitated, brusque, had a devious nature, who were involved in some crime or were absorbed in solving some murder, such stories always had some heart-warming but dangerous beauties who were up to some mischief. These films were in black and white and were made with some big monies and still continue to be made. Some good directors migrated to America only to make good films, like Charlie Chaplin and Alfred Hitchcock, where wealthy businessmen were ready to invest in films. America also readily embraced new advances in technology, films got better and better – from silent to talkies, from black and white to coloured and from two-dimensional to 3D. It influenced film-making all over the world.

Film Noir is known for its black and white cinematographic beauty. The courage of these heroes is not in reaching the desired goal. It is certainly not necessary that the brave be good and victorious always. The credit for the invention of thrillers and *Film Noir* goes hugely to Fritz Lang (1890–1976). He escaped from Germany and fled to America, as he faced the danger from Hitler just before the Second World War. His famous thrillers are: *The Woman in the Window* (1944) and *Scarlet Street* (1945) and these are thought to be the father of *Film Noir*. In the film *The Woman in the Window*, a professor commits a murder in self-defence and then to avoid disrepute and blackmail, tries to hide the body and goes through various kinds of problems. Alfred Hitchcock and

Luis Buñuel decided to take up film directing only after seeing Fritz Lang's *The Weiry Death/Destiny* (1921). It will be a surprise to cine lovers to know that the mad scene outside the hospital, in the film *The Dark Knight*, was written after being influenced by the film *The Testament of Dr. Mabuse*. This film of Fritz Lang was banned by the Nazi Party in Germany.

Some other Noir films where the hero is shown to be rude and sullen are John Houston (1906-87) directed and lead role played by Humphrey Bogart film *The Maltese Falcon* (1941) and *The Treasure of Sierre Madre* (1948). In the film *The Treasure of Sierre Madre*, the hero's greed is shown in the form of his unnatural death. Other famous films of John Houston, such as *The Asphalt Jungle* (1950) and *The African Queen* (1951) deal with heroism and courage.

Celebrated Noir movies of mid-1940s are *Laura* (1944), *Murder My Sweet* (1944), *Mildred Pierce* (1945) and *Detour* (1945) where greed, tight screenplay and obsession were key themes involving detectives and police for solving mysteries. Among the many remarkable Noir films that were made in Hollywood, *Out of the Past* or *Build My Gallows High* (1947) by director Jacques Tourneur (1904-77) is quite outstanding. Billy Wilder's (1906–2002) Noir film, *Double Indemnity* has been remade in Hindi as *Jism* (2003). Director Orson Welles' film *The Lady from Shanghai* (1947) was brutally cut and only a short version was shown to the audience. But the famous "mirror house" scene itself tells the difference between a great and an ordinary director. Another film in which Orson Welles acted and was directed by Britisher Carol Reed (1906-76), *The Third Man* (1949) is rated as one of the finest Noir films, many scenes of this film are a standard in film direction even today. *Night and the City* (1950) and *Kiss Me Deadly* (1955) are other notable films dealing with enthusiasm confronted with moral questions and harsh reality.

In many films, the hero represents the state or due to political reasons is against the state. In the James Bond movies, the hero is devoted to the service of the Queen of England. In Stanley Kubrick's (1928-99), historical epic, *Spartacus* (1960), the hero stands up for the rights of the slaves. Stanley Kubrick, who had made this film under a lot of pressure from the producers and the lead actor Kirk Douglas, doesn't consider it his own film. *Braveheart* (1995) is a film produced and acted in by Mel Gibson, in which he fights for the independence of Scotland. In the film *Gladiator* (2000), an ex-army officer is imprisoned and made to fight with a ferocious lion.

In the opening scene of the Chinese martial arts film *Enter the Dragon* (1973), which was Bruce Lee's last film, his teacher explains to him the philosophy of courageousness. He says that every brave person should use his prowess for warfare and bravery, ethically and justly. The narrative, where the hero using only his prowess, saves the intelligent but weak scientist and defeats the enemy is considered a weak plot according to many parameters. In this film the hero, while thirsting for revenge, manages to defeat his enemies barehanded on an island where arms are prohibited. In the more recent Chinese martial art films like *Crouching Tiger, Hidden Dragon* (2000), *Hero* (2002) and *House of Flying Daggers* (2004) the use of new technology and opulence of the scenes are a beautiful depiction of the irony of bravery. In the film *Crouching Tiger, Hidden Dragon*, directed by Ang Lee (b.1954), the remarkable warrior decides to teach the bad-tempered princess the various methods of warfare, instead of punishing her. In the film *Hero*, directed by Zhang Yimou (b.1951), the gallant hero decides to abort the mission of assassinating the king when he realizes that to do so will be detrimental to the ultimate goal of the unification of China. In another film by the same director, *House of Flying Daggers*, the hero gets entangled between love and duty. In the light of the art of warfare and to describe the enthusiasm sentiment (*utsāha*) very beautifully, it does seem as though films touch on the essence of Vībhatsa Rasa and Bhayānaka Rasa many times. This film takes refuge in Śṛṅgāra Rasa, while its main *rasa* is Vīra Rasa.

Let us also talk of anti-heroes and their bravery. In many films, the hero is shown to be a thief, dacoit or even a ringleader of dacoits. Earlier Hollywood movies of 1930s paved the way for many such gangster-movies. Paul Muni in *Scarface* (1932), Paul Cagney in *The Public Enemy* (1931) and *White Heat* (1949), and Edward G. Robinson in *Little Caesar* (1931) were key stars who portrayed gangsters and won viewers sympathy.

The Godfather, a trilogy (1972, 1974, 1990), made by American director Francis Ford Coppola (b.1939), is the story of a mafia don's ego and pride. The don's ego is turned into an enthusiastic sentiment (*utsāha*). Films made on robbery like *Ocean's Eleven* (1960) and *The Italian Job* (1967) have been remade and are quite popular too. In the famous film *Bonnie and Clyde* (1967), based on a true incident of dacoity, directed by Arthur Penn, the poetess-looter heroine, argues passionately for herself and this scene touches the heart of the audience immensely. The film, *The French Connection* (1971), directed by William Friedkin (b.1935) made on the work of a police officer, has some exclusively shot, but enthusiastic chase scenes.

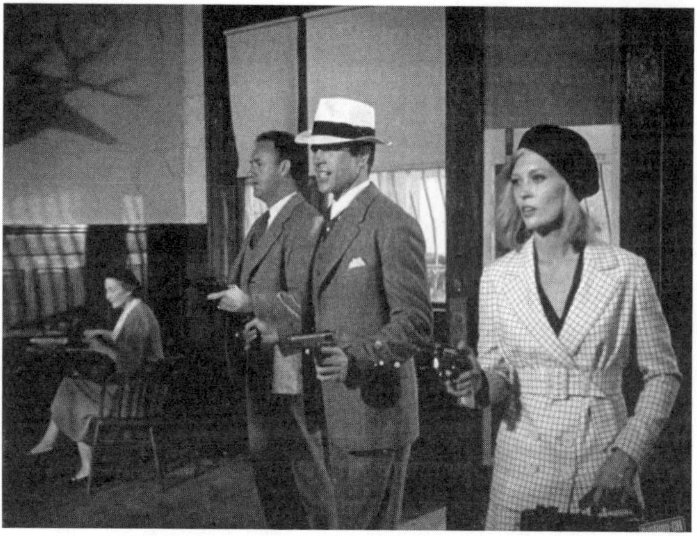

Bonnie and Clyde (1967)

It seems very easy to generalize Vīra Rasa, a lot of weak and tormented people, very easily imagine and identify themselves with the hero of Vīra Rasa. But every great family drama which has hero vs villain fights or an abundance of dance and songs is not always good. It will not be wrong to say that it has been very much generalized and so it has been the most influential. It is nevertheless noteworthy that a versatile spectator is not swayed by ordinary films, on the other hand, after serious discussions they will refuse to accept the films which are not upright, have some or the other shortcomings or have unnecessary feel-good factors.

If we look closely, we find that most film reviews are not about the touching experience of the films but it is more of a discussion on the properiety of various aspects of the film. Our aim is not to show compassion to some and make fun of the likes and dislikes of others, but, to introduce the audience to some artistically great films. If they are not able to appreciate such masterpieces, it is not a great concern. A courageous person should do his duty according to his intellect and good behaviour which will ultimately help him in his life-goal pursuit.

7

Bereavement, Anguish and Duty

Karuṇa Rasa and World Cinema

Scholars of different genres, while discussing the *rasa-siddhānta*, raised a very obvious question – which is the most fundamental of all *rasas*? Kashmiri Śaiva philosopher Abhinavagupta is of the opinion that it is Śānta Rasa. He says just as the waves in the ocean fall back into the ocean itself, all the *rasas* and their *bhāvas* ultimately get integrated into Śānta Rasa. The author of *Sāhityadarpaṇa*, Viśvanātha Kavirāja (approx. 1378–1434), endorses his great-grandfather, Nārāyaṇapaṇḍita's view that Adbhuta Rasa is the root of all the *rasas*. The author of the eighth-century Sanskrit works the *Mālatīmādhava* and *Uttararāmacarita*, Bhavabhūti, says that Karuṇa Rasa is the root of all the *rasas*: According to Bhavabhūti, the psyche is in a solid or frozen state and it needs to be melted before any emotions can be felt and this process of melting the mind can only be done with the manifestation of Karuṇa Rasa. It can only be surmised that the meaning of *karuṇa* here is manifold and can range from simple sorrow and hurt to the heart being wounded badly. Another philosopher Bhoja has deemed that Śṛṅgāra Rasa is the one and only *rasa* and has hence addressed it differently (नगेन्द्र 1969: 253-71).

Bengal resident, Madhusūdan Saraswatī (1540–1640), who

was a philosopher of the Advaita Vedānta school, said this about the psyche:

> The temperament of the psyche is like the sealing wax; tough in appearance, but when exposed to heating elements reaches liquidity, and when these elements cool down, it regains its original nature like the sealing wax. The psyche can be melted and moulded using different objects and subjects and they are the values, desires, feelings and emotions. – पाण्डे 2003: 85

Similarly, great Russian writer, Dostoevsky, says that pain and suffering are always inevitable for a large intelligence and a deep heart. Here, we will have to refute the famous lines from a poem written by renowned Hindi poet Sumitranandan Pant:

> वियोगी होगा पहला कवि, आह से उपजा होगा गान
> निकलकर आँखों से चुपचाप, बही होगी कविता अनजान
>
> *viyogī hogā pahalā kavī, āha se upajā hogā gāna* ।
> *nikalakara āṅkhoṅ se cupacāpa, bahī hogī kavitā anajāna* ॥

The above lines tell of the imagination of the poet wherein the pain in his heart comes out as tears and form a poem thereby making the reader realize the beauty in it. The word *viyoga* denotes the *rati bhāva* and Śṛṅgāra Rasa is starkly different from Karuṇa Rasa. It is believed that the *Vālmīki Rāmāyaṇa* was authored based on this *śloka*:

> मा निषाद प्रतिष्ठां त्वमगमः शाश्वतीः समाः ।
> यत् क्रौञ्चमिथुनादेकमवधीः काममोहितम् ॥
>
> *mā niṣāda pratiṭṣāṁ tvamaga amaḥ śāśvatīḥ samāḥ* ।
> *yat-krauñca-mithunādekamavadhīḥ kāmamohitam* ॥
>
> – Bālakāṇḍa 2.15

This *śloka* explains the grief and distress felt by Ādikavi Vālmīki, when he saw how cruelly a fowler shot an arrow at the male-crane when it was joyously sitting with its female partner.

Śoka is the Sthāyī Bhāva of the Karuṇa Rasa.

Śoka bhāva is not just a normal hurtful feeling or sadness. There is unhappiness when one separates from a lover, there is a hurtful feeling when one is scolded, but, all this is not bereavement or sorrow. Bereavement happens when one loses someone or something irreversibly or irreparably, for example, the death of a loved one.

In this context, a normal question arises as to how sorrow can be justified as a thing of beauty or how manifestation of any *rasa* can be possible by seeing someone in sorrow? The Greek philosopher Aristotle had said that the feelings of fear, sorrow, compassion, etc. which have arisen out of art, bring about a catharsis in the human being, through which we feel stress free. Abhinavagupta adds to this and says that after experiencing such kind of a sorrow, one can speculate in peace with a stable mind, which leads to greater happiness. On the other hand, Viśvanātha Kavirāja opines that tears of sorrow which originate from art do not substantiate unhappiness but are a proof of a compassionate oneness of the heart with the artist. German philosopher, Immanuel Kant, says there is nothing called "aesthetic unhappiness". The sorrow or sadness which emanates from any art form, be it painting, music or even drama, is not sorrow in the real sense, on the other hand, it gives pleasure to the viewer.

The meaning of Karuṇa Rasa is not the feeling one experiences when the hero is injured or laid up, it actually starts after that moment when the hero is injured; the accidents or the tragedies which follow him/her for a seeming lifetime. Frustration, despondency, weakness of body, crying, death, etc. are the transitory emotions or the *sañcārī bhāva*s which lead us to the sentiment of *śoka*. The factors which help in the manifestation of the *śoka bhāva* are: the chagrin felt when cursed, forced separation from a loved one, loss of money, being jailed or held against one's wishes, ouster from one's place of birth or dwelling, accidents or some kind of a misfortune. The *sāttvika bhāva*s (physio-psychological emotions) of Karuṇa Rasa are colour draining from the face, horripilation, fainting, etc.

(द्विवेदी 1992: 170-75, 202).

According to Bharata Muni, as written in the *Nāṭyaśāstra,* Karuṇa Rasa is of three types:

1. Obstacles in following the righteous path.
2. Personal setback like loss of finances.
3. Death of a loved one.

Almost all the notable film-makers of the world have made unforgettable films based on Karuṇa Rasa. Let us look at some of them.

Obstacles in Following the Righteous Path

According to the *Nāṭyaśāstra,* the first type of Karuṇa Rasa is quite intricate. It can be explained in a proper way, by the following excerpt from the famous story of the great Hindi writer, Munshi Premchand's *Būḍhī Kākī.* The excerpt describes the scene where Rūpā, one of the characters, sees the old woman, called Kākī, eating leftovers from used plates:

> Just at that moment, Rūpā woke up and not finding Lāḍalī near her, panicked. She looked here and there, thinking maybe she has fallen off the bed. She finally found her standing near Būḍhī Kākī (Old Aunt), who was picking up the leftovers from the used plates and eating them. Rūpā's heart froze for a moment on seeing such an anguishing scene. A brahmin woman, eating leftovers and that too from used plates! What can be more pathetic than this! It was a sight which would wrench the hearts out of the viewer. It felt as though the earth had suddenly stopped rotating and the sky had started spinning over. Some bad omen would certainly befall the world. Rūpā was not angry, what is anger against grief? Tenderness and fear brought tears to her eyes. Who would partake the blame for such an immoral act? She lifted both her hands towards the heavens and beseeched the gods to have mercy on her children for the injustice that she had committed. She felt that God's wrath will certainly fall upon her.

Munshi Premchand confronts us with a bigger truth; what is anger as opposed to grief? It is quite important to question here, whether the four *rasa*s which are born from the four basic *rasa*s are more forceful than the root *rasa*s? Is pathos stronger than ferocity? Is marvel more forceful than bravery and is fright stronger than disgust? Is comedy more effective than eroticism?

What are the obstacles one can face in the path of righteous behaviour? Many a time, these obstacles become a point of ethical debate. Therefore, most of these impediments are the manifestations of the hero's immaturity or due to some unexplained misfortune. A man is never free of righteousness (*dharma*), prudence (*nīti)*, demeanour (*vyavahāra*), action (*karma*), influence or impact (*prabhāva*) and temperament (*svabhāva*). This is the truth of life and must be introspected upon thoroughly.

Japanese director Akira Kurosawa decided to enter the film-making industry on a note of such a righteous introspection. His film *Rashomon* (1950) was a directorial venture when Japanese films were first noticed by world cinemagoers and it was based on one story out of a collection of short stories by master storyteller, Ryūnosuke Akutagawa (1862–1927). The film is about the murder of a samurai in the forest and the account of the death as given by four different people; the bandit who tried to rob the samurai, the samurai's wife, the samurai himself through a medium and a woodcutter who claims to have witnessed the murder. It appears quite difficult to ascertain the truth after hearing all the four versions and one wonders about the truth at the end. In the duel between truth and righteousness, the spectator is left with a feeling of bereavement for not really knowing the truth.

Akira Kurosawa was influenced by Leo Tolstoy's novel *The Death of Ivan Ilyich* and made *Ikiru* (1952), a film about the struggles of a terminally ill bureaucrat in Tokyo and his quest for the meaning in life. The hero, a middle-aged bureaucrat, realizes he has less than a year to live and decides to find a meaning to his boring, wasted life. He undertakes to convert a cesspool into a children's park, this should not be viewed as a heroic deed of a dying man, instead it is full of pathos because after living a boring life the hero wakes up to find meaning to his life as he realizes that he is dying and wants to do something fulfilling. One of the most touching scenes in the film is the one where the hero is sitting on a swing on a cold night, in the converted park, and singing to his heart's content and the life's lesson he learns from a young female acquaintance. The climax scene of the film is full of pathos just like what we see in the film *Anand* (1971), by Hrishikesh Mukherjee, wherein the death of the hero due to cancer is more anguishing and more readily remembered than the heroism he displayed while alive and struggling to come to terms with his illness. We don't mourn the death of a bad person, we are bereaved only if the person is attached to us. The audience is swayed and naturally gets affected by heroism and righteous behaviour. Therefore, any such obstacle in this path is a reason for our sorrow. Films like *Ikiru* are a symbol of the deep anguish which is shown because of the obstacles in the path of righteous behaviour. It is prudence not to do something unto others, which, by our demeanour, would adversely affect us, somebody close to us or our entire community. But, acting judiciously is not always possible. Every civilization is weighed down by corrupt, arrogant, ill-mannered and dishonest people. This kind of anguish is never ending.

Robert Bresson (1901-99) was a director par excellence and was revered by great film-makers like Andrei Tarkovsky, Jean-Luc Godard and Ingmar Bergman. In a career spanning sixty years, he made just fourteen films: *Diary of a Country Priest* or *Journal d'un curé de Campagne* (1951), *Pickpocket* (1959), *Au Hasard Balthazar* (1966), *The Trial of Joan of Arc* (1962), *Mouchette* (1967), *Le Diable Probablement* (1977) and *L'Argent* or *Money* (1983). Bresson kept himself away from all kinds of publicity events for his films. His films never did make an enormous amount of money and it was always a struggle to garner funds for his films. Many of his films depicted anguish and bereavement and also the righteous conduct to be followed.

Robert Bresson never liked dramatized acting in his films and so, he always took in new, unprofessional actors to play the lead roles in his films. Many critics were of the view that the actors in his films were quite expressionless and that mostly they used various hand gestures or different walking styles to emote. Bresson thought differently and said that he wanted to bring out the natural attraction and exquisite beauty of the actors and therefore asked them to act in that particular way. He differentiated between "cinema" and "movies", according to him, "movies" merely entertain and are filmed version of dramas, whereas "cinema" is much more than this. It is through this new medium of art that we realize new experiences and whose actuality is very different from the reality. He too laid emphasis on perceptions rather than intellect and argument, as is the case with the Indian classical aesthetics. While criticizing acting in films, he says that it is nothing but a deflection, which the actors too understand. Cinema should, in fact, raise the standard of life, not deflect it. Bresson quotes a comment by French writer and thinker, Francois-Rene de Chateaubriand (1748–1848), on contemporary poets, and puts forth similar observation for acting and actors; what they lack is not naturalness, but nature (Morris 2009: 294).

Bresson was an admirer of dramas, yet through his film art he created a new kind of cinema distinguished by his signature approach. His films did not have actors but models who delivered the dialogues without understanding, but with feelings by learning them by rote. Bresson reiterates the statement of writer, Michel Eyquem de Montaigne (1533-92), who said that we appear much more truthful in our expressions and gestures. Some of the traditional Indian aestheticians say that Bresson has given the world a reason to believe that along with greatness of acting through gestures,

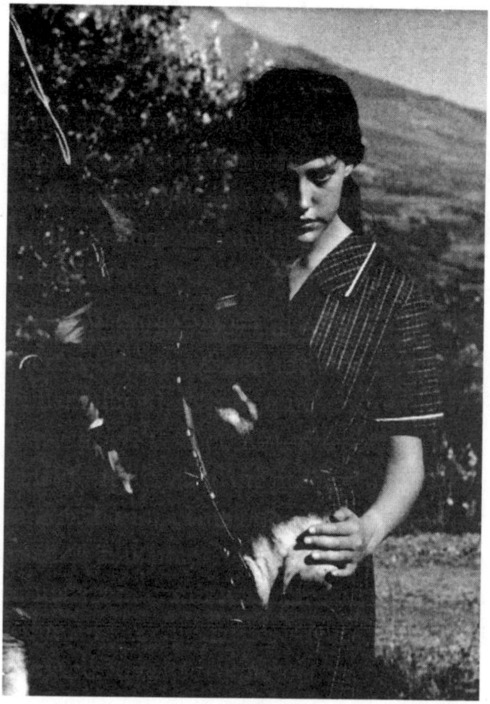

Au Hasard Balthazar (1956)

it is important to remember that the physical expression of the feelings present in the psyche, i.e. the *āṅgika abhinaya* (acting using body parts) is a very important aspect of dramatics, which has been forgotten by people.

The film *Pickpocket* (1959) is the story of a pickpocket who learns the art of picking a pocket and even has to go to jail for the same. The mixture of wrongdoing and then regret for it, the scenes where the pickpocket deftly uses his fingers to pick a pocket or the way he reaches inside the coat to pick a pocket are a treat to watch but, they lead the audience to feel an anguish and sorrow for the hero. The director has very minutely captured on film, what the pickpocket feels. People don't really care to see the way a thief or a dacoit looks at the world. But after the litterateurs, it is only the film-makers who are the true artists; they understand humanity. This film is all about gestures of the hand. Bresson's films are all about acting by using gestures. The film *Au Hasard Balthazar* is a story of a young girl and her donkey. Both of them are used by people, both of them wander around with hurt in their hearts. It is quite difficult to make an animal do any acting, in this respect it is a miraculous film. The film *Mouchette* is again a film to do with director's sparse and minimalistic style. It is a story of a poor girl whose alcoholic and abusive father, ailing and bed-ridden mother have literally abandoned her and she is the butt of all taunts and cruelty in her village. The girl takes all this in her stride till she can take it no more. In the end, she wraps herself in clothes given by somebody and rolls into the lake thereby ending her life. Bresson's film *Le Diable Probablement* or *The Devil Probably* is a film of a nihilistic young man, who hires a gunman to end his life. This film won the Silver Bear – Special Jury Prize at the Twenty-seventh Berlin Film Festival and is considered as Bresson's best. The customs of the modern world were dismissed by the young, intelligent man and this is what he says to his doctor:

> In losing my life, here's what I'd lose; family planning, holiday packages, cultural, sporting and linguistic games, the cultured man's library, all kinds of sports, how to raise a child, parent–teachers meetings, education: schooling: 0 to 7 years, 7 to 14 years, 14 to 17 years, preparation for marriage, military duties, Europe, decorations (honorary insignia), the single woman, paid sickness leave, unpaid leave, being a successful man, tax benefits for the elderly, local rates, rent-purchase, radio and television rentals, credit cards, home repairs, index-linking. VAT and the consumer. ...

According to Bresson's imagination, the prospect of a suicide, seems necessary to do away with the unbearable emptiness of life. There are always interruptions in the way of leading a life of righteousness, in an immoral world. The suicide of an innocent, helpless person is certainly a cause for anguish when such a thing happens. The 1983 film, *L'Argent* or *Money*, is Bresson's last film and is based on Leo Tolstoy's novella *The Forged Coupon*. It won the Director's Prize at the 1983 Cannes Film Festival. The film is a story of how an innocent man has to go through a string of troubles because of a counterfeit note which he accepts unknowingly. He loses his daughter and wife because of penury when he is arrested. He is given shelter by a kind soul, but, he murders everyone in that family in a spate of rage. The sorrow which the protagonist feels after the murders is shown through the barking of a dog. This way of showing grief through an animal is quite a pervasive view of life and nature.

Bresson liked making films because according to him cinema is not immortal like a painting but will be forgotten. He says that things must be destroyed for new things to be created. Newness is the beauty of creation, says Bresson. Jean-Luc Godard has called Bresson as French cinema, just as Dostoevsky is Russian novels and Mozart is German music. The author believes that Bresson's films, with their morality, undercurrents, and human sorrow and anguish will remain embedded in the hearts of filmlovers forever.

Swedish film-maker Ingmar Bergman (1918–2007) did not have too much of a financial struggle to make films. After 1960, most of his films were made on a small island, on a small budget with only eighteen of his trusted associates. He was never bothered about box office success. He thought his films were depressing and disappointing. The classical Indian viewpoint says that his disappointment can be attributed to his atheism, his inability to overcome the fear of death and his mental rebellion. Pity or pathos is much deeper than depression and disappointment. Many of Bergman's films, in spite of this, give an unforgettable rendition of pathos. His film *Wild Strawberries* (1957) is the story of an aged professor who travels to another city to receive an honorary degree from his ex-university. His daughter-in-law, who accompanies him, tells him about his callous and arrogant nature while on the way. Throughout the journey, the professor laments about his lost dreams and discordant marital life. He is forced by recurrent nightmares, daydreams and fear of impending death to revaluate his life. Bergman, in his films, through special cinematography and unparalleled art of storytelling, doesn't let the sorrow be only mournful but he makes it seem more like a delicate and subtle condolence. His excellent film *Persona* (1966) is renowned for the new experimentation and new techniques used in film-making. This film is the story of a stage actress who is recuperating at a seaside resort along with her nurse. She decides to cease speaking. She goes into a depression due to her incapability to accept motherhood and because of her unhappy marital life. The nurse, who cannot accept this predicament, tries to talk to her by telling her about her own experiences, but she too goes into a depression. Philosophical and contemplative problems, if not solved, bring about impediments in the path of righteous behaviour. *Cries and Whispers* (1972), a film set at the end of the nineteenth century, is the story of three sisters who come to live in a huge mansion, to care for the eldest sister, who is on her deathbed. They are not able to give the required care to their sister as they are torn between her impending death and the hope that she dies. The ill sister in the wake of her death begs them for the care denied to her. The sisters are pained at this and the sorrow that ensues touches their psyche. *Fanny and Alexander* (1982) is the longest of Bergman's film, it is five hours long. The director wanted people to watch it uninterrupted. Noted director Alfred Hitchcock was of the view that the length of a film should be directly related to the endurance of the human bladder. *Fanny and Alexander* is a film about two siblings and the ill-treatment they get from their stepfather. Their mother is powerless to do anything and watches in vain. The anguish which the entire family goes through because of the stepfather is something only Bergman could have extracted from his actors. Through this film, Bergman reiterated that even one wrong decision, an unrighteous act and unfulfilled life can become the reason for sorrow and pathos.

Polish director Andrzej Wajda (1926–2016) made three films based on the Second World War: *A Generation* (1954), *Kanal* (1956) and *Popiol I Diament* or *Ashes and Diamonds* (1958). These films are great achievements for Polish cinema. The film *Kanal*, a part of the trilogy, is a story of how a contingent of the army uses the underground sewers to escape the Nazi attackers. Even though the army contingent gets dispersed when inside the sewer, they find it difficult to get out of the sewer and most of them are killed by the Germans. In this story, despondency is the reason for anguish and grief. The film *Ashes and Diamonds* tells the story of the rebellious nature of youth. The duel between a young revolutionary's love interest and his way of thinking is very objectively depicted in the movie. The hero falls in love with a barmaid and keeps staving off his mission which in reality is assassination. This kind of a duel and thought keeps people away from choosing the wrong paths in life.

Les Quartre Cents Coups or *The Four Hundred Blows* (1959) is a French film by director François Truffaut (1932-84). This film tells the story of a young schoolgoing boy, who is thought to be a nuisance both by his teachers and parents alike. He plans to run away from home and, to facilitate that, steals a typewriter from his father's office. He feels a remorse for his act and when he is replacing the stolen article, is caught by his father and sent to jail immediately. This film did quite well commercially, as a part of the La Nouvelle Vague or The French New Wave. It was in a way the director's biography, a picture of his depressing childhood.

American director, Orson Welles, in an interview had declared that if there was any one film on the basis of which he would get entry into heaven; it would be his own film *Chimes at Midnight* (1965). Based on many plays of Shakespeare (most notably – Henry IV), this film is quite close to his personal life. He urged his alcoholic father to give up drinking, by threatening to stop supporting him financially. He even told his father that he would never meet with him if he doesn't stop drinking. A few days later his father died when alone. Welles did not stop berating himself for his father's death and never forgave himself. Similarly, in the film *Chimes at Midnight*, the new king insults his friend and well-wisher Falstaff in front of the entire court and exiles him from the kingdom. Soon after, the friend dies. It does seem that the entire film has been shot for the last scene itself, which is the most gut-wrenching of all. Although the story belongs to Shakespeare, but one must not forget that to bring about an unforgettable effect in cinema, it is not only the plot which holds sway but the editing of the film, music, sets and costumes, selection of the actors, acting, camera angles all play a part in making the film outstanding. All this is, of course, the forte of the director.

Italian director, Michelangelo Antonioni (1912–2007), in many of his films, has depicted the interruptions which come in the way of righteous behaviour due to a modern lifestyle from a purely woman's perspective. In his film *L'Avventura* (1960), Antonioni has beautifully captured the pathos felt by the hero and the heroine when they realize they are in love with each other but are not able to be together as the hero is the heroine's best friend's boyfriend. This immoral behaviour is a cause for sorrow and anguish. *La Notte* (1961) is another film by the same director, it also deals with immoral relationships that a married couple have with other people and how the sorrow of that tears them apart while still keeping them together. The death of their friend leads the heroine to want death for herself too and the anguish she feels when her husband romances another woman in her presence, burns slowly inside her although outwardly she is nonchalant. Both *L'Avventura* and *La Notte* received world acclaim, with the latter receiving the Golden Bear at the German International Film Festival. Antonioni was in the league of great film-makers such as Japanese directors Yasujiro Ozu and Akira Kurosawa, Austrian-German master Fritz Lang and American master John Ford, all of them were not particularly enthusiastic about colour in films, but when the era of coloured films came, they outshone everyone in the business. Antonioni's first colour film, *Red Desert* (1964), tells the story of how a woman can't keep up with the technical advances that happen after the Industrial Revolution and tries to survive despite them. She is shocked to find that her son fakes an illness to talk to her because he thinks that she is completely alienated and alone. The anguish that the woman feels connects her to the audience who empathize with her and grieve with her.

John Cassavetes (1929-89), an actor-director, born in a displaced Greek family, in his first film *Shadows* (1959), has depicted the story of non-acceptability within the society of African–American families and how they suffer the frustration and suffocation dealt to them. His second independent film *Faces* (1968) tells the story of high society American families, their suffocating and pretentious marriages and the anguish and grief arising out of such relationships. His film, *A Woman Under the Influence* (1974), has his wife Gena Rowlands in the lead role, it tells the story of the mental problems undergone by a married woman, who while caring for the children is sent off to a mental asylum by her husband. The sorrow and grief shown touches the heart of the spectator. Another film starred in by Gena Rowlands, *Gloria* (1980), is a praiseworthy thriller wherein the heroine saves the life of a child from the clutches of a confederation of wrong-doers. John Cassavetes will always be remembered for making good quality, independent films with limited resources.

Hungarian director Zoltán Fábri (1917-94) is famous for his epic film, *Húsz óra* or *Twenty Hours* (1965). His film, *Az ötödik pecsét* or *The Fifth Seal* (1976) is quite well known for depicting the anguish felt when a person follows the unrighteous path. In this film, some revolutionaries are plotting a coup against the government and are arrested on the basis of suspicion. One of them is a middle-aged man who runs an orphanage. The police decide to release them on the basis of one condition; that they must slap one hardened revolutionary. His associates do not agree for this, but the middle-aged man agrees as he wants to return to his orphanage.

Andrei Tarkovsky (1932-86) dedicated his last film, *Offret* or *The Sacrifice* (1986), to his friend, director Ingmar Bergman.

This film was unusually complicated and impenetrable. The film is centred on a middle-aged intellectual, who bargains with God that he will give up everything he loves if an impending nuclear holocaust is stopped. The next day he finds that everything is normal and remembers his bargain and sets about destroying everything he loves, he even sets fire to his lovely house. This film received rave reviews for its artistic portrayal and cinematography. It even won the Grand Prix at the Cannes Film Festival. This film, like Tarkovsky's *Nostalghia*, is known for its long and beautiful shots. The director through these films wants to depict the complicated nature of the predominant *rasa*s.

Spanish director, Pedro Almodovar (b.1949), is well known for new types of cinema. His three films, *Mujeres al borde de un ataque denervios* or *Woman on the Verge of a Nervous Breakdown* (1988), *Todo sobre mi Madre* or *All About My Mother* (1999) and *Hable con ella* or *Talk to Her* (2002) depict the depressing lives of the people who are not able to synchronize their lives according to the changes in the modern-day Western and pop culture. In the film, *Hable con ella*, a male nurse falls in love with a young girl who is in coma. Despite his friend's repeated advice, he doesn't relent and finally commits suicide, unable to take the harassment the young girl is undergoing. His friend's unrighteous behaviour becomes a reason for anguish in the film. Pedro Almodovar brings in the new age problems faced by the modern world into his films. It is important that a great deal of attention be paid to this.

There could also be situations where the righteous path is often coupled with a person's own desire but that has been checked by society or some other external factors. Luis Buñuel often explored destiny as a major theme in his works. This can be seen in the following two examples before concluding this subsection:

- The American movie *I Am a Fugitive from a Chain Gang* (1932) is one such tale-based on real life incidents where the wrongly convicted protagonist is forced to spend a torturous life in jail and even after his escape and subsequent marriage there is no end to his troubles. Versatile actor Paul Muni (1895–1967) in the leading role has immortalized the end scene of the movie; when his lover, who finds him hiding from the police for about a year, asks, "How do you live?" he answers, "I steal". The decision to avoid the righteous path was probably the only way that appeared correct to the protagonist.

- Film essayist and film director Chris Marker (1921–2012) made an interesting science-fiction featurette *La Jetée* (1962) that was entirely constructed from still photographs about a post-nuclear war world. This experimental movie explored the idea of time-travel and romantic relationships developed in such a scenario marred by destiny.

We must also remember that according to the *rasa-siddhānta*, a person who is humane and compassionate must possess the same feelings as in the creator's heart, i.e. he must be able to imagine the same way as the poet or author or director does, his thoughts must be in total harmony with that of the creator.

Leon Bloy (1846–1917), a French poet, said that the only real sadness, the only real failure, the only great tragedy in life is not to become a saint. Philosophers like Bharata Muni and Abhinavagupta would have certainly applauded him.

Loss of Wealth

One more reason to feel anguish or sorrow is the loss of wealth. It is then a moral question to ask what is wealth and how much loss would qualify for bereavement? With reference to this context, there is a *śloka* in Sanskrit:

सर्वनाशे समुत्पन्ने ह्यर्धं त्यजति पण्डितः ।
अर्धेन कुरुते कार्यं सर्वनाशः हि दुःसहः ॥

sarvanāśe samutpanne hyardhaṁ tyajati paṇḍitaḥ ।

ardhena kurute kāryaṁ sarvanāśaḥ hi duḥusaḥ ॥

When the time for total loss is near then an intelligent person readily sacrifices half of what he has, knowing fully well that life can be lead very frugally, but losing everything is quite cumbersome and heart wrenching.

The film *The Grapes of Wrath* (1940) was based on Nobel Laureate, John Steinbeck's Pulitzer Prize-winning novel of the same name. It was directed by John Ford (1894–1973) and depicted the acute financial setbacks that people had to undergo because of the economic depression in the Americas during 1930s. The story is about a joint family which has to leave its hometown and travel more than a thousand miles in search of livelihood.

Ladri di Biciclette or *Bicycle Thieves* (1948), directed by Italian Vittorio De Sica (1901-74), has been counted as one of the most outstanding films in world cinema. Noted for neorealism, this film is preceded by De Sica's other film, *Sciuscia* or *Shoeshine* (1946). It follows two shoeshine boys, who try to earn enough money to buy a horse but are falsely trapped by thugs and are imprisoned.

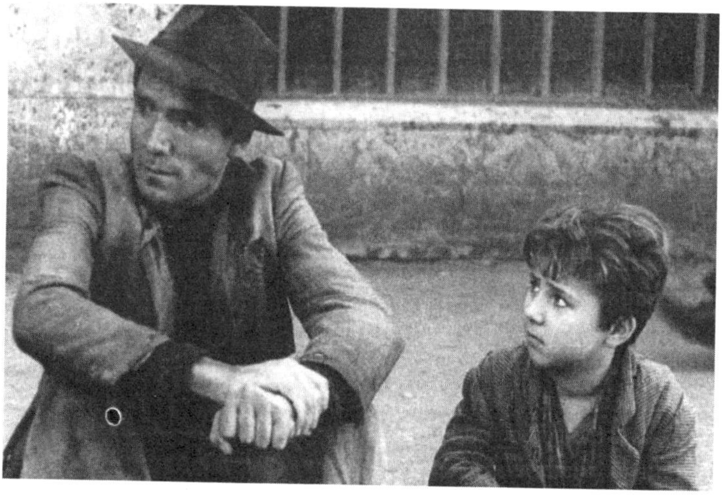

Bicycle Thieves (1948)

Loss of wealth, abject poverty and the anguish arising out of this is the mainstay of De Sica's films. The film *Ladri di Biciclette* is a prime example of Italian Neo-Realism and enjoys the status of being a recurring contender for the greatest movie ever made. The film follows a poor, unemployed father's quest for a job to keep his family. He gets a job of pasting advertisement bills, but the prerequisite is a cycle. The couple pawn their bed-linen to get back their pawned cycle. On the first day itself, the bicycle is stolen and the father–son pair set about searching for it. They are unable to find it anywhere. The bicycle is their only possession and means to a livelihood. The hopelessness felt by the father and son is a must watch. I recollect the time when this film was screened in the common room of my hostel, not one student was left dry-eyed after watching the last scene. A cinema lover must see this film, if not done already. Director Vittorio De Sica's next film, *Umberto D* (1951), follows the tragic story of an old man and his dog who have been evicted from their house. This was one of director Ingmar Bergman's favourite films.

Los Olvidados (1950) is a Mexican film made by Spanish director Luis Buñuel (1900-83), which is a favourite of many great writers, for example, Nobel Laureate Mario Vargas Losa. It follows the story of some poor boys that are also wicked and beat up a beggar. Their devilish pranks are portrayed and filmed with brutal, realistic settings. This film depicts all kinds of anguish and sorrow like immorality, debauchery, loss of some amount of wealth and death. Being poor as well as an orphan brings with it, its own tragedies, and this has been beautifully portrayed in the film. The famous films of Luis Buñuel like *Viridiana* (1961), *Tristana* (1970), *The Discreet Charm of the Bourgeoisie* (1972), *The Phantom of Liberty* (1974) and *That Obscure Object of Desire* (1977) do not depict any one particular *rasa*, but is an amalgamation of many *rasa*s and *bhāva*s, and Luis Buñuel, through his films, wanted people to know his views on important matters and wanted that people should think on their own based on the art depicted in the films. He knew that experience is very vital, and explained that the spectator's intelligence and his keenness to understand the message of the film were very important. The kind of diversity that Luis Buñuel has depicted in his films, in a long and illustrious career, no other director comes even close to it. He has never advertised his films, nor has he tried to explain his works or give any justification for them. Even when he was pressurized to accept an Oscar, he did so reticently. He wore large shades and a wig to collect the award.

Federico Fellini (1920-93) started off as an assistant to Roberto Rossellini, and then went on to become one of the famous directors of the world. *8½* or *Otto e Mezzo* (1963) is his career's most unique film which divides his entire work into pre-*8½* and post-*8½*. Films like *I Vitteloni* (1953), *La Strada* (1954), *Nights of Cabiria* (1957) and *La Dolce Vita* (1960) are all pre-*8½*. They tell the stories

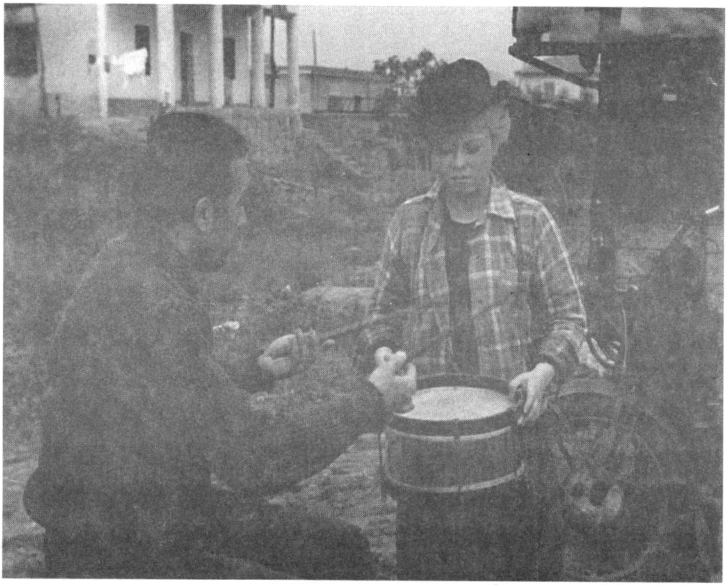

La Strada (1954)

of absurdities and tragedies in society. The post-*8½* films are: *Satyricon* (1969) and *Amarcord* (1973). These films were starkly different from the earlier ones, they depicted dream sequences, memoires, musicals and celebrations. At the end of his career, Fellini started losing people's respect. Film audiences saw his last few films out of sheer respect and nothing else.

Two of his films are noteworthy for the Karuṇa Rasa depicted in them: *La Strada* and *Nights of Cabiria.* Both the films are women-centric and the lead role was essayed by Fellini's wife Giulietta Masina. Both the films won the Best Film in a Foreign Language Award at the Oscars. Giulietta Masina got the Best Actress award for *Nights of Cabiria* at the Cannes Film Festival. The film *La Strada,* follows the story of Zampano, a street performer, who buys his dead wife's sister from his mother-in-law to perform alongside him. The young girl, played by Masina, does not enjoy performing on the streets, but has no choice. The film ends on a very tragic note where, Zampano abandons her, but when he comes to know that she has wasted away and died, he feels immense remorse and cries.

Fellini suffered a nervous breakdown whilst making this film due to financial setbacks. Critics had called this film worthless, but today it is counted among the best films worldwide. The heroine, Masina, received countless letters from poor and abandoned women, world over, who claimed that after seeing this film, their husbands returned home. Cinema is truly miraculous and art has the wherewithal to show the path of truth and righteousness to people.

The film *Nights of Cabiria* tells the story of a prostitute Cabiria, who is taken advantage of by her boyfriend-lover. He tries to kill her and vanishes with her money. She is made fun of and laughed at, in a magician's show, where she is hypnotized and her real feelings and desires of living a normal life are known. People laugh at how a prostitute can dream of marrying and having a family. While walking the streets she sees the reality of life, where a young man is drawn to her and wants to marry her, but again, it is only for her money. Both the films are well known for their memorable climax scenes.

Greek–American director, Elia Kazan (1909–2003), made a film called *A Street Car Named Desire* (1951), in which a very poor, alcoholic young girl has to take refuge in her sister and brother-in-law's home. She gets insulted for her habit of showing off unnecessarily. The tragic and anguishing film ends when, after a nervous breakdown, some officials come to take her off to an institution. The protagonist remarks in the concluding scene about her pitiful situation, "Whoever you are, I have always depended on the kindness of strangers". It is a purely sorrowful film which has all the ramblings of woefulness and shows how poverty can reduce one to a very pitiful state. Director Woody Allen made *Blue Jasmine* (2013), a much-talked about film with a similar story. Elia Kazan's other noteworthy movies are *On the Waterfront* (1954) and *East of Eden* (1955).

Sunset Boulevard (1950) is a magnificent film about a silent era actress who wants a second innings at acting. The film is a harsh depiction of how life treats a successful actress who has lost her looks. The film directed by Billy Wilder is very poignant and unforgettable.

It is quite unimaginable to fathom the condition of an emperor, who has been stripped of his kingdom and thrown into a prison. When he is released from prison, he has to work as a gardener for a living. Such is the story of the epic film, *The Last Emperor* (1987), directed by Italian Bernardo Bertolucci (1941–2018). It has won nine Academy awards and is based on the life story of the last Chinese Emperor Aisin-Gioro Puyi (1906-67). The history of China is flashed through the story of this film. Loss of wealth and loss of power are very humbling and this has been very effectively shown through the life story of Puyi. Bernardo Bertolucci's other films *The Conformist* (1970) and *Last Tango in Paris* (1972) are noteworthy and watchable.

The two films of Theo Angelopoulos (1935–2012); *Ulysses' Gaze* (1995) and *Eternity and a Day* (1998) are remembered for the hopelessness which is born out of a disregard for worldly objects. The film shows the impact that Antonioni, Tarkovsky, Orson Welles and Kenji Mizoguchi had on Angelopoulos. These films do not show the actual loss of wealth, but show the erosion of beautiful memories, desires and even our age-old traditions. Our culture and traditions are after all our wealth, which when lost do hurt us immensely. In the film *Eternity and a Day*, the hero who is on the verge of death, gets very attached to all the material objects which he will lose otherwise.

Gloom Born Out of Death

The sorrow and pain arising out of the death of a dear person is a distressing experience. The truth of life is death and there are many philosophical thoughts that are put forth on this. Even the thought of a dear one dying brings great pain to us, but it is the infallible truth that anyone who is born has to die. Such bereavement is generally seen in connection with someone's untimely death. A person's death at a hundred years or more is celebrated as it happens rarely. Untimely death happens for the following reasons: war, illness, murder, death at childbirth, accidents, suicide, natural disasters, etc. All these are causes for grief and bereavement.

All Quiet on the Western Front (1930) is a film based on a novel of the same name and is a much talked about and awarded film which shows the atrocities and futility of war. The film starts when a teacher in a school gives an impassioned speech on the virtues of fighting for the country, some of the students enrol for the war. But, their romance with uniforms and guns is shattered when they are on the front and see dead and mutilated bodies of their own friends strewn around. The horrors of war are enough to disillusion them completely. The last scene gives a ray of hope when the protagonist stretches his hand toward a butterfly, hoping to catch it, but instead he is caught in the cross-hairs of a sniper and is shot dead. This movie should be shown in senior secondary schools for anti-war sentiments, where students can contemplate that unchannelled anger and hasty decisions can plunge them into situations unimagined.

French director, Jean Renoir (1894–1979), made a film against the backdrop of Bengal called *The River* (1951). Renowned director Satyajit Ray was so profoundly inspired by Renoir that he decided to adapt Bibhutibhushan Bandhopadyay's novel into the film *Pather Panchali* (1955). He had to pawn his wife's jewellery to get the film going, the West Bengal government too helped with a loan for the film, through the road improvement department, a reference to film's title. In my opinion Satyajit Ray's cinematic works can be used to explain the *rasa-siddhānta* effectively. For his camera movements and simultaneous background scores often constitute laudable determinants (*vibhāva*s) and consequents (*anubhāva*s). His first ever film created an immense excitement world over. This film with its every scene be it Apu and his sister looking at a train for the first time, or their grandmother's death or the scene where his mother and father cry at the death of Durgā or even Apu getting drenched in the rain, are scenes which bring out the intense subtlety of Karuṇa Rasa. His other films, *Aparajito* (1956) and *Apur Sansaar* (1959) too have Karuṇa Rasa as the main *rasa*. These very *rasa* determinants or *vibhāva*s and the actor's consequents or *anubhāva*s are prominently seen in the films *Ashani Sanket* (1973) and *Aranyer Din Ratri* (1999).

Film director Ritwik Ghatak made three very poignant films based on the partition of Bengal: *Meghe Dhaka Tara* (1960), *Komal Gandhar* (1961) and *Subarnarekha* (1963). Although the films don't explicitly depict the dreadful after-effect of the partition, but the sacrifice, death, murder which happened in the society at that time are very realistically depicted. The end of each of these films is emotional and a milestone for Bengali cinema. In the film *Meghe Dhaka Tara*, the elder sister, takes on the responsibility of the entire household without even a stray word. She happily provides for them and even endures their exigencies. She even gives up her love to be of service to the family, but in the end contracts tuberculosis and is almost on the verge of death when her brother takes her to a sanatorium for treatment. The film, *Subarnarekha* follows the story of a woman, who, due to financial problems takes to prostitution. She commits suicide when she finds that her first customer is her own brother who is totally drunk. This last scene is so anguishing and tragic that not a dry eye was seen in the theatre. The last scene of *Meghe Dhaka Tara*, where the heroine's brother leaves her in the sanatorium and returns is so poignant and full of pathos that it is difficult to remain unemotional.

Satyajit Ray and Ritwik Ghatak are by far the most celebrated and respected directors in India. It is imperative to note that both these directors had a very keen ear for music and they were writers par excellence. Ritwik Ghatak even wrote the story of *Madhumati* (1958). They both worked extensively on the storyline and the screenplay of the film. In fact, Satyajit Ray wrote the storyline for all his films. Very few directors have depicted scenes as beautifully or as artistically as him. He had a mastery over editing, directing and an unprecedented vision to bring a newness into every shot. Both these directors lifted cinema above the level of technicalities or commercial successes, they respected cinema as an art, the purest form. They lay emphasis on their own experiences, on traditional values and gave their due to foreign artists, value to their time and in their field contributed most readily and magnanimously.

Sergei Bondarchuk (1920-94) made an ambitious four-part film series: *Voyna i Mir* or *War and Peace* (1966, 1967), based on

Leo Tolstoy's novel, *War and Peace*. This film, sponsored by the Soviet government, was the most expensive film made till then. This film was the Soviet Union's answer to the American–Italian film *War and Peace* made in 1959 by director King Wallis Vidor (1894–1982), it won many prestigious awards and is a film which depicts the worsening condition of Russia after Napoleon's attack. It shows the horrors of war, fights and duels to appease the false ego and unnecessary arson all these tragic scenes make the film an example of Karuṇa Rasa. As Tolstoy identified himself with Pierre Bezukhov, a side character in the novel, Sergei Bondarchuk played this role of a dull outcast nobleman trying to be a part of high society.

We have discussed the painful and tragic film *Ivan's Childhood*, directed by famous Russian director Andrei Tarkovsky. Now, we discuss his Italian film *Nostalghia* (1983). Tarkovsky was very adept at showing extreme grief which cannot be spoken but can only be felt. In this film, he tells the story of a writer, who, after being separated from his country, meets with a strange man. This man has, due to the fear of the world, imprisoned his own wife and children in his house. When the police come to release them after seven years, his children run out of the house like drowning rats. Meanwhile this very strange man, plays the fourth movement of Beethoven's Ninth Symphony and gives a speech on world fraternity and commits suicide by immolating himself. The end of the film, where dogs bark and many dream-like scenes of the strange man lend a very sorrowful and tragic emotion to the film. The death of the hero is much more complicated as compared to simple death and sorrow.

The film, *Il Fiore Delle Mille e Una Notte* or *The Flower of 1001 Nights* or *Arabian Nights*, did not contain the famous stories of the *Arabian Nights* like Alif–Lailā's famous stories, Allādīn and the magic lamp, Alībābā and the forty thieves and Sindbād the sailor, but had other less prominent stories. One such story is the love story of Aziz and Aziza. Italian director Pier Paolo Pasolini (1922-75), who directed this film, gave a complete makeover to a village for this film. He removed everything machine made in the village to give it an authentic eighth-century Arab feel. In the film Aziz falls in love with a beautiful woman just before the wedding with Aziza and stops eating and drinking in remembrance of her. Aziza vows to help him win over the extremely intelligent and mysterious girl. The film ends on a tragic note when, overcome with sadness, Aziza commits suicide. The storyline of the film is based on Arab sensibilities and depicts the culture beautifully.

Hotaru no Haka or *Grave of Fireflies* (1988) is a film directed by Isao Takahata and animated by Studio Ghibli, a famous Japanese institute for making animated films. It is an autobiography of a ten-year old boy and his little, four-year old sister, whose parents are killed during the Second World War. The afflictions and anguish the boy and his little sister undergo when they are forced to stay with relatives are truly a cause for sorrow. There are many scenes filled with pathos like the boy being beaten up by the police and both the brother and sister living on the shores of a lake, etc. This film is an important and effective document against the war. The writer of the novel on which this film is based did not agree for

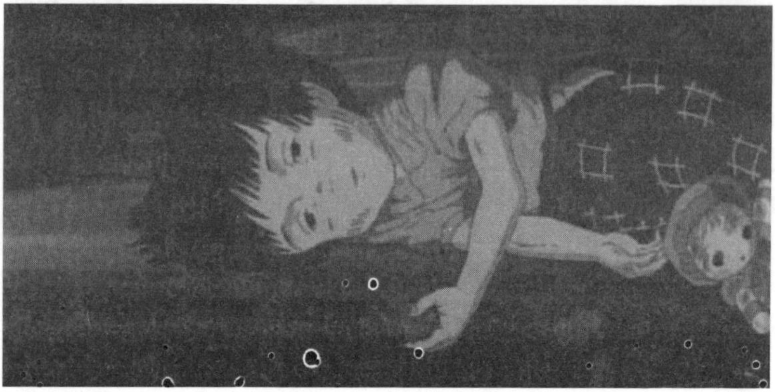

Grave of Fireflies (1988)

making it into a film for a long time, stating that a film will not be able to do justice to the delicate emotions enumerated in the book, but when he was shown the story-board for the animated version, he agreed as it was the nearest to his own imaginations. The animated film was able to do all that which was not possible in a regular film like making a fly drone on a dead body in a particular way. It is impossible to direct flies.

The Seventh Continent (1989) is a tragic film following the story of a middle-class family's enmasse suicide for unknown reasons. Directed by Austrian, Michael Haneke (b.1942), the story is about a family whose head starts selling off all the objects in the house and states that the family is moving off to the seventh continent: Australia. He flushes off the money got from the sale into the toilet. Just as the director had envisioned, the audience finds it difficult to accept the destruction of money rather than the destruction of human life. This depiction of harsh reality is a direct assault on the power of contemplation of the audience.

Polish director Krzysztof Kieslowski (1941-96) made many films based on Karuṇa Rasa. His main films like *The Decalogue* (1989) – a ten-part television series, *The Double Life of Veronique* (1991) and *The Three Colours* trilogy (1993-94), which has three parts: *Three Colours – Blue* (1993), *Three Colours – White* (1994) and *Three Colours – Red* (1994), are considered great films of world cinema. The standard of the ten-part television series was so high that a director of eminence like Stanley Kubrick also designated it to be a rare work of art. The very first episode of *The Decalogue* is tragic as it depicts the death of a twelve-year old boy. The second episode shows that after the death of his wife and newborn son in a bomb attack, a doctor profoundly understands the importance of life.

Sometimes, man leaves behind tragedy and disappointment and looks toward emancipation. In the film *Three Colours – Blue,* the protagonist, a musician, drowns herself in sorrow following the death of her husband and daughter in a car accident. She tries to search for comfort. In the end, she realizes her folly and follows the path of duty. Thus, even the permanent expressions of sorrow and grief also change with time and circumstances.

Peace always reigns after sorrow and grief.

8

Anger and Ferocity

Important Films of the Raudra Rasa

The *Nāṭyaśāstra*, authored by Bharata Muni, enumerates anger (*krodha*) as the *sthāyī bhāva* of Raudra Rasa. The constituent factors which result in *raudra* (ferocity) are anger, rape, abuses, insults, falsehood, warning, revenge, jealously, etc. The transitory feelings (*vyabhicārī bhāvas*) which help manifest Raudra Rasa are pride, envy, ardour, impulsiveness, arrogance, inconsistency, ferocity, sweating, trembling, horripilation, feebleness of the voice, etc. (द्विवेदी 1992: 175).

Anger can be of five types:

1. caused by the enemy,
2. caused by a noble person,
3. caused by a lover,
4. caused by employees, and
5. false anger.

Anger, in drama, is depicted by reddening of the eyes, shooting up of the eyebrows, biting of the lips, clutching of one hand with the other, etc. In the *Nāṭyaśāstra,* depiction of Raudra Rasa is generally used to characterize demons and evil beings. This is probably how the Sanskrit dramas were directed. The *Nāṭyaśāstra* is silent on the interpretation of its theories, apart from directions to form an opinion, nothing else is forthcoming.

Prima facie, it is very difficult to point out the actual manifestation of Raudra Rasa and the manifestation of the feeling of anger. In our earlier discussions, we have seen that anger is the emotion which leads into Vīra Rasa and Vībhatsa Rasa. We know that anger is the *sthāyī bhāva* of Raudra Rasa, but it is difficult to ascertain when this turns into a full-fledged *rasa* or how long it remains in the *sthāyī bhāva* itself. With reference to the complications which arise in the manifestation of the *rasa*, it is quite significant to mention here the example of a folk dance of Kerala: Kathakali, a description of the killing of Duḥśāsana by Pāṇḍava prince Bhīma. Based on the *Veṇīsaṁhāra,* a play by the eighth-century Sanskrit scholar Bhaṭṭa Nārāyaṇa, when Bhīma goes to kill Duḥśāsana, the expression on his face and the body language show Raudra Rasa, this quickly changes into Vīra Rasa once the fight commences. It further changes into Vībhatsa Rasa when Bhīma gruesomely kills Duḥśāsana by tearing apart his arm and chest and drinks blood from him torn chest. This Vībhatsa Rasa changes into Śṛṅgāra Rasa, when he washes Draupadī's hair with the blood from Duḥśāsana's body. It does seem, according to the *rasa-siddhānta*, the understanding and relishing of the *rasa*s along with the help of the determinant feelings (*vibhāvas*), consequents (*anubhāvas*) and the transitory feelings (*vyabhicārī bhāvas*) maybe an easy accomplishment, but in truth it is extremely complex in nature. World cinema has many great works which bear a mute testimony to this.

Arthur Schopenhauer may have conceptualized beauty when he was impressed by the Indian classical aesthetic theory. It is said that the usefulness of our intellect is only ascertained when we are able to bring forth conclusive proofs to our assumptions of space, time and causality. But the concept of beauty takes away any arguments of the intellectual self. Here, we can also use psyche, instead of intellect, and instead of self-realization, we can say it is the psyche which is in the awareness mode. It is imperative to understand that German philosopher, Schopenhauer, doesn't merely appreciate beauty but, reconstructs the reactions, and does survey on the psyche which is completely soaked in the essence of beauty. Apart from art, our mental disposition is attached to our selfish interests too, but with reference to art, the connoisseur is unbiased. Nevertheless, every philosopher has certain clear thoughts on the metaphysical and epistemological guidelines, without which that philosophical tradition is next to impossible. It is because of the inherent difference between the metaphysical and epistemological views that philosophies appear so greatly varied.

How is anger defined? According to Baruch Spinoza, anger is a desire whereby through hatred, we are induced to injure the one we hate. If this injury is because of some hurt we have faced personally, then it is called revenge or retribution. We are discussing Spinoza here because nobody has described feelings as beautifully or as effectively as him. Anybody who is seriously interested and curious about life must read his book *Ethics*. I would go so far in saying that a person, who has not read *Ethics*, should think a hundred times before venturing into an argument as the uninformed are most prone to be contradictory. It is just like, although somebody does not know Euclidian Geometry, but has a yearning to learn Riemannian Geometry. We do come across people debating on various issues but most of them are baseless or blank. An advice for the curious, if anyone wants to debate or argue, then make sure you prepare yourself well on the subject or else enjoy the peace which is always beneficial.

Abhinavagupta says that Raudra Rasa is mainly manifested whenever injustice is done (द्विवेदी 1992: 175-86). People everywhere want to punish the perpetrator of injustice. It has been proven that injustice is the main cause of anger. The anger is mainly targeted toward the person who is responsible for the unjust act and people are even willing to kill for that.

Let us look at the example of what Mahākavi Bhāsa, has said:

> Neither is it the Tretā Yuga, nor is it the devoted place of Lord Rāma, neither is Sītā present nor is there the soft-hearted Lord Rāma, even then, people would not be sated if they kill Rāvaṇa just as mercilessly.
>
> – द्विवेदी 1992: 175

When Raudra Rasa is manifested, it is in the form of exasperation. In his treatise, the *Abhinavabhāratī*, Abhinavagupta clarifies that demons and monsters are by nature ferocious, they have an inherent craving for violence, they are hence called overbearing. Due to this impertinent nature itself, Bhīma was able to make such an improper vow of drinking the blood of Duḥśāsana after killing him. Anger is not the correct motive for any war. The determinants (*vibhāvas*) which help realize Raudra Rasa are: other person's anger, contempt of women, telling lies, torturing the elders of the house, the desire to hit or kill someone instantly, finding faults in another's good nature, etc. Anger is not the prerogative of demons and monsters, but they are thought to be the masters of it due to their ferocious nature. How do the people in a society get angry or show resentment when they see demons? Abhinavagupta says that when the intended meaning gets communicated to the heart, it is called realization of the *rasa*. In anger, the heart identifies with the dark-natured people of the society. That is why persons who have a compassionate heart cannot tolerate anybody perpetrating injustice and show their wrath toward them. This cannot be termed as a fault.

The Greek Tragedy *Medea* is about a revenge taken by a former princess, Medea. She brutally kills both her sons to teach a lesson to her wayward husband so that he mends his ways. This drama shows the emotions of anger till they end up in anguish. This is an example which shows us that many such emotions are attached to anger and ire. We will concentrate on those works of world cinema which show anger or wrath as the main sentiment as compared to Vībhatsa Rasa, Karuṇa Rasa and Vīra Rasa which have been delegated to the background. Danish film director Lars von Trier directed *Medea* (1988) based on Carl Dreyer's adaptation of this Greek tragedy.

Rage is normally considered to be destructive, it is said to deprive one of intellect. An angry person ends up forgetting the difference between right or wrong. Director of silent movies, D.W. Griffith (1875–1947), made an American film, *Broken Blossoms* (1919), in which the famous actress, Lilian Gish has enacted the role of a small girl who gets beaten up by her boxer father for no apparent reason. To escape from the daily beatings, the girl locks herself up in a small room, but her exasperated father, takes an axe and hacks down the door of the room and drags the young girl outside and beats her brutally with a cane. This film is remembered for the acting of an angry man and the acting skills of an afflicted young girl.

Cinema has been many a time used for propaganda too. The film *Triumph des Willens* or *Triumph of the Will* (1935), a Nazi Party film, was made solely to promote Hitler as a leader of the masses and a messiah. Cinema is used negatively, when it is thought that to awaken the anger and resentment in viewers, one should show the injustice done. It is always in anger that man loses control of his intellectual faculties and is prone to be misused or misappropriated. Gautama Buddha says that just as it is impossible to see one's face clearly in a pot of boiling water, it is also impossible to take a clear or correct decision when one is angry. It is imperative to keep in mind that these dictums are valid for anger targeted toward an enemy and not toward parents or teachers who scold you in anger or anger shown by a lover or anger shown to an employee by the boss or employer or even falsely shown anger.

Is anger bad or showing any type of anger, dangerous? An old fable has it that a venomous snake was once advised by a hermit to give up biting people. When people came to know, they started throwing stones to injure the snake. The snake took its grievances to the hermit, who listened carefully and then told the snake that he had told him not to bite, but he had never told him not to bare his fangs and scare people. It is neither natural nor is it customary, that anger be done away with totally. The circumstances of anger have to be understood correctly. Every now and then, for political gains, many publicity stunts and vicious propaganda are used to agitate and anger people. People are still ready to kill and maim in the name of anger.

The silent and black and white era film, *Battleship Potemkin* (1925), directed by Russian film-maker Sergei Eisenstein (1898–1948), is considered as a noteworthy film in the history of world cinema. The most talked about scene of this film is the massacre on the steps of Odessa, which people believe to be a historical event, but which is only imagined in the film. In the film, the sailor's revolt, the revolutionary's anger and the wanton crowd's backing for the revolutionaries are like a double-edged sword. Some critics call it the glorification of the revolutionaries and some say it is a picturization of the madness of a crowd. This film is remembered for its marvellous montage of the various scenes. Montages offer a

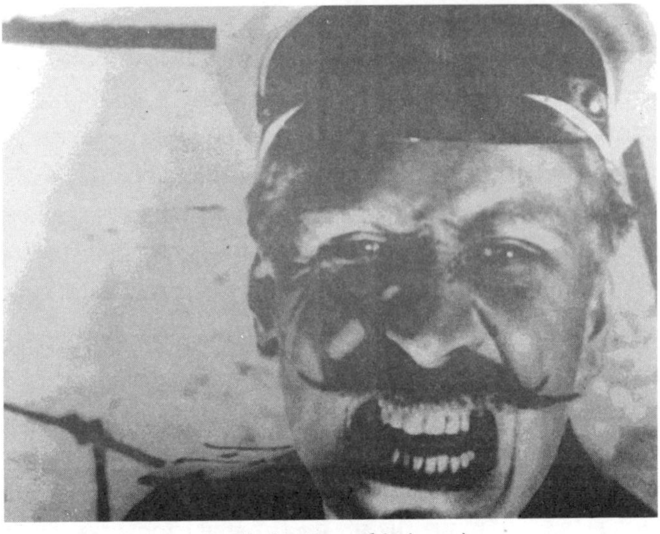

Battleship Potemkin (1925)

complicated problem to the *rasa-siddhānta* for creating a tension between determinants and consequents. Often, rapid montages are depicted for determinants and consequents tend to be slower to manifest the relative permanence and boosting *sthāyī bhāva*. It can be very well observed toward the end of the Odessa steps sequence, when a lady dies, her child's trolley rolls down the steps in comparison to the beginning of the sequence.

Crowd mentality and crowd anger have been superbly directed and filmed by German director Fritz Lang (1890–1976) in his films *M* (1931) and *Fury* (1936). Both the films are noteworthy and historical. They are as relevant today as they were about eighty-five years ago.

The film *M* is about a serial killer of children, who has been escaping the police dragnet. The criminal underworld and the local goons decide to take matters into their own hands, and with the help of beggars on the street, manage to catch the killer. He is produced in front of a Kangaroo court for a trial. The killer's attempt to prove himself innocent when faced with the wrath of the underworld is truly remarkable. In the film *Fury*, an innocent man is imprisoned on the mistaken suspicion that he is a kidnapper. The

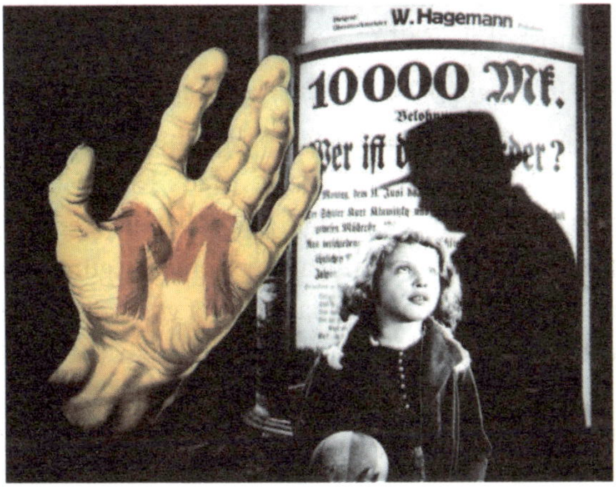

Fritz Lang's M (1931)

rumours of this reach the people of the city and they burn down the Mayor's office so that the kidnapper may be killed. Such an unruly and trigger-happy crowd can be seen, even today, in every city, every street, everywhere, and we will continue finding such a crowd and will go on searching for such a human being till their moral standards do not rise. The second half of the film shows that a trial is being conducted on twenty-two people of a crowd for killing one innocent man. The film shows a court scene where, during the trial, the prosecutor produces a newsreel as hard evidence to prove the members of the crowd guilty.

Orson Welles, the great American director, once challenged a producer, to bring him the worst possible script and that he would make a great movie out of the same. The script was in the form of a novel called *Badge of Evil*. Welles made the film *Touch of Evil* (1958), which was a film noir and went on to become a huge success and a much talked about film. Orson Welles played the role of a police inspector, whose pent-up and simmering anger is the soul of the film. This film is a great example that a film is not just dependent on an outstanding script, but on camera angles, dialogues, imagination of the scenes to be shot, choosing the right location, choosing the right actors, etc. Some of these parameters may go awry sometimes but do work most of the time.

Agurrie, The Wrath of God (1972) is a fine example of Raudra Rasa in films. Made by German director, Werner Herzog (b.1942), this film casts famous German actor, Klaus Kinski (1926-91), known for his temper and tantrums, as a sixteenth-century cruel and aggressive commander of the armed forces. Agurrie leads an expedition to search for the legendary city of gold, El Dorado and becomes an undisputed but tyrannical leader in the jungles of Amazon. He kills mercilessly and says this about himself during a conversation:

> If I Aguirre, command the birds to fall off the tree and die, they

> do my bidding. I am the wrath of God. The earth too trembles where I set foot. Those of you who follow the river and me, will find immense wealth, but if anyone betrays me. ...

This film is not just about one man's pride, snobbishness and rage at all, but a document about the wrath of nature and the unforgiving destiny. The actor Kinski's tantrums while shooting is legendary. Rumour has it that Kinski was as temperamental and full of resentment even in real life. His daughter, irked by his growing popularity, let know that she was sexually abused by him, twenty-two years after his death.

The four films of famous film-maker, Martin Scorsese (b.1942) – *Taxi Driver* (1976), *Raging Bull* (1980), *Goodfellas* (1990) and *Gangs of New York* (2002) – reveal that he has always been mesmerized by Raudra Rasa. In all these films, the actor is shown to have a simmering anger just beneath the surface, who doesn't hesitate to even kill someone at the slightest pretext. These characters show the images of a crime-infested society in America. Many a time, crime is the reason for anger, but anger is not always the character of the offender. Temptation, frustration and barbarism are sometimes the reason for offences. Every act of violence is not perpetrated by anger, but anger toward an enemy is always violent. Violence makes an unwilling person do acts which are against his mind and will either by strength or by force and which cause injury or harm to someone. Sometimes, violence becomes ambitious and uses intellect instead of mere anger.

The film *Taxi Driver* is the story of a retired war veteran who after returning home drives a taxi for survival. Despite being frustrated in his own life, he tries to free a young girl from the throes of prostitution. He buys a gun and practises hitting at hidden or unknown targets, so as to be ready when the time comes. To offset his anger, he tries to search for new targets and new enemies, such enemies whom he can kill legally. The film *Raging Bull* has a professional boxer, who, in anger, fights with his own wife and brother and so becomes the reason for his own downfall. Ace actor Robert De Niro was highly praised for his roles in both the films.

Goodfellas is a movie about the world of organized crime, in which the murder is committed on a very trivial issue of an insult. A gangster kills someone as he gets agitated over the use of an abuse. The film *Gangs of New York* has a father tell his son that the blood stays on the blade, which is an indication of an angry person's violent streak.

What is the meaning of insult or dishonour? It is not as if a person's honour diminishes with just one abusive word. The intention is to disregard or disgrace a person. This contempt or disregard can trigger immense anger in a person. But why, it is a question which requires an extensive thought.

What is the difference between anger, jealousy and envy? The pain one feels on seeing another person's success is called envy; when you feel that the same success and prosperity you could also have had, because you were as capable as the other person. The pain of jealousy is when the other person gets the person or object you love or desire and you start to envy that person. This pain may even give birth to anger and in anger one might try to harm the other person, although it is not imperative that this will happen.

The film *Raise the Red Lantern* (1991), directed by Zhang Yimou, is well known for its fetching scenes. According to some critics, this film was an allegory to the despotic government of the time and so was banned in China for a while. The story is of a nineteen-year old girl who marries an old man after her father's death. The old man already has three wives, who live in a large palace befitted with all luxuries. But, the young girl is tormented by the infighting between all the three wives, various conspiracies being hatched and the ambitiousness of all the wives of the old man. The heroine, instead of keeping quiet, gets angry and starts to find answers for the various problems besetting her. Her anger and powerlessness are her waterloo. Her end in the film is quite saddening. The film was internationally acclaimed and won many awards. Zhang Yimou's other film, *Huozhe* or *To Live* (1994), was awarded the Grand Prix at the Cannes Film Festival. This film was banned in China on the account of its anti-Maoist sentiments.

Urged by the success of the film, *Raise the Red Lantern*, director Chen Kaige (b.1952), made *Farewell My Concubine* (1993), which depicts the fifty-three-year old history of China. This film was honoured at the Cannes Film Festival and also won other international awards. This film follows the story of two friends, who play the parts of "king" and "queen" in dramas. One of the friends gets married and this creates a tension between all three of them, their problems follow with the history of China. This story is the story of envy and jealousy rather than anger and is well remembered for its costumes and set decorations. Leslie Cheung, the singer, actor, music director is closely associated with this film. He is considered as great a musician as Michael Jackson and the Beatles. He later committed suicide.

Many directors over-rate Raudra Rasa, whenever a bullet is fired, it is shown as though a bomb has exploded and when a bomb explodes, it is shown that an atom bomb has exploded. This exaggeration can be traced to a famous Western movie – *Shane* (1953). Quentin Tarantino (b.1963), the American director par excellence, is credited to show violence in the correct way in all his films, be it *Reservoir Dogs* (1992), *Pulp Fiction* (1994), *Kill Bill: Volume 1* (2003), *Kill Bill: Volume 2* (2004), *Inglourious Basterds* (2009) or *Django Unchained* (2012). Of these, the *Kill Bill* series is the epitome for depicting Raudra Rasa, wherein a homage has been paid to Western spaghetti films, the Hong Kong martial arts films, samurai films, etc. *Kill Bill* is the story of a woman, who plans to assassinate all the members of a terrorist gang after they leave her for dead, when she was pregnant about four years back. She goes about meticulously killing them one by one and shows her intense anger and ferocity in the process. She cuts off the arm of one girl and decapitates the head of one member of the gang called O-Ren-Ishii. The films *Inglourious Basterds* and *Django Unchained* too have similar scenes of violence which depict Raudra Rasa. In the modern world, it is quite difficult to show killing as it is inhumane, unpalatable and very harsh. The horror can only be dramatized or filmed and shown to audiences to explain to them the dreadfulness of killing. Quentin Tarantino has been known to use long and engaging dialogues, as *vibhāvas* (determinants). Feelings like insult, anger, hatred, envy and pride are shown here. Even the music which is used to inflame the violence shown on screen is from the Western classical operas.

Noted directors Stanley Kubrick and Jean-Luc Godard also use Western classical music to show some emotions in their works. The Hindi film industry is sadly lacking in the use of India's great classical music heritage and we don't get to hear any pure *rāgas* in film music nowadays. People in the Western countries take pains to learn classical music like Bach, Beethoven, Mozart, Vivaldi, Tchaikovsky and Dvorak, while we despite having a rich heritage of classical music, tend to ignore and forget it. Only a very few people show an interest in learning the classical *rāgas* and correctly identify them. The Hindi film industry can name only a very few music directors who were keen to use the traditional music and the folk music in their compositions. The names of Naushad, Madan Mohan, Jaidev, Shankar Jaikishan, Khayyam, Bhupen Hazarika are etched in gold as those who were inspired by our classical and folk music.

The films made by the Coen Brothers (Joel and Ethan Coen): – *Barton Fink* (1991), *Fargo* (1996) and *No Country for Old Men* (2007) – describe angry offenders. The film *Barton Fink* touches on various subjects like lack of dialogue and interaction between the intelligentsia and the common people, the world wars, anger, crime, murder and mysteries. The film's identity is the anger of the villain. Similarly, in the film *Fargo*, two kidnappers blame their uncontrollable anger as the reason for the various murders they commit during their work. The 2007 film, *No Country for Old Men*, tells the story of an assassin, who has absolutely no hesitation to kill anybody and will go to any length to finish whatever job he has undertaken. This film has been adapted from a novel and its story and acting by the lead actors is worth mentioning.

The discovery of oil wells at the end of the nineteenth century (the fights for them) and the angry ambitions of capitalism are the basis for the film, *There Will Be Blood* (2007), made by director, Paul Thomas Anderson (b.1970). A young priest's ambition clashes with the wish of a businessman who wants to buy an oil well. The businessman is by temperament an angry and crafty person, gets afflicted many times and also afflicts the others.

A *śloka* from *Śrīmad-Bhagavadgītā* II.62 is as follows:

ध्यायतो विषयान्पुंसः संगस्तेषूपजायते ।
संगात्सञ्जायते कामः कामात्क्रोधोऽभिजायते ॥

dhyāyato viśayānpuṁsaḥ saṅgasteśūpajāyate ।
saṅgātsañjāyate kāmaḥ kāmātkrodho'bhijāyate ॥

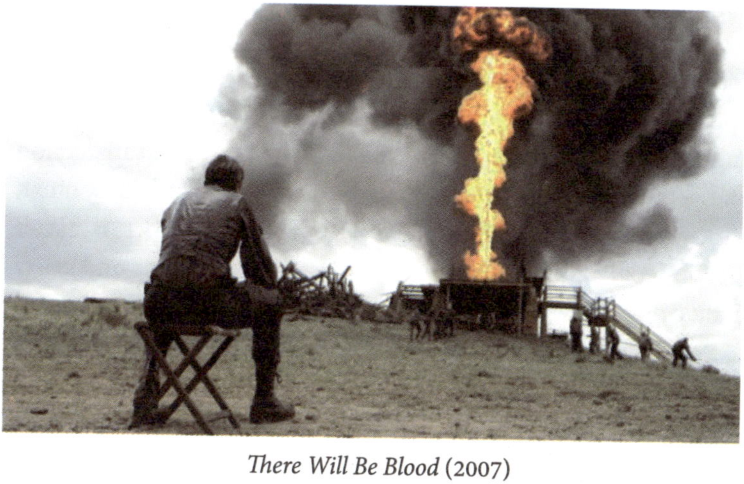

There Will Be Blood (2007)

> One gets attached or infatuated if one thinks about a subject (here it should be understood in the limited sense as a subject of desires), it is this infatuation that arouses the desires and it is these desires that arouse the anger in a person.

According to Abhinavagupta, Raudra Rasa teaches one how to master one of the four goals (*puruṣārthas*) of man, i.e. *arth*. Here, *artha* has a different meaning from the conventional prosperity, it means the effort made to achieve something or accumulate something. The desire to win over someone or to enslave someone is also termed as *artha*.

It is quite thought provoking that all the examples of films made on Raudra Rasa have been admired by cine critics. There is not one among them that discredits the anger shown by a virtuous character. The protagonists of many of the films of Raudra Rasa are shown to be vindictive in nature, they can be called as demons and monsters also.

It is quite important to bring to fore this discussion about *puruṣārtha* that a man's moral conduct is a matter of philosophical debate. Indian philosopher Goswami Shyam Manohar-ji, says that it is concerned with our soul and self-awareness. The self-awareness is that, one should be aware that beyond the call of duty, there lies another duty and that is toward oneself. Whatever duty one is called upon to do is *dharma*, the resources for it to be done is called *artha* and the desire to do the duty is called *kāma* and the satisfaction one gets after the duty is done is *mokṣa*. In the Indian context, philosophers build upon the maxim from *Manusmṛti* 4.176 that all the four goals should be supportive of each other. *Kāma* and *artha* against *dharma* will not bring harmony and similarly, *dharma* and *kāma* against *artha* should not be acceptable (गोस्वामी 2011: 51).

9

Laughter, Fun and Satire

Unparalleled Examples of the Hāsya Rasa in World Cinema

At THE outset, it is pertinent to understand that the mental association between the words laughing and weeping doesn't imply any kind of theoretical collocation between them, such as being contrary to each other. Whatever theories or standards are used to measure laughter, the opposite of that can't be the rule for grieving. The following tale will explain the concept more clearly; a speaker regaled his audience with a great joke and had them in splits. He repeated the joke and the number of people who laughed decreased; he repeated it again and again till no one laughed. He then asked the audience, that when the joke which had them in splits previously was repeated, no one laughed, why then do people cry remembering the same sad episode again and again. The motive of the speaker is not under question here, but what needs to be ascertained is that laughter denotes the feeling of happiness, but it is not the sole expression. The smiling faces seen on happy occasions are not *hāsa bhāva*, but only a display of pleasure. In the same way, weeping is not symbolic to grieving. Tears can also be of happiness. To call laughing and weeping as opposites of each other is nothing but a common error and one must steer clear of it, otherwise it may lead to improper speculation which may further lead to incongruous thoughts and actions.

According to Bharata Muni, the origin of Hāsya Rasa is in the *hāsa sthāyī bhāva*. He says that this *rasa* has taken the form of the *bhāva*, i.e. the *rasa* is exactly like the *hāsa bhāva*. Śr̥ṅgāra Rasa shows the *rati sthāyī bhāva*, while Karuṇa Rasa depicts the *śoka sthāyī bhāva*. All the other *rasa*s follow the *sthāyī bhāva* of their own family. The immense sorrow of *śoka bhāva* gives rise to grief in experiencing the Karuṇa Rasa, and the delight of meeting in *rati bhāva* gives rise to happiness in the spectator while experiencing the Śr̥ṅgāra Rasa.

The determinant causes (*vibhāva*s) for the realization of Hāsya Rasa are inappropriate clothing or ornaments, rude behaviour, greed, petty fights, ill-formed or deformed body parts, use of words out of the context, description of different kinds of defects, etc. The *vyabhicārī bhāva*s (transitory feelings) leading to Hāsya Rasa are laziness, sleepiness, dreamy state, ill-health or ill-spirit, sleeplessness, etc. The consequent effects (*anubhāva*s) are trembling and twitching of the lips, nose and cheeks, dilation and contraction of the eyes, change in the colour of the face and profuse sweating, etc. (द्विवेदी 1992: 159-69).

Hāsa bhāva is of two types:

1. *ātmastha hāsa* (laughing at oneself), and
2. *parastha hāsa* (laughing at others).

Bharata Muni explains *ātmastha hāsa* as laughing at oneself and *parastha hāsa* as laughing at others. Abhinavagupta suggested a correction to this definition and said that *ātmastha hāsa* is the result of the above-mentioned *vibhāva*s, while *parastha hāsa* is the laughter which happens when you see others laugh and the reason for the mirth is known later on. Laughter by virtue is infectious, while love (*rati*), sorrow (*śoka*) and anger (*krodha*) are non-infectious. It is human nature to laugh whenever we see another person laugh (पारेख 1974: 91).

Hāsya Rasa has been divided into three types to facilitate acting: body movements, costumes and use of words and sentences. In the *Nāṭyaśāstra*, according to the rank and nature of the character, laughter has been classified under three heads:

1. *Uttama* – *smita* and *hasita*
2. *Madhyama* – *vihasita* and *upahasita*
3. *Adhama* – *apahasita* and *atihāsita*

Whereas, scholar Keshavadas has described only four types, i.e. *mandahāsa, kalahāsa, atihāsa* and *parihāsa*. In the *Nāṭyaśāstra,* it has been written that the persons of upper class are supposed to use *smita* and *hasita,* where the laughter is subtle and the facial expression shows only a slight curve of the lips and dilation of the eyes. The middle category of the people is to use *vihasita,* where the sound of laughter is heard and *upahasita*, which is used to make fun of others. The lower class of people are to use *apahasita,* where the laughter is very loud and tears flow from the eyes while laughing, and *atihasita*, where the whole body shakes due to laughter.

Just as in the *Nāṭyaśāstra*, Greek dramas too have allocated tragedies for the upper class and comedies for the lower class. Greek philosopher, Aristotle, has also chosen the *hāsa bhāva* for its universal appeal, in his epic book *Poetics*. The second part of this book, in which there is a mention of *hāsa bhāva,* is now unavailable. Western scholar, Henri Bergson (1859–1941), who was the Nobel laureate for literature, wrote an essay on laughter and the meaning of the comic, which even today is referred to as a standard in the discussion of the comic genre. Underlining the difference between tragedy and comedy, Bergson says that tragedy is specific to an individual while comedy specifically points to a class, even though both are enacted in a very special way (Bergson 1901).

Dutch philosopher of Portguese origin, Baruch Spinoza (1632-

77), associated laughter with bodily modifications and omitted it among his list of emotions. According to Spinoza's definition, emotions are quite akin to dormant sentiments and Bharata Muni defines it differently. This difference in the two philosophers' thinking, creates a huge lacuna in their individual theories. Seventh-century poet and philosopher, Bhartṛhari opines in his book *Vākyapadīya*: "The knowledge of what should be done in this world, depends on a word". Based on the importance of languages, it can be interpreted that the word is not merely recognized for its meaning but is also very much instrumental for the direction it gives to our lives.

The important aspect for any debate on the identification of *rasa* and the stable state or the *sthāyī bhāva* is that *sthāyī bhāva* is centred around its stimulus and gives rise to (worldly) functional activities (*arthakriyā*) (Visuvalingam 1983: chap. 7).

Functional activities are a set of activities that determine the meaning of any action. There are two forms of this: outer (*bāhya*) and inner (*āntarika*). The outer functional activities consist of the observable physical activities, for example, a fire must burn the wood. It is by burning, there is a meaning attached to the worldly functional activity. On the other hand, inner functional activities are merely psychological.

Abhinavagupta distinguishes aesthetic functional activities from worldly functional activities by specifying that the former is restricted by being essentially internal. The relishing or self-repose accompanied with pleasure is inner functional activity (*āntarika arthakriyā*) associated with *rasa* relishment. During *rasa* relishing, these inner functional activities can be sometimes identified in a spectator by related reflexive actions such as tears, laughter and horripilation, etc.

While explaining Abhinavagupta's stand, Sunthar Visuvalingam asserts that Abhinavagupta subscribes to Bharata Muni's observations that it is a trivial emotion appealing mostly to women, children and the vulgar. French anthropologist and ethnologist Claude Lévi-Strauss (1908–2009) noted that this "repressive" attitude to laughter has been shared by all traditional cultures, starting with the so-called "primitive" societies, where adult males, particularly the initiated, rarely even smile.

Hāsya Rasa in many ways is an offbeat and quaint *rasa*. Western scholars also do not have consensus culminating into one binding theory to define laughter, fun, satire, comedy and jest. Hāsya Rasa is quite similar to its *hāsa bhāva*, just as Bhayānaka Rasa is similar to the *bhaya bhāva*. Let us now understand the difference and similarities between the *rasa* and the *sthāyī bhāva*. We know that the *rasa* is ultimately relished only when the heart of the spectator becomes one with the heart of the creator (i.e. they become *sahṛdaya* to each other). It is the *sthāyī bhāva* alone, which, with the help of the supporting reasons (*ālambana*), is able to immerse the viewer and help him absorb the *vibhāva*s and bring about the realization or the relishing of the appropriate *rasa*.

Bhayānaka Rasa takes refuge in demons and evil spirits, so as to depict the *bhaya bhāva*, Vīra Rasa has the heroic persons, Karuṇa Rasa takes the support of the victim or the downtrodden to show the *śoka bhāva*, Śṛṅgāra Rasa easily takes cover behind the lovers to show the *rati bhāva*, but what does Hāsya Rasa have as a resort or refuge to depict the *hāsa bhāva*. In fact, *hāsa bhāva* and *jugupsā bhāva* are the only two *sthāyī bhāva*s which do not require any support for the identification of their corresponding *rasa*. Wherever the *vibhāva*s are unusually great, the supporting factors themselves help in engrossing the viewer. In case of *hāsa bhāva* and *jugupsā bhāva*, there is no need for any normal or worldly support from the determinant causes. One of the scholarly views states that at the time of the relishing of the *rasa*, the viewer, who is now a *sahṛdaya*, himself becomes the refuge or the support, however many scholars reject this.

Abhinavagupta distinguishes *hāsa-sthāyī* as self-subsisting in the world (*siddha/laukika*) and provoked by common (*sādhāraṇa*) stimulus, whereas *hāsya* is to be brought into being by a transcendental act of relishing (*sādhya/alaukika*) through a transposed stimulus (*vibhāva*) that is uncommon (*asādhāraṇa*).

The case of *hāsa bhāva* and Hāsya Rasa is problematic. The most empirically verifiable criterion for distinguishing a *rasa* from its *sthāyī* is that the latter gives rise to (worldly) purposive activity (*arthakriyā*) centred around the stimulus, whereas the enjoyment of the former involves no such activity. But *hāsa* stands apart in that its resulting laughter is not so much a purposive activity but release of energies that would otherwise have sustained a purposive attitude (*arthakriyā-kāritva*). And *hāsya* though a *rasa* may well be accompanied by the same laughter that is characteristic of *hāsa*. Since *hāsa* is not accompanied by purposive activity and *hāsya* is not exclusive of laughter, this important criterion is invalid for this pair and the distinction between them becomes much more blurred here than for the other *rasa/sthāyī* pairs. That is why jokes and witticisms seem to form a separate genre having a quasi-independent existence, somewhere on the borderline between the aesthetic and the worldly domains. So, we must turn to the "exclusive determinant" (*asādhāraṇa-vibhāva*) for re-establishing the crucial distinction (Visuvalingam 1983: chap. 7).

Abhinavagupta's most important and innovative contribution is his declaration that all the *rasa* can be understood through Hāsya Rasa. Theoretically seen, if the *sthāyī bhāva* is experienced along with propriety, it becomes a *rasa* and when any *vyabhicārī bhāva* is experienced with uprightness, it remains a *bhāva*, and does not become a *sthāyī bhāva*. If the same *bhāva*s are presented with impropriety, then it gives rise to *rasa* resemblance. For example, the one-sided love/lust displayed by Rāvaṇa for Sītā cannot be perceived as *śṛṅgāra*, but only as *hāsya*. If the viewer does not perceive this lust as inappropriate, then it cannot be deemed as *hāsya*, but if it is seen as absurd, then it is the reason for laughter

(Visuvalingam 1983: chaps 3 and 7).

Sunthar Visuvalingam further explains Abhinavagupta's statement – *sarve rasā hāsye 'ntarbhūtā* – that all the (aesthetic) emotions (*rasa*) are included in humour (*hāsya*) because it is a binary (bisociative) structure resulting from the mutual neutralization of two sharply opposed cognitive and emotional fields. Behaviour that provokes laughter is in effect being (socially) censured (as per Henri Bergson) and this is how humour can be introduced in theatre (and cinema) to promote the proper (*aucitya*) pursuit of legitimate human goals (*puruṣārtha*).

The transitory feelings or the *vyabhicārī bhāvas* which are opposite in nature to the determinants (*vibhāvas*) and improper consequents (*anubhāvas*) tend to become the determinant or the *vibhāvas* for laughter. The *rasa* awareness which is got by such impropriety can be thought of as laughableness. The awareness of the *rasa* can be thought of as a reason for laughter. For example, at the time of the farewell of the bride from her parental home, if the bridegroom also starts crying along with bride (as though identifying himself with the sorrow of bride or her family), then it is seen as a perfect reason for laughter. Wherever the determinant feelings of the *rasa* are crude or unseemly, the *rasa* resemblance is the genesis of laughter. This is a question of *rasa* resemblance for laughter. It can be understood as poor depiction or incongruence in the determinants.

It seems relevant to mention here that Abhinavagupta's student, Ācārya Kṣemendra in his book *Aucitya-Vicāra-Carcā* has propounded the theory of appropriateness. It has been suggested that the *rasa-siddhānta* is much older than Bharata Muni's *Nāṭyaśāstra*. Three prominent scholars of Kashmir have made everlasting contributions to poetics, they are: philosopher Abhinavagupta, who wrote *Abhinavabhāratī*, his commentary on *rasa-siddhānta* as proposed by Bharata Muni's *Nāṭyaśāstra*;

Ācārya Ānandavardhana through *dhvani-siddhānta* and Ācārya Kṣemendra through his *aucitya-siddhānta.* (See Annexure for details.)

It is extremely necessary to contemplate that a serene demeanour or a smiling face is not necessarily the *hāsa bhāva.* Amazement, incredulity, love, joy, etc. cause gaiety but the markers like a widespread smile or mirth do not point out to Hāsya Rasa. For example, seeing a garden full of fragrant flowers does bring a smile to our faces, but that is not Hāsya Rasa, only a serene feeling. *Hāsa bhāva* is evoked when mimicry of others is done, tomfoolery is done or even when illogical, incoherent and absurd words are spoken. When a young girl sees her naughty beloved as he pops-out from behind a bush in the park and smiles, or even a small child's tantrums can evoke the *hāsa bhāva.* Many a time very ordinary happenings of the world can be associated with the *hāsa bhāva.*

Let us discuss in detail the differences between Hāsya Rasa and *hāsa bhāva.*

According to Abhinavagupta, the very concept of absurdity or even the inkling of two opposite or even comparable reactions can be predictive of Hāsya Rasa. Citing the example of a clown or jester, Abhinavagupta brings out the ingrained inner conflict in them. On one hand, the viewers scorn the efforts of a jester, they feel humiliated to be associated with that person and on the other they pity the jester and even laugh at his antics.

It is imperative here to keep in mind that the *rasa-siddhānta* has been formulated by Bharata Muni for drama and we use it as a part of our daily lives and to understand philosophy. Traditionally, in Indian dramas, it was the jester who made the audience laugh. In Mahākavi Kālidāsa's works *Vikramorvaśīyam* and *Mālavikāgnimitra*, the clown plays a very important role. This trend continued in Hindi films for quite some time. Later on, in the 1970s, the jester slowly started disappearing from the commercial Hindi movies and the role and responsibility of the jester fell on the hero's shoulder.

It will not be wrong if we say that in films, the jester is the momentary support for the realization of Hāsya Rasa.

Hāsya Rasa and the Jester

The (ritual) clown (*vidūṣaka*), who is the prime focus of laughter in Indian classical aesthetics, is indeed a (if not the) central character, alongside the hero (*nāyaka*). Through him the deepest principles and understanding of theatre (and life) as (Vedic) sacrifice is communicated and conserved across generations. However, we laugh at him precisely because we do not grasp his "non-sense" and it is our "collective unconscious" that remains receptive to the truths he repetitively conveys. His *hāsya* is ultimately (only) a semblance (*ābhāsa*).

The character of the jester is quite famous in world cinema too, the films where the jester plays a central role have gone on to become lauded and remarkable films. The jester has contributed hugely to make the cinema universally acceptable and popular. The first name on this list is the world- renowned actor, Sir Charles Spencer Chaplin or simply Charlie Chaplin. His life story is nothing less than an incredible movie itself, his childhood was spent in abject poverty. A child of separated parents, at the age of fourteen, he saw his mother admitted to a mental asylum. He made his mark on stage by working in a drama company. In 1914, he became a household name with the character "Tramp". The "Tramp" was unemployed, homeless and poor, but a man with a heart of gold, to make ends meet, he did odd jobs. The common man's aspirations and desires were very well picturized through the quick-witted and clever "Tramp". Charlie Chaplin, through this character, gained immense popularity world over. Baggy pants, a toothbrush moustache, a waddling gait because of over-sized shoes, casual old clothes, hat and walking stick became his distinct identity. A time came when there was none as famous as Charlie

Chaplin as in the whole world.

Apart from many small films, Charlie Chaplin made a few full-length feature films too. For many years even after the talkies were introduced, he went onto make great silent films, but in the end, he accepted that it is the talkies which will enhance the characters he wants to portray. Some of the full-length films acted in and directed by Charlie Chaplin are *The Kid* (1921), *The Gold Rush* (1925), *The Circus* (1928), *City Lights* (1931), *Modern Times* (1936) and a satire on his look alike, German dictator Adolf Hitler, *The Great Dictator* (1940). These films are counted among the greatest films of the world. According to Henri Bergson, whenever a jester laughs at himself, he is playing two characters; one he is consciously laughing, but this is totally different from the person being laughed at. He also reiterates that the comedy demands a momentary anaesthesia of the heart. But the philosophers who study the works of Abhinavagupta, discard this notion of momentary anaesthesia. The spectator does at some point in time identify with these feelings.

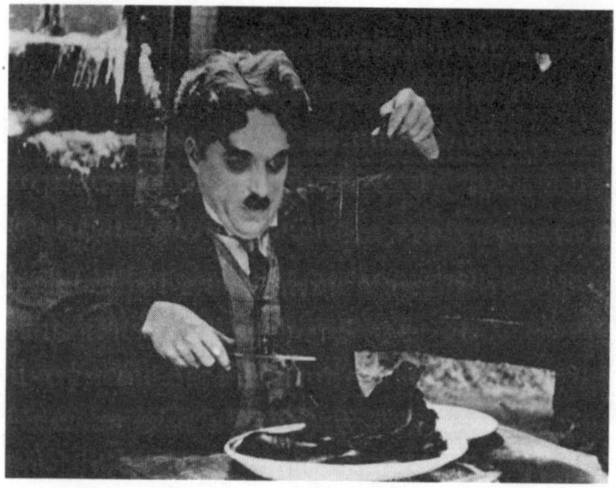

Charlie Chaplin in *The Gold Rush* (1925)

The film *The Gold Rush* has some scenes wherein the contradictions in the minds of the audience are exposed through many incongruencies due to the different innate nature among the spectators. While trying to search for gold in Alaska, the "Tramp" is caught in a snow-storm and has to spend a few days without food in a hut, along with another person named Big Jim. Unable to bear his hunger, the Tramp eats his shoe seasoned with salt. His companion, also mad with hunger, imagines the Tramp to be a chicken and chases him around. Even after his hallucination breaks he decides to kill him and eat him. Of all the hilarious scenes in the film, this satirical scene is remembered as a symbol of hunger and poverty in world cinema. Bengali writer and my friend, Bhairavi Chatterji, questions with a surprise, as to why, a scene which is so full of pathos, has been relished as funny and comical by a large number of people?

Charlie Chaplin and his contemporaries, Buster Keaton (1895–1966), Stan Laurel (1890–1965), Oliver Hardy (1892–1957) and Marx Brothers, are very well known for slapstick comedy. In these films, apart from body movements, attitude and basic understanding, the exaggerated incongruencies like slipping on floors, knocking out another person, jumping and kicking, which are enough to make the audience laugh and enjoy themselves. This sort of a tradition to use slapstick comedy, was started by French silent film actors Max Linder (1883–1925) and Charles Prince (1872–1933). Sir Charles Chaplin's early films bear testimony to that.

Mimicry is an unparalleled determinant cause of laughter. The question which arises here is, why do we laugh when someone's mimicry is done? If we seriously think about it, we find that every copy or mere imitation is not worth laughing at. Cinema has always given importance to "mirror images" and many-a-film has been made to show case that. Max Linder's silent film, *Seven Years Bad Luck* (1921) and Marx Brothers' film *Duck Soup* (1933) have got the much discussed "mirror images" scenes. These films are a mimicry of possible mirror images alone, it was only in the talkies that mimicry of the talking style was shown. By seeing these famous scenes, one can understand how without using any mirrors, an artist can mime and repeat each and every action and reaction and feelings so unbelievingly without wasting any precious minutes.

This repetition with its inane absurdities gives birth to Hāsya Rasa through the *hāsa bhāva*.

Great mathematician Pascal remarked:

> Two faces that are alike, although neither of them excites laughter by itself, make us laugh when together, on account of their likeness.

This is so because there are no repetitions in nature, and this in itself is incongruous. *Difference et Repetition* (1968), a book written by French philosopher, Gilles Deleuze, which deals with repetitions, is a must read. Deleuze argues that it is impossible to have total repetition in nature.

It is extremely important to moderately revise the *hāsa bhāva*. Karl Marx had said that history repeats itself, first as tragedy, second as farce. Charlie Chaplin administers repetition very systematically in the process of laughter; the repetition is seen in music, in scenes, in jokes and so on and so forth. But he never ever repeats it the third or the fourth time, for example the scene in *City Lights*, where he drowns in the water along with the rich man, or the scene where he hides behind the referee during a boxing match, or the scene in *The Kid*, where he breaks the glass of the windows along with the kids and the scene in *The Gold Rush*, where he is stranded in a snowstorm; none of these scenes is repeated more than twice and hence increases the laughter quotient many times.

The penultimate scene of *Modern Times* is a prime example of laughter born out of unrestrained blabbering or non-sensical talk. The "Tramp" is asked to sing a song by his beloved, but unfortunately, he misplaces the lyrics that was written on a note. To salvage the situation, he starts singing some incomprehensible, insensible song. This alone is not the cause for laughter, but the physical acting (*āṅgika abhinaya*), the wit and astuteness displayed, all are responsible for the *hāsa bhāva* which ultimately gets manifested into Hāsya Rasa. Sir Charlie's comprehension of laughter, comes to the fore with a great panache in two films: *Monsieur Verdoux* (1947) made on the story suggested by Orson Welles and a political satire, *A King in New York* (1957).

It is said that the realization of *rasa* is "sudden" or *taḍit-tulya* (lightning-like), akin to the formation of butter while churning cream. *Rasa* realization happens unexpectedly, this lightening like phenomenon is the relishing of the *rasa*. Thomas Hobbes (1588–1679), claimed, *whatsoever it be that moveth laughter, it must be new and unexpected*. In other words, he believes that it is not sufficient to have a new or unexpected thing for anyone to laugh at, but it is most necessary. This, in itself, is food for thought and enough to realize that children do not laugh without a reason.

Abhinavagupta, while differentiating between *hāsa bhāva* and Hāsya Rasa says that the determining causes could be ordinary for the former, the supporting causes have to be exceptional for the latter. The *hāsa bhāva* is proven and established by ordinary determination, but Hāsya Rasa is attainable only through a "reflective cognition" or a reflective observation (*anu-vyavasāya*). Our sense organs help us perceive but the mind apprehends and analyses this knowledge through an introspective awareness (*anu-vyavasāya*). For example, in one film, actor Harold Lloyd climbs up a pipe up to the twelfth floor, to escape the wrath of the police, this in itself is quite ordinary, but the realization that it is quite dangerous is exceptional and comes only after a reflective observation. It should be noted that such reflective cognition is specific to spectators. This is an example where the determinants are not largely generalized. If the viewer does not find an incongruity worthy laughing or consider it heroic, he will not relish the scene.

Discussing in the same line of discourse, Harold Lloyd (1893–1971), in his famous work *Safety Last* (1923) and the comedian duo of Laurel and Hardy famous for slapstick comedy, were only able to bring out a semblance of laughter in the audience and not even the actual *hāsa bhāva* in the best of their works. The reason could be that the intelligentsia found the *hāsa bhāva* to be inappropriate. The three main films of Laurel and Hardy – *Big Business* (1926), *The Music Box* (1932) and *Sons of the Desert* (1932) – were serenaded by the general public, but not by the critics.

To understand the intricacies of the introspective awareness necessary to deal with the support or cover used by Hāsya Rasa, we must look into the story *Anamdas ka Potha* by noted Hindi novelist, literary historian and scholar, Acharya Hazariprasad Dwivedi:

> A few days ago, I met an acquaintance. He had made up his mind to write something. He wanted some advice from me. Within a few minutes I realized that it was not advice, but approval that he was seeking. He told me that God had given human beings alone a lifespan of a hundred years. Some people die early because of the sins they committed in their previous lives and some others live a long life because of the good work they do in this life. He said that those who live to be 66-67 years, their past life sins are not very severe. According to traditions, they live their mid-life and then enter their old age. My friend also informed me that he is on the threshold of old age. I did ask him as to why he is so unsure of this, to which he replied that he would finally be sure after ten days. He said that according to the lunar calendar, he has already stepped into old age, but according to the solar calendar he is ten days away. He, very seriously, added that the god of death, Yamarāja, always followed the lunar calendar, whereas his creator, God, always followed the solar calendar. He told me that Yamarāja always believed in the ancestral traditions and Brahmā, the creator believed in the tradition of serving the gods. He also clarified that sometimes the calculations in the offices of Yamarāja and Brahmā get mixed up, but the discretion always lies with Brahmā. He said that in the midst of all this, it is the dying person who has to suffer the most because Yamarāja's servants are ever ready to take away the dead, while Brahmā has not yet signalled his acquiesance. It is apparently this knowledge which has made my acquaintance

> speak in very doubtful tones. He reassured me that ten days is not a huge gap and they will also pass without any obstruction, because his good deeds have been done and proved. He said that although he trusts the gods totally, he still is calculative.

The incongruity here is that Anamdas does not have any inkling of the certainty of his age, and he gives vague and superstitious reasons like solar calculations and lunar calculations for calendar. It is therefore imperative here that the reader has an in-depth knowledge of mythological stories and stories of Yamarāja and his ways of calculation. An introspective awareness or a reflective cognition is really helpful in piecing together the inane impropriety as depicted by Anamdas.

Our discussion on the role of jesters in silent films is incomplete without the mention of ace film-maker and actor, Buster Keaton. His films *Our Hospitality* (1923), *Sherlock Junior* (1924) and *The General* (1926) are heritage of world cinema. Keaton, known for his deadpan expression and round bowler hat, wrote his own gags and performed his own stunts, however difficult they were. Some wrong and unprofitable decisions, taken while working in the talkies sent his career on a downward spiral, but he bounced back and made a decent comeback in the evening of his life. A contemporary of Charlie Chaplin, Buster Keaton, played a small role in Chaplin's film *Limelight* (1952), in which the two-great jester-actors entertained the audience paired as old friends. Orson Welles, a great fan of Buster Keaton, has anointed *The General*, as one of the greatest comedies ever made. A scene in this film, wherein a train falls into the water, is one

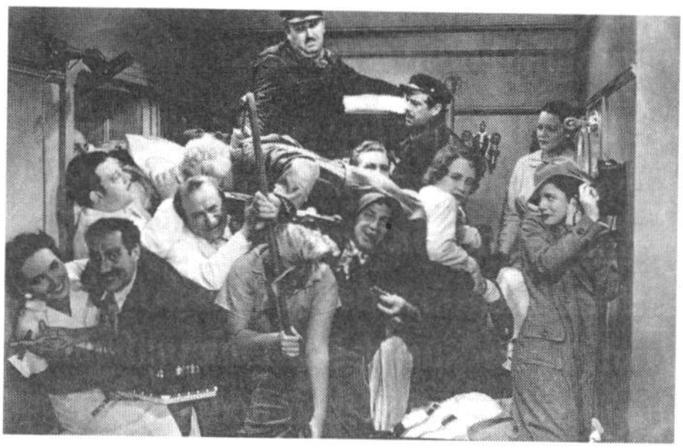

Marx Brother in *A Night at the Opera* (1935)

of the most expensive scenes filmed for a silent movie. This film was written off by the critics and spectators when it was released, but today it is considered amongst the greatest films of the world. Buster Keaton was well known for performing his own stunts, sometimes to his own peril. In films like *The General* and *Sherlock Junior*, while doing stunts he got injured, even breaking his neck, but this never deterred him from giving the audience the best. His films are an amalgamation of Vīra Rasa, Hāsya Rasa and Adbhuta Rasa, and a must watch for every film aficionado.

Marx Brothers were five siblings, at least three or four of them acted in any of the films they made and created a laugh riot. These siblings were all accomplished musicians as they belonged to an artistic family. Chico Marx played the piano, quiet Harpo played the Harp, quick-witted and strange Groucho played the guitar and sang and the youngest Zeppo was a singer. From childhood itself these brothers would give music programmes. Theatre and the Talkies made them very popular. Groucho Marx was famous for using greasepaint in place of moustache and had a strange slouched gait. He was well known for his quick wit and rare sarcasm, for example, "I don't want to belong to any club that will accept people like me as a member," etc. Four films, in which Marx Brothers played a part, which are unforgettable are *Monkey Business* (1931), *Duck Soup* (1933), *A Night at the Opera* (1935) and *A Day at the Races* (1937). In the films starring these siblings, to relish Hāsya Rasa, one has to acquaint one with similar attitude of Marx Brothers because many a time their jokes and incongruities are a part of their cultural environment, it is sometimes a swipe at the society and many a time it is quite an unrestrained view of the societal happenings. A scene from the film *A Night at the Opera* explains it rather well; a small stateroom on board a ship is filled with people who are all shown to be doing their assigned duties as they come and go and when Groucho Marx enters and he says: "Is it my imagination, or is it getting crowded in here".

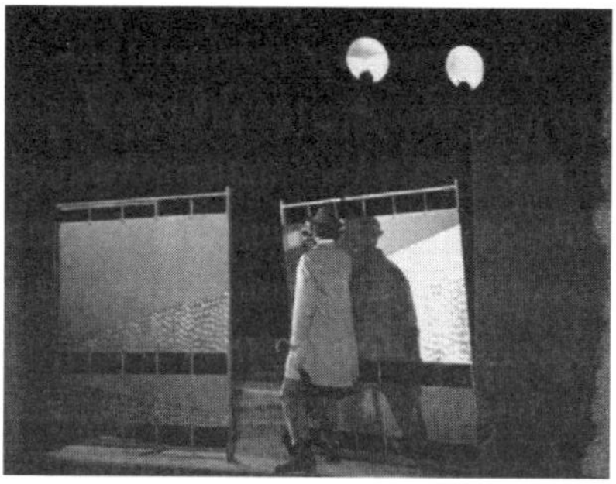

Mon Oncle (1958)

Jacques Tati (1907–82), a French actor-director had an unmatched and special vision to showcase laughter. His artistic commentary on form, colour, expressions, dramatic gestures, civility and class differences give an acute insight toward the extraordinary talent he possessed. His film *Les Vacances de M. Hulot* (1953) is counted as one of the most successful films of the French cinema. The film is a description of a seaside holiday taken by the innocent and lovable Monsieur Hulot (played by Tati himself). The film superbly shows the incongruities in the ways and means of the daily lives of the common man. Two more of his films *Mon Oncle* (1958) and *Playtime* (1967) are heritage films for world cinema. *Mon Oncle* represents an important turn in his career as a film-maker and actor. In this film he has courteously and sarcastically criticized the modern society's need for copying others, showing off their wealth and materialistic attitude. The film plays down the spoken dialogues while giving a fillip to other normal sounds like sounds of footsteps, sounds of some object falling and breaking and vehicular sounds. Showcasing the materialistic world of consumerism, this film has many comical scenes which bear the Tati stamp, in a scene filmed at night, the geometrical ultra-modern, fully automated and impersonal house belonging to M. Hulot's sister is seen as a huge face and his sister's and brother-in-law's faces are seen as huge pupils of the eyes.

Playtime was Tati's most aspirational film for which he got made many expensive sets. It was one of the costliest French film of that time. He subordinated his role substantially unlike Chaplin and the Marx Brothers who were the heroes and repeated their characters. This film took nine years in making. The film bombed at the box office and as a result Jacques Tati became bankrupt. The director emphasized that even if he would have hired the then prominent Hollywood actress for the film, it would have cost just as much. This film is appreciated for its exclusive sets, wonderful technicalities, vision, satire on society and a vaguely perceptible sarcasm. I have an extreme fondness for this film. The film is an intelligence test as well as illusionary as it has been filmed entirely from the street looking into the houses and offices having huge windows. An exceptionally talented and pure-hearted individual can relish these films which use the "*smita* and *hasita*" form of Hāsya Rasa, in which the laughter is subtle and not gregarious. A film lover must watch these films again and again.

A unique example of intellectual resourcefulness and an uncanny ability to bring out the laughter in a given situation can be seen in the American director Woody Allen (b.1935). *Annie Hall* (1977) and *Manhattan* (1979) are not only different kinds of films, but they mark the educational and developmental journey of the director too. In one of the scenes in the film, a man is shown to be standing in a queue to buy cinema tickets and also contemplating on movies like Fellini's *La Strada* and on philosopher Marshall McLuhan. Suddenly, Woody Allen brings on the screen the philosopher McLuhan himself, who berates the man standing in the queue for misunderstanding his work. Woody Allen was able to, through this scene, bring the discussions of great minds amidst common people.

Laughter is recognized and blatantly relished when the incongruity of the mysterious or profound thoughts are ungracefully put across. Common man is accursed to live with it.

Great Works of Other Stalwarts Pertaining to Hāsya Rasa

According to Abhinavagupta, Hāsya Rasa is attainable through reflective cognition (*anu-vyavasāya*) (Visuvalingam 1983: chap. 7). We use the term reflective cognition or an introspective awareness (*anu-vyavasāya*) instead of cognition because it means that the act is described by a poet, played on the stage, sung by a singer, and perceived by the spectator having oneness with the heart of the poet is recreated or reassessed by the latter. Abhinavagupta reasons that when a play or drama is reassessed, laughter or Hāsya Rasa is perceived but only if the basis of the reassessment is incongruency. Therefore, to experience the feeling of laughter it is utmost necessary to establish what the incongruency is.

A question very casually comes to the mind when we study Indian philosophy and that is where is this incongruency established? Which part of our consciousness does this re-assessment pertain to? According to the *Śārīrikopaniṣad*, our consciousness has four parts: mind, intellect, inner psyche (*citta*) and ego. It is argued in certain philosophical traditions that memory resides in the inner psyche (*citta*) and this is the haven or refuge for all awareness or disturbances. Our intellect helps us differentiate between good and bad. Then logically, incongruities should have been taken care of by our intellect?

Indian philosophers keep using the term inner consciousness (*citta*). On researching the meaning of *citta*, we find that every philosophy takes a different form of its meaning for their use. There are twenty-five entities in the Sāṁkhya *Darśana*.

- *Prakṛti* (Nature), mind (*manas*), intellect (*buddhi*) and ego-sense (*ahaṁkāra*).
- Five external sense organs or *pañca-jñānendriya.*
- Five motor sense organs or *pañca-karmendriya.*
- Five *tanmatrās* or *pañca-tanmātra* (subtle elements).
- Five gross elements (earth, water, fire, air and space) or *pañca-mahābhūtas.*

These twenty-four entities along with the conscious *Puruṣa* make up the twenty-five elements of Sāṁkhya *Darśana*. There is no mention of inner consciousness (*citta*) here at all. In Yoga Darśana, the inner consciousness (*citta*) is made up of the mind, intellect and ego; these three together form the unconscious mind. In Vaiśeṣika Darśana, the mind along with eight other elements – the five elements of nature, time, direction and the soul – are taken into consideration. Here too there is no mention of the inner consciousness. In Nyāya Darśana, the word mind follows the advice as in Vaiśeṣika Darśana. In Mīmāṁsā too, the elements are as described as in Vaiśeṣika. In the metaphysical aspect of the Advaita Vedānta, there is no mention of any other entity other than *Brahman* (शर्मा 1995). In Śaiva philosophy, there are thirty-six basic entities. Abhinavagupta, through his treatise *Abhinavabhāratī*, interprets the concept of *rasa* in the realm of Kashmiri Non-Dualistic philosophy. According to this philosophy, the inner consciousness (*citta*) can be thought of as the consciousness of the individualized soul or an embodiment of power. In Abhinavagupta's metaphysics, the inner consciousness comprises of our mind, intellect and ego (Deshpande 1989: 51).

There is a confusion on the use of words. A question arises as to what did Bharata Muni, Kavirāja Viśvanātha, Mammaṭa Bhaṭṭa, Ācārya Kṣemendra and other scholars mean by the word "inner consciousness"? The metaphysical aspects of various philosophies are very different from one another. That could be the reason why the discussions and interpretations of these scholars on the *rasa-siddhānta* are so varied.

In this regard, the modern-day scholars of the Indian poetics and aesthetics argue that the incongruities, shown and relished as part of Hāsya Rasa, cannot be a decision of the intellect alone, it has to involve certain category of the awareness and trepidations of the inner consciousness too. Here the inner consciousness includes the mind, intellect and ego, each of these has a unique function. This character of the consciousness has been borrowed from Sāṁkhya Darśana into Kashmiri Non-Dualistic philosophy with added nuances. The seeds of the *sthāyī bhāva* are present in the inner consciousness, therefore, it is the inner consciousness which is capable of understanding the intricacies and incongruities of the *hāsa bhāva*. This rationale that can be held that the intellect is used to differentiate between the good and the bad and not for the mental disposition. It is food for thought as to what a neurologist would say about this, as the analytical philosophy tends to find a process or structure to explain a phenomenon. According to Kashmiri Non-Dualistic philosophy, this can be discussed on the same level as our consciousness, thereafter it is not just conscious effort or a determined decision, but an easily understandable awareness, for which one doesn't have to make an effort. Introspective awareness (*anu-vyavasāya*) can be explained with a simple example; when we see an object, we understand what it is and can name it as in "it is a pot", when somebody is adamant about the description, we can say it is a clay pot, further we can add that colourful flowers have been painted on it. All these three perceptions happen at once, but we answer specifically only when questioned (रस्तोगी 2012: 263-64). The decision taken by our subconscious to call it a clay pot with flowers painted on it is called introspective awareness or cognition. We do not need any preparation for it, it happens automatically, as if without any mental process. Similarly, reappraisal of the incongruities also happens automatically. With reference to art, it is called trans-empirical savouring.

The *hāsa bhāva* is the transient feeling or the *vyabhicārī bhāva* for Śṛṅgāra Rasa. Some scenes of the films depicting Hāsya Rasa show a dominance of Śṛṅgāra Rasa. We will discuss them with reference to Śṛṅgāra Rasa. There are some other films which depict Hāsya Rasa through the laughter evolved in the storyline. The film *The Thin Man* (1934), made by W.S. Van Dyke (1889–1943), the maker of swashbuckling and adventurous films, is a film on murder investigation. It is laced with humour mixed with eroticism. There were eight films in this series, the first three were noteworthy and remarkable. *After the Thin Man* (1936) and *Another Thin Man* (1939) are other two memorable films of this series.

Jean Renoir (1894–1979), after the success of *The Grand Illusion* (1937), made the most expensive film of that time, *La Règle du Jeu* (1939). A satire on the society at that time, it was negated by spectators and critics alike. Today, it is present in every "Best Film of the World" list because of its very special style of direction. In his autobiography, Renoir wrote that the common man doesn't like to be told the truth. It lays a constraint on them because sarcastic humour brings them face to face with the bitter truth.

Henri Bergson says that the main objective of laughing and making others laugh is to acquaint people of their drawbacks and then point out to them the appropriate behaviour (Bergson 1901). A similar thought exists in Abhinavagupta's theories, but he doesn't disregard the negative aspects of sarcasm. Experience teaches us that sarcasm can give excruciating pain to an individual.

German–American director, Ernst Lubitsch (1892–1947), was well known for his cultured and skilfully portrayed humour. His

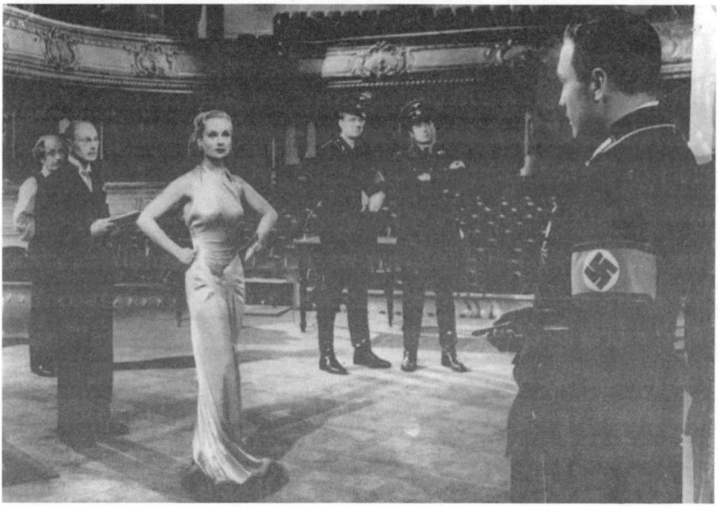

To Be or Not to Be (1942)

films like *Trouble in Paradise* (1932), *The Merry Widow* (1934), *Ninotchka* (1939), *The Shop Around the Corner* (1940), *To Be or Not to Be* (1942) and *Heaven Can Wait* (1943) are filled with sophisticated humour and have been serenaded by many directors around the world. The famous director Billy Wilder was associated with Lubitsch as a co-writer for the film *Ninotchka* much before he shot to fame himself. The famous actress Greta Garbo played the lead role in this film. This film was banned in the erstwhile Soviet Union and its associate countries because their hard-line policies were ridiculed in this film. The film *To Be or Not to Be* faced antagonism when Poland was attacked without a reason by Hitler. The dictator was thought to be a danger to world peace by the director. How automation and blindly following orders in a dictatorship can lead to comical situations has been ably dealt within this film. The film has reference to the soliloquy "To Be or Not to Be" of the Shakespearean drama *Hamlet*.

According to the theory of Henri Bergson, rigidity, automation, absent-mindedness and unsociability are the reasons which help the realization of the *hāsa bhāva*. His very apt saying about laughter is that one can laugh at the incongruities of human alone and not at animals or non-living things, unless they resemble humans. The same explanation holds true for man's mechanical activity. We tend to laugh at the machine-like actions of man, for example, when somebody falls and bounces like a ball, this evokes laughter rather than when a person falls with a support (Bergson 1901).

Apart from Robert Bresson and Andrei Tarkovsky, nearly all great directors have, at one time or the other, made films of the comic genre or at least had some elements of laughter in them. Luis Buñuel tasted commercial success with the film *El Gran Calavera/The Great Madcap* (1949). The film is about a rich man's spend thrift habits and how his jobless family members sponge on him and yet are irritated by his ways. Buñuel had a quaint way of depicting comedy, which can be seen in his surrealistic films *The Discreet*

Charm of the Bourgeoisie (1972) and *The Phantom of Liberty* (1974).

Federico Fellini (1920-93), the maker of *La Strada*, made many comedy films based on scripts of Michelangelo Antonioni. His writing prowess came to the fore with his independently directed film *The White Sheik* (1952), which tells the story of a newly-wed couple who come to roam in Rome. The bride goes off on a rendezvous with the hero of a photo strip soap opera, leaving behind her embarrassed husband to cover up her absence in front of relatives. Woody Allen has used the same plot in his film *To Rome with Love* (2012). Fellini must have been a very jovial person; his gaiety and ebullience can be seen in all his films. The film *Amarcord* (1973) is a tribute to his childhood memories and hometown and has many memorable scenes filled with fun and laughter.

Laughter depends upon its acceptability in the social fabric. Ingmar Bergman directed *Smiles of a Summer Night* (1955), which is a film, in the comic genre, based on the incongruities seen in many marital relationships. A middle-aged man marries a nineteen-year old girl, who is of the same age as the man's son. The man's son secretly likes his stepmother but is unable to do anything. The man unable to form a lasting relationship with his young wife, has an affair with a beautiful stage actress. In a dialogue, the man says to his wife that he can tolerate his wife's infidelity but if anyone touches his lover, his animal instinct will take over. In another shot, he says to his lover that he can tolerate his lover's infidelity, but if anyone touches his wife the animal in him will have to be faced. This duplicity in character and values is the determining cause for laughter. The actresses of all Bergman's films were adept at acting, full of self-confidence and attractive to boot. The film *The Magic Flute* (1975), based on Mozart's opera, shows the transient feelings required for women to realize Hāsya Rasa. These feelings, be it the happiness in the heart or thoughts, are very cleverly hidden. The film makes a beautiful use of this *vyabhicārī bhāva*, which is seldom seen.

It is virtually impossible to imagine a film-maker, who has dealt with murders, mysteries and fear all his career, make a comedy, but after leaving Britain and settling in Hollywood, master film-maker Alfred Hitchcock, made his maiden comedy *Mr. and Mrs. Smith* (1941). The film turned out to be mediocre, not liked by Hitchcock himself. Another one of his romantic comedies with thriller overtones is *The Trouble with Harry* (1955). The film is about the dead body of Harry found on a hillside by the town people, four of whom believe that it was their folly that killed Harry. In their quest to find what really killed Harry, they try to evade the town sheriff, try to bury the body unnoticed and also fall in love with each other. The movie is an easy-going romance and nobody seems overly bothered about poor Harry who is dead. The film was not a runaway success.

Billy Wilder (1906–2002), a film-maker known for his drama films like *Double Indemnity* (1944) and *Sunset Boulevard* (1950), was originally known for his writing talent, making films of the laughter genre and his rendering of the comic emotion. His two films with the ethereal beauty Marilyn Monroe *Seven Year Itch* (1955) and *Some Like It Hot* (1959) are rated as greats in the comic genre of world cinema. Apart from these two, other films *The Apartment* (1960) and *Irma La Douce* (1963) have also been recognized as extraordinary films. Indian actor-director Shammi Kapoor was influenced by the drama version of this film and he made it into a film called *Manoranjan* (1974). We can see the example of automation in the rank and file of the police and bureaucracy in this film.

The film *Seven Year Itch* uses incoherent and inconsistent talks as determinant causes and laziness and sleepiness as its consequents. It is a story of a good-hearted and very imaginative artist, who shows an interest in his beautiful neighbour, after his wife and son go away on a vacation. The heroine too keeps coming to his house on the pretext of using the air conditioner. This film is remembered for its peerless dialogues even today. The film *Some Like It Hot* tells the story of two musician friends who are faced with unemployment. They find that a young girls' band has vacancies and cross dress to get hired. The hero falls in love

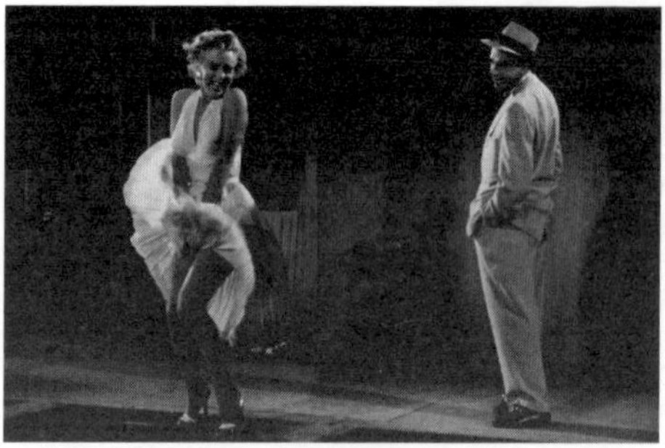

Seven Year Itch (1955)

with the beautiful lead singer, played by Marilyn Monroe and his friend keeps getting into trouble, while trying to help them meet. The Hindi film *Rafoo Chakkar* (1975), starring Rishi Kapoor and Neetu Singh, is a remake of this film. The story of the film *The Apartment*, is that a hard-working bachelor, lends his apartment for the enjoyment of high officials of his firm. The hero has morally high standards, even though a lot of unchaste sentiments are portrayed in the film. The film spreads a beautiful message about trust in relationships and love. This is the aim of drama according to Indian tradition, endearing persuasion.

Sophisticated humour has been a part of the films directed by Jean-Luc Godard (b.1930), during the time of the French new wave. His prominent films are *A Bout de Soufflé* or *Breathless* (1960), *Une Femme est Une Femme* or *A Woman Is a Woman* (1961), *Bande à part* or *Band of Outsiders* (1964) and *Pierrot le Fou* (1965). The film *A Woman Is a Woman* is a homage to the musical films of Hollywood and in a unique way shows a

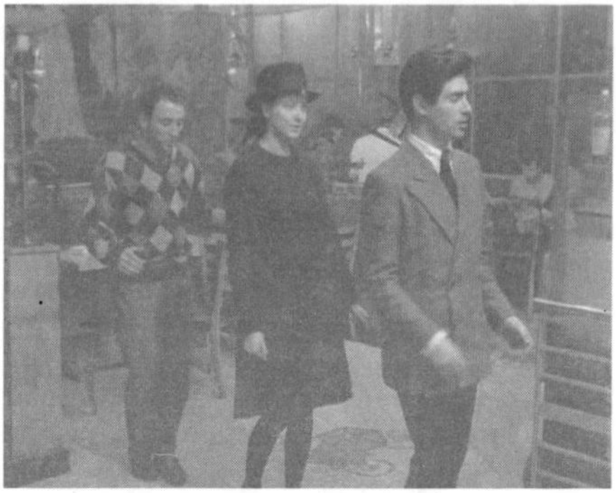

Bande à part (1964)

very distinctive kind of laughter through it. The film is about an unmarried couple who are in love, the woman wants to conceive a love-child while the man is reluctant to do so. Godard's films do have an element of laughter in them, but in these films, it is quite prominently seen.

Director Satyajit Ray, although well known for his serious and socially relevant cinema, was also known to have a funny bone in him. His films *Pather Panchali*, *Aparajito*, *Jalsaghar* and *Apur Sansaar* did become world famous, but his engrossing film *Paras Patthar* (1958), which tells the story of how, when an ordinary bank clerk gets hold of the philosopher's stone all hell breaks loose in his town. The film is an introduction to Satyajit Ray's acute sense of humour. Another film in this genre is *Mahapurush* (1965), it tells the story of an imposter in the guise of a sage. Ray is able to bring out very subtly the humour in this film. A film, which uses the silliness and inane beliefs about magic, ghosts and spirits to bring on humour and laughter, is *Gopi Gaine Bagha Baine* (1969). The humorous streak in Satyajit Ray's personality comes to the fore in two of his thrillers *Sonar Kella* (1974) and *Joi Baba Felunath* (1979).

Pietro Germi (1914-74) made films with a sarcastic twist on marital relationships and sexual lust of the upper echelons of the then Italian society. His film *Divorce, Italian Style* or *Divorzio all'Italiana* (1961) is one such film. It has all the usual sound effects and elements required for a culturally acceptable film like good sounding adjectives and an adept storyteller. The story is of a rich nobleman who wants to get rid of his unattractive wife so that he can marry his beautiful distant cousin. He keeps thinking of ways to kill her or do away with her. He tries to involve her in an extra-marital affair for the same. The film won the Academy award for foreign films and so received international honour. His next two films too were based on immoral and incorrect wants and fantasies which bring out the laughter quotient in the film. Film *Sedotta e Abbandonata* or *Seduced and Abandoned* (1964) is a dark satire on the then Sicilian social customs and honour laws. It tells about "bride kidnapping" and "rehabilitation marriages". The film *Signore and Signori* or *The Birds, the Bees and the Italians* (1966) is an example of licentiousness in marital relationships and the director's sarcastic vision. The film *Signore and Signori* exposes the duplicity and hypocrisy of the society, it won the "Grand Prix" at the Cannes Film Festival that year.

Vittorio De Sica, the maker of the intensely tragic film, *Bicycle Thieves*, made a film, making fun of the directors lusting after awards, *After the Fox* (1966). After reading the script, he saw that the story had a deep concept which gave out a social message – money has the power to corrupt even art. The film's British actor, Peter Sellers and its Italian director, de Sica were not able to see eye to eye and the critics too were divided over the excellence of the film. By and large it was a simple and praiseworthy film. The Hindi remake of this film was *Tees Maar Khan* (2010), directed by Farah Khan. It is at best a shoddy copy of the original. Laughter has always been very intellectual to Orson Welles. The dialogues in his films are always very systematic and tactful. *Too Much Johnson* (1938) was a short film of the comic genre made by Orson Welles. It was thought to be destroyed by a fire but was luckily found in the original negative form in Italy. It was a tribute to the laughter expressed in the films of the silent era and was dedicated to the public in a ceremony in 2013.

Miloš Forman (1932–2018), was a Czech born director who immigrated to America for personal reasons. He made well-known and prestigious films like: *One Flew Over the Cuckoo's Nest* (1975) and *Amadeus* (1975). These films won many awards too. *Loves of a Blonde* (1965) and *The Fireman's Ball* (1967) were remarkable films of the comic genre. The films are a critical satire on the incongruities born out of political decisions. *Loves of a Blonde* is a story based in a small-town shoe factory where the people work. The ratio of women to men is 16:1. The supervisor decides that to increase the production capacity, he must introduce the women to more men. So, he organizes a ball and invites army men to it. A young and beautiful sixteen-year old girl is pursued by a forty-year old married man. The young girl is secretly in love with a young musician at the ball and is tormented at being with the old man. The film captures this agony in a very realistic way. The film *The Fireman's Ball* is a farewell party given by the workers of the fire department for their chairman on his retirement. The party is ill organized, many of the gifts get stolen and there is general mayhem caused. This prompted the Czech government to ban the film permanently, calling it a sarcasm on the government.

Jiri Menzel (b.1938), an important film-maker of the "Czech New Wave", made some memorable films: *Closely Watched Trains* or Czech: *Ostře Sledované Vlaky* (1966), *My Sweet Little Village* or Czech: *Vesničko Má Středisková* (1986) and *Larks on a String* or Czech: *Skřivánci na niti* (1969). The film *Closely Watched Trains* won the Best Foreign Film at the Oscars. The story revolves around the love interest of a come-of-age, young boy who has been appointed as a station guard and the political revolt taking place in German-occupied Czechoslovakia during Second World War. *My Sweet Little Village* is the story of a mentally challenged orphan and life around him in his village. He works for a truck driver who is exasperated with him and wants to send him away to the capital Prague. The villagers succeed to send him off, but also bring him back when they miss him. The movie is joyful from the beginning to the end. It is the most popular Czech comedy in history. The film *Larks on a String* was banned by the Communist regime of Czechoslovakia and was only released after the fall of the regime in 1990. It won the Golden Bear at the Berlin International Film Festival. All these films bring out the laughter and mirth in a very subtle and sophisticated way.

Croatian director Kreso Golik (1922-96) also made films with subtle and subdued mirth. *One Song a Day Takes Mischief Away* or

Tko Pjeva Zlo ne Misli (1970) is a great Croatian comedy/drama which tells the story of a dandy who tries to flirt with and seduce the wife of another man in his very presence. These kind of films, show the widespread and the real meaning of the comic/joyous genre, where the laughter is not constrained to loud or raucous, but engulfs pure fun and joyous laughter.

Examples of sarcastic and black humour are not seen in ancient Sanskrit dramas as most of them have a happy ending. How can one perceive this in the Indian context? When derision or laughing at others is shown to be laughing at the oddities or at things which are taboo or not permitted, then blood-letting, murder, man-slaughter, etc. are shown as black humour. The determining causes for such a humour are definitely insatiable greed, hunger for indomitable power and blind following of orders. Charlie Chaplin's top-notch film *The Great Dictator* is a satire on Hitler and Mussolini. Legend has it that Chaplin sent the film for the dictator to watch and Hitler watched it twice. Chaplin was quite curious to know the dictator's reaction. At the end of the film when the dictator and his look-alike barber exchange places, the barber turned dictator, sends out a message to the world fraternity:

> Soldiers! Don't give yourselves to brutes – men who despise you and enslave you – who regiment your lives – tell you what to do – what to think and what to feel! Who drill you – diet you – treat you like cattle, use you as cannon fodder. Don't give yourselves to these unnatural men – machine men with machine minds and machine hearts! You are not machines! You are not cattle! You are men! You have the love of humanity in your hearts. You don't hate, only the unloved hate – the unloved and the unnatural! Soldiers! Don't fight for slavery! Fight for liberty!

Two British films, based on murder, are quite renowned for Hāsya Rasa (joyous sentiment) they portray. The film *Kind Hearts and Coronets* (1949) tells the story of a girl of a royal family marrying a common musician. The death of her husband leaves her desolate and no one from her royal family come forward to help her. Her son with an eye on the throne ingrains himself into the royal family and starts killing people one by one. This film shows the rudiments of the *hāsya rasa*, but is well known for its great dialogues, direction and the eight-character roles played by Sir Alec Guinness (1914–2000). In the second film, *The Ladykillers* (1955), Sir Alec played the lead role. It is a story of an old lady who lives alone and thinks up various situations so that the police can help her, who end up humouring her. Her house is rented by a gang of dacoits planning a heist. She is made to get involved in the end and the gang decide to kill her, but get killed instead by each other, she takes the loot to the police and they being wary of her ask her to keep it. Special costumes, great dialogues, superb acting and efficient photography have made it a very entertaining film. This film was remade by Coen Brothers in 2004. The film's script was written by William Rose, who claimed that he dreamed the entire story, just as Organic Chemist August Kekule had claimed that he had dreamed the ring structure of Benzene.The other films written by Rose and which are famous for the laughter and comic sentiments are *It's a Mad, Mad, Mad, Mad, World* (1963), *The Russians Are Coming, the Russians Are Coming* (1966) and *Look Who Is Coming to Dinner* (1967). The Hindi remake of *It's a Mad, Mad, Mad, Mad, World* is the film *Dhamaal* (2007).

The film made on the lives of doctors during a war: *MASH* (1970), by director Robert Altman (1925–2006), reminds us of the novel *Catch-22*, by writer Joseph Heller. The toughness of the characters, automation and the not-able-to-mix with anyone type of an attitude of the character have become the targets for the comic sentiment of the film. This film was bestowed the Palme d'Or at the Cannes Film Festival. Two other notable films of Robert Altman are *McCabe and Mrs. Miller* (1971) and *Nashville* (1975).

American director, Stanley Kubrick's film *Dr. Strangelove or How I Learned to Stop Worrying and Love the Bomb* (1964) is a political satire, black comedy that shows the inherent dangers of nuclear warfare during the period of the Cold War. The film questions as to how some people can make such a destructive bomb that it will destroy the most beautiful creation – Earth. The film ends with a nuclear bomb destroying the whole world. The hero of the film is Peter Sellers in a triple role.

Brazil (1985) is Britisher Terry Gilliam's satire on the bureaucratic and very dysfunctional industrial world. It bears resemblance to the George Orwell's novel – *1984*. It is a sarcastic take on the wishes and problems of man and how the bureaucracy pays no heed to it, in a way taking away a man's freedom and oppressing him.

The films of Coen Brothers – Joel Coen (b.1954) and Ethan Coen (b.1957) – *The Big Lebowski* (1998), *O Brother, Where Art Thou* (2000) and *Burn After Reading* (2007) are crime comedies and black comedies, satirizing the then American society on the concept of humour and its determinant causes. The film *The Big Lebowski* is about a simple man getting sucked into the affairs of greedy and crooked men. It is known for its idiosyncratic characters, dream sequences and unconventional dialogues. *O Brother Where Art Thou* is a sarcasm on Homer's epic work *Odyssey*. Three convicts escape from prison to search for a hidden treasure and keep getting into one fracas after another. Interestingly this movie borrows the title and plot from American director Preston Sturges's (1898–1959) comedy film *Sullivan's Travels* (1941). In this black and white classic, a Hollywood director refuses to make another comedy named "O Brother Where Art Thou" during economic depression and runs away to experience hardship and poverty himself. Coen Brothers picked up cues and paid tribute to this classic.

Philosophers argue that laughing is a social activity. People tend to laugh more in each other's company. As laughter is infectious, it is advised to watch the films of Hāsya Rasa in the company of friends or like-minded people. Abhinavagupta says that the relishing of *nāṭya* (as *nāṭya* itself is *rasa*) is a social endeavour and that the joy multiplies in good company. Citing an example, he says that when one singer after another is singing or when many singers are singing in a chorus, the listeners are totally engrossed compared to listening to just one. One can derive complete satisfaction from relishing such an assembly over art spectacle (रस्तोगी 2012: 302).

10

Love, Separation and Union

Great Films of Śṛṅgāra Rasa in World Cinema

Most Sanskrit words are made up of three parts: a main root, a prefix and a suffix. The root of any word is verb-centric. An Indologist and a Sanskrit scholar Navjivan Rastogi has used the √*ram* the √*rañj* root words to illustrate the aesthetics in this field. The √*ram* root word takes its meaning from active participation in any activity, be it sports or delighting or indulging oneself in any play (*krīḍā)* and the √*rañj* root word has its connotation in the ability to be affected or relishing the action done or actively appreciating the action (*rāga*). The words gracious (*ramaṇīya*), elegant (*ramya*) and charming (*ramaṇīka*) are derived from the root word √*ram* and the words passion (*rāga*), delighting (*rañjana*), colouring (*rañjaka*), calamity (*uparāga*) and liking something so much that one is bonded with it (*raktatā*) are derived from the root √*rañj*. These words have been used to denote many emotions and the personality of the word (*anekārthakatā*) and its inherent playfulness is used to convey the natural meaning (*svābhāvika artha*) of the word. The guilelessness or the naivety in the word *krīḍā*, which denotes playing or active participation, emerges from the different moods of the root word √*ram*. In the same way, the different words of the root word √*rañj* also show two feelings; one is the objective side of the action done (*vastupakṣa*) and the other is the knower's side (*pramātṛpakṣa*) in which the doer is bonded with the action and derives immense enjoyment or satisfaction from it (*anurakti*).

The traditional Indian reflective philosophy believes that passions and sentiments are the propensity and the attributes of the mind and the intellect, but the Kashmiri non-dualistic philosophy argues that such an individualized passionate propensity (*rāga*) is the defining element of a personality. *Rāga* (passionate propensity) is the main cause for the fulfilment of desire and through it, mental satisfaction. This attitude leads to attachment (*āsakti*), which is the gateway to the rapt engrossment (रस्तोगी 2012: 252).

> स वै नैव रेमे तस्मादेकाकी न रमते स द्वितीयमैच्छत् स हैतावानास यथा स्त्रीपुमाँसौ संपरिष्वक्तौ स इममेवाऽऽत्मानं द्वेधाऽपातयत्ततः पतिश्च पत्नी चाभवतां तस्मादिदमर्धबृगलमिव स्व इति ह स्माह याज्ञवल्क्यस्तस्मादयमाकाशः स्त्रिया पूर्यत एव ताँ समभवत्ततो मनुष्या अजायन्त ॥
>
> *sa vai naiva reme tasmādekākī na ramate sa dvitīyamaicchat sa haitāvānāsa yathā strīpumāṁsau saṁpariṣvaktau sa imamevā tmānaṁ dvedhā pātayattataḥ patiśca patnī cābhavatāṁ tasmādidamardhabṛgalamiva sva iti ha smāha yājñavalkyastasmādayamākāśaḥ striyā pūryata eva tāṁ samabhavattato manuṣyā ajāyanta* ||
>
> –*Bṛhadāraṇyakopaniṣad* 1.4.3
>
> He did not indulge, as alone it is not possible to indulge or play. He desired for a companion to play. But he was, at that time, in an embrace, just as a man and woman are in an embrace. He was split into two and the husband and wife were formed. But this was one half of the whole, just as peas are the half of a pod. This was said by Ācārya Yājñavalkya. The emptiness of the other half is filled by women. And so men were born.

It is difficult for a person to be engaged or absorbed or immersed in his passions all the time. A lone man cannot play, even in the literal sense of the word. According to the tenets of the Kashmiri non-dualistic philosophy, the playful predisposition a man has toward certain charming activities or elegant surroundings gives rise to indulgence. This indulgence is the reason of attitude toward rapt immersion during art spectating. The eleventh-century scholar, Bhoja, in his works *Sarasvatī-Kaṇṭhābharaṇa* and *Śṛṅgāra-Prakāśa,* while contemplating on *rasa,* has declared that Śṛṅgāra Rasa is the only *rasa*. He is of the view that the basis of all *rasa*s is human consciousness, which can also be called as the self (*aham*). Considering this explanation, one can completely agree to the fact that Śṛṅgāra Rasa is the basic and true *rasa* and all other *rasa*s have been the offshoots of it. Man's pride is the reason for his self-love.

In the earlier chapters, we have seen that a similar assertion was made by Kavirāja Viśvanātha for Adbhuta Rasa, by Bhavabhūti for Karuṇa Rasa and by Abhinavagupta for Śānta Rasa. This could easily be blamed on the "what-maybe" (Syādvāda) or the "assertion of the various possibilities" philosophy of Jainism. Ācārya Dhanañjaya, a tenth-century scholar and author of the dramaturgy treatise *Daśarūpaka*, which exemplifies the special qualities and characteristics of the ten different elements of the Sanskrit drama, says that consciousness is believed to be in four stages: progress (*vikāsa*), extent or scope (*vistāra*), turbulence (*vikṣobha*) and aberration (*vikṣepa*).

Śṛṅgāra Rasa and Hāsya Rasa are a part of the growth and progress of our consciousness, Vīra Rasa and Adbhuta Rasa are a part of the extent of consciousness, Vībhatsa Rasa and Bhayānaka Rasa are a part of the turbulence felt by consciousness and Raudra Rasa and Karuṇa Rasa are a part of the aberrations felt by consciousness. Ācārya Dhanañjaya says that Śṛṅgāra Rasa and Hāsya Rasa are the only two *rasa*s which take the support of compassionate heart (*sahṛdaya*) and become identical to it. This in reality means that a spectator sees himself as the heroic actor or an actor playing the role of a lover. This doesn't happen with the other *rasas*, here the supporting reasons which help in the *rasa* manifestation themselves help the viewer's heart become one with the poet, no external help is needed. Therefore, it is quite easy to generalize both Śṛṅgāra Rasa and Vīra Rasa. Ācārya Dhanañjaya says that the development and spread of our consciousness is pleasurable, while its turbulence and aberration are painful (द्विवेदी और द्विवेदी 1963: 46).

The *sthāyī bhāva* of Śṛṅgāra Rasa is love (*rati*). The word *śṛṅgāra* has been attributed a very colloquial use, as it is quite natural to want to beautify one-self, wear shining beautiful clothes and be ready to play the field or enchant the world. According to Bharata Muni, desire is to denote the man–woman relationship and good youthful nature. The meaning of desire in Śṛṅgāra Rasa is not merely sexual but pertains to the mutual pleasure derived from devotion and faith having indulgent propensity. The appentence of sexual desire is the *vyabhicārī bhāva* of Śṛṅgāra Rasa. In Śṛṅgāra Rasa, the wishfulness to meet and the pleasure of meeting a beloved is called *śṛṅgāra* in union while the pain of separation is called *śṛṅgāra* in separation (द्विवेदी 1992: 124-58).

Let us make it very clear that at the outset that every love story doesn't subscribe to Śṛṅgāra Rasa. Let us take two very opulent and path-breaking films in world cinema to exemplify this: *Gone with the Wind* (1939), directed by Victor Fleming, is the love story of a young girl during the American Civil War. Although, a love story, the magnificent sets and the war scenes in the film all point toward Adbhuta Rasa and not Śṛṅgāra Rasa. Similarly, the film *Les Enfants du Paradis* or *Children of Paradise* (1945), directed by Marcel Carne (1906-96), who also directed, *Le Quai du Brumes* or *Port of Shadows* (1938), the first French noir film, is the story of a woman pursued by four men. The plot shows several love angles, plots and subplots, etc. which cannot be categorized as Śṛṅgāra Rasa. To term both these films as films of Śṛṅgāra Rasa will be akin to calling the *Rāmāyaṇa* as the love story of Lord Rāma and Sītā. The main reason for not attributing Śṛṅgāra Rasa to these films is the lack of mutual devotion between the male and female protagonists. Albeit it being written in Leo Tolstoy's novel *Anna Karenina*, that "If it is true that there are as many minds as there are heads, then there are as many kinds of love as there are hearts".

Many films like George Cukor's *The Philadelphia Story* (1940) and Howard Hawks' *Bringing up Baby* (1938) and *His Girl Friday* (1940) and Preston Sturges's *The Lady Eve* (1941) are love stories and tell a good story, they all point toward the feeling of pleasure and desire, while depicting the *hāsa bhāva* yet the stress on mutual devotion takes a back seat. These are classic examples of Śṛṅgāra Rasa supported by Hāsya Rasa. No doubt, these are great films; they score on technique, cinematography, new ways of storytelling, etc.

Clarifying Bharata Muni's stand, Abhinavagupta says that *śṛṅgāra* in union and *śṛṅgāra* in separation are two states in Śṛṅgāra Rasa. Although we can identify a cow on the basis of its being coloured or not, it doesn't make much difference as it will remain a cow despite the varied colour, so also there is no difference between the above two states. For example, one can differentiate between a rainy day and a hot day, but day and night are stages of a calendar day and not differences. The two states of Śṛṅgāra Rasa are interconvertible, i.e. in *śṛṅgāra* in union there is a fear of losing a partner and in *śṛṅgāra* in separation there is a hope of reunion. This in itself is the main feature of Śṛṅgāra Rasa (द्विवेदी 1992: 124-30; पारेख 1974). Our aspirations, jealousies, journeys and such-like conditions are all immanent in it. All feelings apart from laziness, acrimony and disgust are the *vyabhicārī bhāva* of this *rasa*. The *anubhāvas* (determinants) for *śṛṅgāra* in union are the astuteness seen in the eyes and brows, the sweet voice between the two lovers, mild movements of limbs, etc. The determinants (*anubhavas*) for *śṛṅgāra* in separation are fear, jealousy, resignation, eagerness, epilepsy, inertia and death.

Both stages of *śṛṅgāra* – union and separation – form the background for the intense and spectacular love story, *Titanic* (1997), directed by James Cameron. It is a lavishly made film which was a box office hit and was the most expensive movie of that time. The hero, a poor lad, saves the rich heroine from committing suicide and both fall in love. Tender love words, beautiful picturesque sets, opulent costumes, music and dance are all enough to stimulate and incite Śṛṅgāra Rasa. The hero dies when the ill-fated ship collides with a massive iceberg. The heroine who survives the accident tells her love story in a flashback, when in her old age and hopes to meet her lover even after death. This is reminiscent of the traditional Sanskrit dramas where the hero and the heroine hope that at least their souls will meet after death, makes the pain of separation in Śṛṅgāra Rasa very different from the pathos of Karuṇa Rasa. The concluding scene in this film is very similar to old Hindi movies where the separated love birds are shown to meet in the sky as soul mates. Jack and Rose, the eternal lovers, are shown to be destined to meet where the Titanic sank, thus manifesting the Śṛṅgāra Rasa.

The pain of parting, mutual trust and the hope of meeting again are the backdrop of the cult film *Casablanca* (1942), directed by Michael Curtiz. Based on a very famous play, this film has Humphrey Bogart and Ingrid Bergman in stellar roles. The film tells the story of two ex-lovers who meet accidentally in *Casablanca*, Morocco, during the Second World War, they remember with pain and regret their love and promises made to each other while being caught in their present lives and duties. This film is counted as one of the greatest in world cinema because of its cinematography, superb acting and huge popularity.

It is certainly not without reason that most films are based on Śṛṅgāra Rasa and they are very successful too. The attraction of these films is worldwide and mainly poignant. It is therefore quite correct to say that Śṛṅgāra Rasa is undisputedly the king of all *rasa*s.

In his commentary *Abhinavabhāratī*, Abhinavagupta describes three types of Śṛṅgāra Rasa from the acting point of view: (a) *vacanātmaka* (through words), (b) *veśātmaka* (through dress), and (c) *kriyātmaka* (through action) (द्विवेदी 1992: 202). Abhinavagupta connects the four basic *rasas* to the *puruṣārtha* (life-pursuits) which is advised to a social being so that he/she can live a balanced and fulfilling life and divides Śṛṅgāra Rasa into three types; primarily desire (*kāma*) and secondarily, means and duty (*artha* and *dharma*) with reference to *Nāṭyaśāstra* 18.72 (पारेख 1974: 53). These differences have been more explicitly explained in the *Nāṭyadarpaṇa* and *Śṛṅgāra-Prakāśa* authored by Bhoja, but through the ages, these differences have ceased to exist independently, and their identity too has been negated by scholars (नागेन्द्र 1969: 247; गुप्ता 1972). We can understand Śṛṅgāra Rasa through the eyes of Abhinavagupta and through his *puruṣārtha* theory.

Artha Śṛṅgāra

Abhinavagupta explains, and we have noted in Raudra Rasa, that the meaning of *artha* is the effort a person puts in and the means he has to achieve something. The duty takes the form of *dharma* here. The means (not necessarily financial) to achieve this duty is *artha*, the desire to fulfil the duty is *kāma*. Sometimes this desire to achieve something brings a feeling of being a burden on another being. It is quite natural for *artha śṛṅgāra* to occur when one is angry or in grief too. When the desired love is not easily got, then the besotted lover tries all means to get the attention of the sought, but rarely it is in the form of love. We do meet people who resort to all kinds of methods to get their love. In the film *The Phantom of Opera* (1925), the hero abducts the beautiful heroine in order to get her love, but no such thing happens because the heroine lacks any kind of a desire toward the hero. This film is more of an example of Bhayānaka Rasa than Śṛṅgāra Rasa, as the heroine is scared of the Phantom. Other scholars have defined artha Śṛṅgāra

Rasa basically as: "where for or because of money the actor desires the woman belonging to another man or tries to form a relationship with her" (गुप्ता 1972).

American director William Wyler made a film, *Wuthering Heights* (1939), which is a beautiful example of *artha śṛṅgāra*. The film, an adaptation of the novel of the same name by Emily Brontë, is the story of Heathcliff and Cathy, two childhood friends turned lovers. In order to spite and show Cathy down, Heathcliff marries another woman, but is unable to forget her. The film is remembered for its unequalled cinematography and stellar performances by the actors. It won many awards too. A Hindi remake, starring Dilip Kumar, *Dil Diya Dard Liya* (1966), was not a commercial hit.

The film *Vertigo* (1958), directed by Alfred Hitchcock, which was adjudged as the greatest film ever made by film critics all over the world in the year 2012, is the story of a retired police officer who falls in love with his friend's wife while snooping on her. His one-sided desire becomes an obsession. The film is famous for its new direction techniques like dolly zoom, magnificent opening background music, etc. In spite of this, the film was not commercially successful, but is remembered by people for its mystery factor and narration. Mystery, which is a genre of story narration, points to its *sthāyī bhāva* and authenticates the lunatic desire of the hero, James Stewart.

Roman Polanski's film, *Knife in the Water* (1962), is also based on *artha śṛṅgāra* and has been appreciated world over. A couple's sailing expedition turns into an ego tussle, when the husband and another youth who goes with them vie for the attention of the woman by showing off their skills. The woman is sexually attracted to the other man and this changes the equation at the end. François Truffaut's (1932-84) film, *Jules et Jim* (1962) too is a love triangle, where the heroine marries each of her suitors turn by turn but remains unsatiated and in the end, commits suicide. This film has been termed as a great achievement for French cinema.

In the same vein is Carl Dreyer's last film, *Gertrud* (1964). Gertrud is a woman who believes in love without any unjustified condition with her husband as well as her lovers. She does not compromise on her desire for sex and love. She finally goes her own way leaving behind everyone. She does not have any remorse as she looks back on her life. It brings up an essential question; should we incorporate such values into our life or should we stay away from them?

Luis Buñuel is one director who has made films on a variety of subjects and encompassing a variety of *rasa*s. We have seen in our study up to now, that directors tend to get associated with one or two main *rasa*s. Luis Buñuel has made a great many film on *artha śr̥ṅgāra*. Film *El – This Strange Passion* (1953) is the story of a rich man who is successful in attracting the fiancée of his friend and marrying her. He then starts doubting her and this obsession with his mistrust grows to such heights that he contemplates sewing body parts of his wife after tying her. He keeps failing and ends up being taken in by the monks.

Luis Buñuel had a fetish for guns, but he never shot down game with them. He would design the guns as well as the bullets for them. He once decided to make a bullet which would disintegrate on coming in contact with clothes and not harm the person wearing the clothes. After months of relentless work, he succeeded in making the bullet. To test it he placed a few old dictionaries and telephone directories in the room and fired. The bullet tore through the books and went into his neighbour's house. He would often manipulate and play with the stories of his films in the same way. His films *Viridiana* (1961) and *Tristana* (1970), associated with the *artha śr̥ṅgāra*, are such scary bullets which bring out the unfathomed aspects of the human nature. It is important here to mention two of Buñuel's films, one is *Belle de Jour* or *Beauty of the Day* (1968), which is the story of a rich woman who is in love with her husband, yet during the day does prostitution to calm her

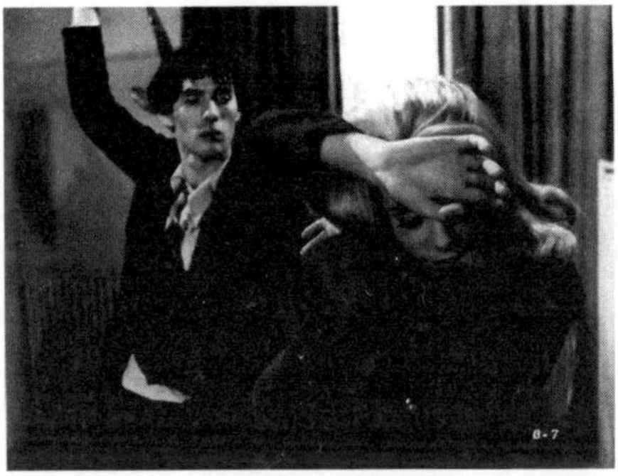

Belle de Jour (1968)

strange sexual urges. She doesn't do it for money or because she is taking revenge on her husband or even for lust. She does it to achieve something unknown. This is not desire, but a kind of emancipation she seeks from love and life.

There are two popular complexes related to lust and they are: sadism (where hurting another person gives sexual pleasure) and masochism (where hurting oneself gives sexual pleasure). We have learnt about the first one in Vībhatsa Rasa through the novel *The 120 Days of Sodom* (1789) by the French writer, Marquis de Sade. Masochism can be understood through the novel *Venus in Furs* (1870), written by an Austrian, Leopold von Sacher Masoch (1836-95). Their argumentative analysis is seen in the form of a kind of psychological heat.

The film *That Obscure Object of Desire* (1977), made by Luis Buñuel, is based on the novel – *Le Femme et le pantin* or *The Woman and the Puppet* (1898), written by Pierre Louÿs. This film shows a peculiar type of psychological pain and indecisiveness. A rich and middle-aged man falls in love with an eighteen-year-old unmarried girl but is unable to ascertain whether she loves him in return or not. The speciality of the film is that two actresses have played the role of the same girl and in every scene the face of the girl changes by changing the actresses.

Let us talk about French director François Truffaut's less discussed film *The Man Who Loved Women* or *L'Homme qui aimait les femmes* (1977). It is a peculiar story of a middle-aged man, who is attracted to and dreams of settling down in an imaginary island inhabited only by women. He ogles at the naked legs of women and is always hankering for sex with them. The man is not evil in anyway, he values kindness, love and peace. He writes his memoires and dies an untimely death. His funeral is attended only by his lovers and girlfriends.

Another film based on *artha śṛṅgāra* is Polish director Krzysztof Kieslowski's (1941-96) film, *A Short Story about Love* (1988). In this film a nineteen-year-old young man falls in love with a thirty-year old, beautiful woman. He keeps a tab on her through his telescope for a year and when he finally declares his love for her, she dismisses it by saying that the only truth in the world is lust and love is mere stupidity. This film was an improvisation of the sixth episode of the television series *Decalogue*. Love and dejection are deeply related to each other, especially if love is in the *artha śṛṅgāra* fame. Famous Hungarian director Bela Tarr's (b.1955) black and white film, *Damnation* or *Karhozat* (1987) is a prime example of this. A common man, arrested for falling in love with a married singer, tries all tricks in the book to eliminate her husband from being in the way, but unsuccessfully. His failure leads him to believe that he is worse than a dog. In the last scene of the film, he is shown to be barking just like a dog, in front of one and near a pot-hole filled with muddy slush. This is seen as a sign of his failure turning into despair. Other famous films of this director are *Sátántangó* (1994) and *Werckmeister Harmonies* (2000).

Dharma Śṛṅgāra

The activities or duties done for self-development or for one's own good is called *dharma*. The relationship a man establishes with his wife for the creation of a family life is defined as *dharma śṛṅgāra* by some scholars. The righteous way to demonstrate love and affection has been categorized in three ways by Abhinavagupta:

a. fondness (*sneha*) – the mutual love between people of same status,

b. devotion (*bhakti*) – the affection youngsters have toward their elders, and

c. affection (*vātsalya*) – the affection elders have toward their children, etc. (पारेख 1974: 110).

As we can see, the generality of *dharma śṛṅgāra* increases when we understand its meaning comprehensively. Through this perspective Sākhya Rasa, Bhakti Rasa and Vātsalya Rasa get merged into Śṛṅgāra Rasa.

The world-famous example of *dharma śṛṅgāra* is the film *The Sound of Music* (1965). Directed by Robert Wise (1914–2005), this film set a new bar for box office success. The story is of a young girl who gave up being a nun to become a governess to seven young, motherless children, it has all the determinants which qualify for the *dharma śṛṅgāra;* fondness (*sneha*), devotion and affection (*vātsalya*). The determinants for Śṛṅgāra Rasa like enjoyable

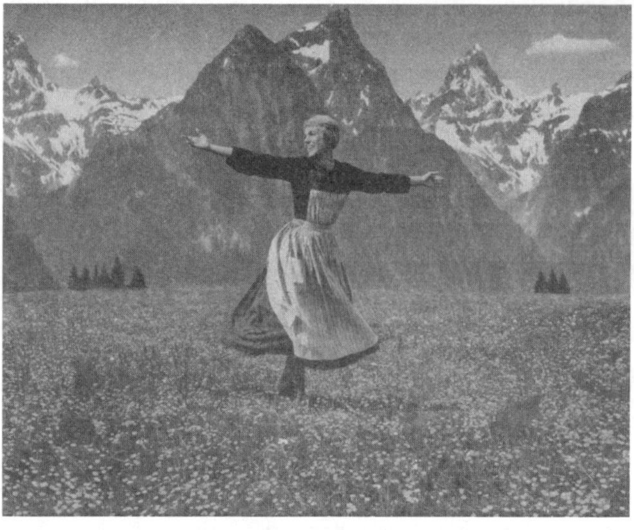

The Sound of Music (1965)

weather, actors wearing delectable costumes and jewellery, playing or walking in gardens, sailing on water and the company of the beloved are all very skilfully shown in the film. The very melodious and catchy songs and the stellar acting by all the actors make this film memorable even today. The director Robert Wise started his career as an assistant and editor to Orson Welles in his films: *Citizen Kane* and *The Magnificent Ambersons*. He also directed a critically acclaimed musical based on the drama Romeo and Juliet, *West Side Story* (1961).

Sneha Śṛṅgāra

The fondness between people of the same age or status is called as *sneha*. The sentiments of friendship are intrinsic to this. We have seen all along that Abhinavagupta has said that according to the Pratyabhijñā school (the idealistic monistic and theistic school of philosophy which says that Śiva is the only supreme power), all the emotions or moods are present in their nascent form in our consciousness itself. This is also the definition of our desires and yearnings. Desire is that state of our consciousness in which the subject is understood intrinsically. Similarly, we can say that desire is that state of our consciousness, wherein our knowledge, our action and our feelings are present in a nascent but complex seed-like form. A further analysis is the subject matter of epistemology (Jñāna-Mīmāṁsā). The desire for self-repose is relished like miracle. This savoury relishing is miracle, but *rasa* is not a miracle in itself (रस्तोगी 2012: 258, 260).

Typically, desire is defined and understood as the absence of a desired thing, however, this does not explain the sexual curiosity such as the desire of merely seeing a naked body.

In the film *Rebel without a Cause* (1955), directed by Nicholas Ray (1911-79), a despondency born out of drifting away from parental love and care has brought together three delinquent teenagers, two boys and an young girl. A strange friendship grows

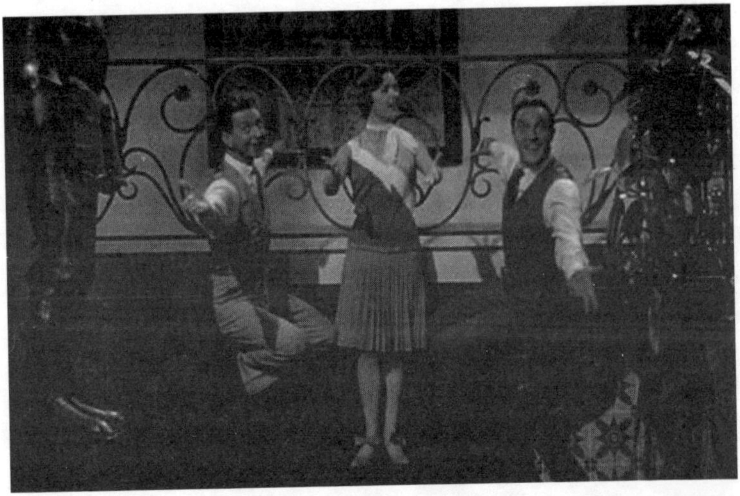

Singin' in the Rain (1952)

among them. The film shows the problems faced by the teenagers and is an example of *sneha śṛṅgāra*, rather than anger.

Fred Zinnemann (1907-97) directed film, *From Here to Eternity* (1953), is a perfect example of victory of love over anger. The film's mainstay is the bonds of friendship formed between the soldiers fighting in the Second World War.

American director, Stanley Donen (b.1924), co-directed the musical, *Singin' in the Rain* (1952) and directed the musical *Seven Brides for Seven Brothers* (1954), which are acclaimed films of the *sneha śṛṅgāra*. The film *Singin' in the Rain* uses the hit songs of old American movies to show the lasting friendships formed between actors and the film industry's transition from the silent era to the talkies. The film is remembered till date for its exclusive song and dance sequences. The film *Seven Brides for Seven Brothers* is based on an ancient Roman folklore wherein seven brothers kidnap girls for themselves. The love, affection and fondness displayed by the brothers toward their sister-in-laws and by the kidnapped girls toward the eldest sister-in-law are phenomenal and is *sneha śṛṅgāra* in its pure form.

Bhakti Śṛṅgāra

The devotion displayed by young people toward their elders is portrayed in a very special and different way in Śṛṅgāra Rasa. There are only a handful of films in the world cinema which have been able to bring out this speciality. It is seldom that people of the young age understand elders and are able to conduct themselves accordingly. It is seemingly easy for elders to show affection toward their young because of the tolerance they have for their limited knowledge and experience. Young people have respect for their teachers because of the vast knowledge and capability they have. Parents have an edge because of the mutual love and affection they show each other.

Devotion is commonly understood as the love for God. But it is difficult for God to come and show the love He has for one and all, so if there is no mutuality then where from is the love? Understanding that devotion is supernatural. Sriroop Swami has deigned that devotion (*bhakti*) should be given the status of a *mūla rasa*. Abhinavagupta is convinced that devotion toward God pertains to Śānta Rasa. We will discuss this aspect here itself, since keeping in mind the Sanskrit dramas, a detailed discussion on Śānta Rasa is not possible.

The scholars, who believe that devotion or Bhakti Rasa is a basic *rasa*, also believe that Śṛṅgāra Rasa is absolutely a subject matter of the objective world. They believe that the supreme power of God is the only source of inspiration and the realization of that is the only *rasa*. Ordinarily, we see conscious and insentient things all around us. Some schools of learning believe that the conscious things are the only truth and the unconscious are only a seeming perception. Some other thoughts point out that all the conscious elements are related to the supreme power. Modern science subscribes to materialism and argues that consciousness is nothing but a derivative of matter. It can be said without a debate that if the supremacy of God has not been experienced first-hand or if there is any doubt in one's mind regarding any thoughts, then there is no harm whatsoever in listening to and contemplating on various viewpoints by being an eager beaver. The very aim of studying and gaining knowledge is to broaden one's vision and horizon. The devotee sees the manifestation of the supreme power in the *rasa* and thereby relishes the devotion.

The film *My Fair Lady* (1964), directed by George Cukor, adapted from the famous novel, *Pygmalion* by George Bernard Shaw, showcases the *dharma śṛṅgāra* in a very beautiful way. The film portrays that language, social conduct, pronunciation and class differences are all very deeply entrenched in the societal fabric. All this can be criticized but that is not within our scope. A professor of phonetics agrees to transform a cockney-accented flower seller into a socially acceptable diva after he loses a bet with a friend. The flower seller's devotion sans lust/desire toward the professor is worth mentioning. The film is outstanding and is remembered in history for its beautiful dialogues, great display of acting skills, etc.

Sworn atheist, Italian director Pier Paolo Pasolini, was to meet with the Pope, but for some reason the meeting could not take place. On returning to the hotel, Pasolini picked up the Bible kept there and read through it. He was so impressed by the gospel and God's word that he made a film based on the life story of Jesus Christ, *The Gospel According to St. Matthew* (1964). This film totally flabbergasted people; they were not able to comprehend as to how a person who was an atheist, a Marxist and a homosexual could understand devotion toward God and make a film which was loaded with Christian values. Many film festivals appreciated the film. The followers of Christ looked

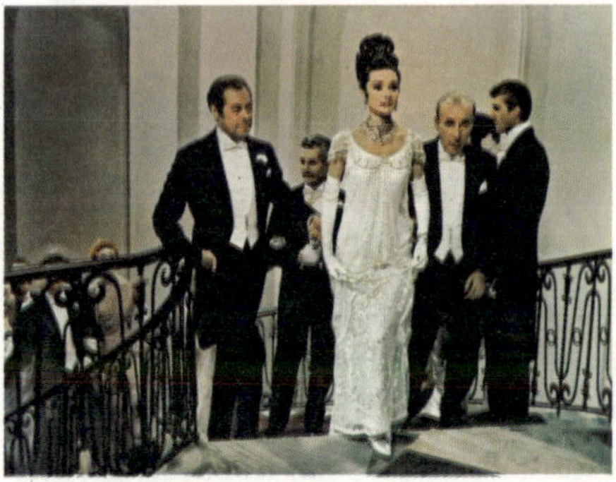

My Fair Lady (1964)

up to him with devotion and fondness. God's own word resonate in the baptism scene: "This is My beloved Son, in whom I am well pleased!".

To call *Andrei Rublev* (1966), a film by Andrei Tarkovsky, a Russian film-maker, based on the *dharma śṛṅgāra,* is quite strange. The film is filled with opposite feelings like friendship which has elements of doubt in it, devotion toward God, perfidy by friends, murder, etc. which show that the film is majorly of Karuṇa Rasa. The story pertains to the life of the fifteenth-century famous painter Andrei Rublev. It was an awarded and much discussed and appreciated film, whose beautiful scenes and artistic expressions were amazing. Rublev's friends never thought of him as an equal and always bowed down to his supremacy. Even though some were jealous of his fame, they became his fans once they recognized his talent. Andrei Rublev's last decision shows the victory of devotion for his followers. This artistic film says a lot on many levels, it is remembered for its beautiful expressions, the supporting and fortifying expressions and the miracle-like manifestation of the various expressions.

Through this film and its multitude of expressions, we realize that finding the name of the *rasa* is not the aim of *rasa-siddhānta* but the pleasurable immersion is, as there are examples of multiple chief (*aṅgī*) *rasa*s in celebrated dramas. Moreover, not all movies pertain to immediate *rasa* relishment for all individuals, but it may be instrumental in shaping aesthetic sensibilities through contemplation.

Vātsalya Śṛṅgāra

Yasujiro Ozu (1903-63) is a very revered name in the history of world cinema. This great Japanese film-maker has made numerous films pertaining to the *dharma śṛṅgāra.* His films have explored all kinds of family relationships: father–daughter, father–son, mother–son, husband–wife, etc. He remained unmarried throughout his life and stayed with his mother till her death. He too died two years after. He made notable films in all categories: silent, talkies and colour. In the evening of his career his camera went still, i.e. he adopted the *tatami shot*. This technique of shooting involves keeping the camera on the ground, facing the actors and taking the shot. It feels as though a man sitting on the floor is watching the scene unfold. The films like *Banshun* or *Late Spring* (1949), *Ochazuke no aji* or *The Flavour of Green Tea over Rice* (1952), *Bakushu* or *Early Summer* (1951), *Tokyo Monogatari* or *Tokyo Story* (1953), *Higanbana* or *Equinox Flower* (1958) and *Ukigusa* or *Floating Weeds* (1959) bring in a sense of peace through the *dharma śṛṅgāra* and are quite loved and appreciated by the cinephiles.

Japanese etiquettes and culture have been greatly influenced by India. Indian audiences find an affinity with most of the films. Familial values and the affection felt for the young people (*vātsalya*) are seldom seen in Western films. Yasujiro Ozu, like many of his contemporaries, was averse to making colour films, but he made *Equinox Flower* and *Floating Weeds* in colour. Since then these films have acted as an ideal in the use of colour for other film-makers. This is proof enough of his genius.

Film *Banshun* is adapted from a novel – *Father and Daughter*. Setsuko Hara, a great Japanese actress, plays the role of a twenty-seven-year old girl, who decides to remain unmarried so as to take care of her widower father. The story revolves around how the father tries to convince the daughter to get married. Films like *Banshun* are like the fresh and cool breeze on a hot summer morning. Actress, Setsuko Hara has also played the role of a widowed daughter-in-law in the film *Tokyo Story*. An old couple come to visit their children in Tokyo, but the children do not have time for the old parents and think of them as an encumbrance in their lives. They book them on a city tour and shift them to a hotel to get rid of them. The affection shown by the old father-in-law toward the widowed daughter-in-law is heart wrenching and unforgettable. The film, *Floating Weeds*, is a tragic story of a middle-aged man working in a travelling theatre company who goes to meet his son from an extramarital affair. The son, however, refuses to acknowledge the father.

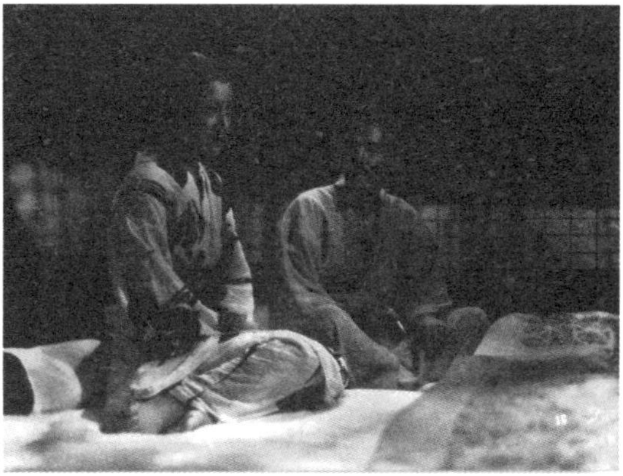

Banshun (1949)

Yasujiro Ozu's films are like expensive and exotic perfumes, whose fragrance stays with you for days to come and keep reminding you of the occasion for which it was worn.

American actor-singer Bing Crosby (1903-77), along with director Leo McCarey (1898–1969) made two films which are great films and apt examples for *dharma śṛṅgāra*. *Going My Way* (1944) and its sequel *The Bells at St. Mary's* (1945) tell the story of a young priest who goes to take over the responsibility of a church from the older priest. The devotion and respect the young priest shows the older one is exemplary. He takes under his wing the orphaned children of the town and teaches them to sing, the American public loved this character and showered him with utmost love and affection. Actress Ingrid Bergman plays a nun in the sequel, *The Bells at St. Mary's*, who also teaches small children. The film portrays the love and affection elders have for the youngsters and also shows that in life it does good to have a peaceful and benevolent nature.

Film-maker Satyajit Ray's name cannot be left behind when we discuss films of the *dharma śṛṅgāra*. His films *Aparojito* (1956) and *Apur Sansar* (1959) beautifully portray the relationship between the mother and son and the father and son. The films, which have

Pt. Ravishankar's *sitār* score as a background music, have been appreciated in film festivals all over the world.

Italian director, Giuseppe Tornatore's (b.1956) film *Cinema Paradiso* (1988) is the story of a small boy's deep friendship with the local cinema hall's projectionist. The boy grows up in the shadow of the projectionist, and on his advice, goes on to Rome and becomes a director. The story is in flashback from the time of the projectionist's death. The film has been awarded many times and has in many ways brought Italian cinema back to life. Roberto Benigni (b.1952), a fellow Italian director made a film, *Life Is Beautiful* (1997), wherein, he tells the story of a father and son in the Nazi labour camps. The love and affection (*vātsalya*) depicted between them is praiseworthy. This story bears resemblance to the director's father's life story. In the film, the gutsy Jewish hero, while in the concentration camp, convincingly tells his young son that all this is like a game and at the end of it whoever wins will get a tank as a prize. The love and sacrifice that his father did for the family dawns on the son after he grows up.

The Legend of Suram Fortress (1985) is Russian–Armenian film-maker, Sergei Parajanov's (1924-90) gift to *dharma śṛṅgāra.* In the film, the heroine who has been jilted in love, turns into a fortune-teller and orders that her lover's son be buried alive in the fortress. She, out of love and affection for the dead boy, goes to place a wreath at the burial site and tells her sad life story to the boy whom she feels is her own. This scene somehow epitomizes the affection (*vātsalya*) felt by the heroine but turns tragic at the end.

These films point out that affection (*vātsalya*) are not the sentiments expressed whenever you are with someone, they can also be expressed when you are separated. Separation and union are the two aspects of love and so must be accepted so as to have a positive outlook and a happy life. It also decides the policies and procedure in life.

Kāma Śṛṅgāra

The thirty-ninth and fortieth *ślokas* of the third chapter of the *Śrīmad-Bhagavadgītā* have this to say about desire (*kāma*):

> आवृतं ज्ञानमेतेन ज्ञानिनो नित्यवैरिणा।
> कामरूपेण कौन्तेय दुष्पूरेणानलेन च ॥३९॥
>
> *āvṛtaṁ jñānametena jñānino nityavairiṇā* ।
> *kāmarūpeṇa kaunteya duṣpūreṇānalena ca* ॥39॥
>
> Lord Kṛṣṇa addresses the Pāṇḍava prince, "Oh Arjuna! Just as fire is insatiable, so also is desire, which covers knowledge almost like an eternal enemy of the wise."
>
> इन्द्रियाणि मनो बुद्धिरस्याधिष्ठानमुच्यते।
> एतैर्विमोहयत्येष ज्ञानमावृत्य देहिनम् ॥४०॥
>
> *indriyāṇi mano buddhirasyādhiṣṭhānamucyate* ।
> *etairvimohayatyeṣa jñānamāvṛtya dehinam* ॥40॥
>
> The senses, the mind and the intellect are declared to be the seat of this desire, covering the knowledge, desire eludes the embodied soul.

The desire mentioned in these verses of the *Gītā* denotes the word in a broad context and not merely as sexual desire. In other words, desire here means what attracts people toward consumption of whatever can be consumed or relished in the objective world. In ancient Indian thinking, desire is the want of immediate, perceptual and corpulent happiness. Man is attracted to whatever is achievable by him, the source of this attraction is none but the supreme power. The outward form of this attraction is manifested as desire. This is the happiness we feel whenever our desires or wants are fulfilled.

This indigenous meaning of desire shows that Śṛṅgāra is the one and only *rasa*. If we adhere to Bharata Muni's and Abhinavagupta's version, our implication for the word desire will be very limited. The subject of our study is the emotional madness or frenzy which happens in a man–woman relationship, which is called as *kāma śr̥ṅgāra*. Bharata Muni has interpreted Śr̥ṅgāra Rasa as chiefly pertaining to desire. The great scholar, Vātsyāyana says that sexual desire is addressed to the opposite. Bharata Muni says sexual desire is assiduity toward opposite. This in turn brings us to the question as to how we would define homosexuality?

To understand the nuances of love and desire, one must attempt to read the epic work *Kādambarī*, written by seventh-century poet, Mahākavi Bāṇabhaṭṭa. Its greatness can be incurred from the fact that the word *kādambarī* has been taken from the Kannada and Marathi language for novels. Vasudev Sharan Agarwal (1904-66), a scholar on Indian history, culture, art, literature and ancient knowledge, has this to say as a commentary on *Kādambarī*:

> Desire (*kāma*) is present in two forms – the higher form is love, while the baser one is lust. Bāṇabhaṭṭa has described the lust and a similar mad pursuit for a woman as false desire (*kāma*). The feelings of a human being are similar to water. Water by nature flows, similarly, the mind too is full of free-flowing feelings. When these feelings flow upward it is called devotion. Devotion is generally towards teachers and elders. Towards youngsters this feeling of affection is called *vātsalya*. Here the flow of feelings is downwards. When these feelings flow between people of the same age or status it is called fondness (*sneha*), for example towards friends. Devotion, affection (*vātsalya*) and fondness (*sneha*) when dedicated to one person it should be understood as sexual desire (*kāma*). The purview of desire is the woman. Desire is generally towards one person. The same, when it is conferred in totality, is called love. The attachment to a physical base form is lust. Lust is nothing but a bond or chain which has a selfish nature. Love is supposed to be uphill and lust, downhill. Love is eternal but lust not so. The fruit of love is happiness while the fruit of lust is sorrow. The emancipation from this sorrow makes the mind clean and fills it with happiness. Love is far from curses, is boundless and fills our consciousness with a happy feeling. – अग्रवाल 1988: 349, 378

In the above commentary, the assimilation of the *dharma śṛṅgāra* into *kāma śṛṅgāra* is in accordance with the *puruṣārtha siddhānta* of philosopher, Acharya Goswami Shyammanohar-ji. According to which, *kāma puruṣārtha* should be complementary to *dharma*, *artha* and *mokṣa puruṣārthas*. In the *Śrīmad-Bhagavadgītā*, Śrī Kṛṣṇa says to Arjuna:

> बलं बलवतां चाहं कामरागविवर्जितम् ।
> धर्माविरुद्धो भूतेषु कामोऽस्मि भरतर्षभ ॥
>
> *balaṁ balavatāṁ cāhaṁ kāmarāgavivarjitam* ।
> *dharmāviruddho bhūteṣu kāmo 'smi bharatarṣabha* ॥
>
> – VII.11

> Oh, Mighty Arjuna! I am the might, free from passion and desire. In beings I am the sexual desire not at all conflicting with virtuous or scriptural injunctions.

Śṛṅgāra in Union

Bharata Muni says that there are ten phases of desire – appentence, reflection, remembrance, speaking of merits, agitation, rambling, frenzy, extreme anger or fever, inertia and death. These phases are in the increasing order more painful than the previous one. In both cases when desire is in reality present, then these phases become a part of *śṛṅgāra*, otherwise they remain independent of each other (द्विवेदी 1992: 149; पारेख 1974).

Enjoying good weather, wearing flowers, applying fragrant oils, wearing fine jewellery, going for walks in the garden, seeing beautiful, big buildings or gardens, the company of a beloved, etc. are documented as determinants for relishing Śṛṅgāra Rasa, according to Bharata Muni. Abhinavagupta, while clarifying this, says that for *śṛṅgāra* in union, the man and woman are determinants enough for each other. The other above-mentioned determinants are only meant to be enhancers.

It is quite easy to establish an identity with the help of the determinant props of Śṛṅgāra Rasa. Therefore, many films use this *rasa* to put forward their point. One of the most expensive and commercially successful films of its time was *Way Down East* (1920), directed by the director of silent films, D.W. Griffith. He used to make films with a simple moral story, where a few characters were immoral and the hero–heroine would be troubled by them. In the film *Way Down East* the heroine, a simple village girl who has been traumatized by the goons, but in the end, finds true love. In the climax, the unconscious heroine is to flow down an icy waterfall but is saved by the very heroic actor. This dangerous stunt was performed by the actors themselves without using any body doubles. It is one of the most unforgettable scenes of the film. The actresses' hair and fingers and the director's face were frozen from the icy water during filming.

The American silent film, *Sunrise: A Song of Two Humans* (1927), is the beautiful story which describes the love between a husband and wife. It was directed by German director, F.W. Murnau (1888–1931), also famous for his film *Nosferatu* (1922). Many scholars have termed marital love as *dharma śṛṅgāra* and attraction to other women, i.e. either other's wives or prostitutes, as *artha śṛṅgāra*. This thought is extremely narrow-minded. Every universal theory should be broad-minded and courageous enough to define and discuss all possibilities in a decent way. Such narrow-minded thoughts ignorantly make the *rasa-siddhānta*, insensitive and harsh to understand.

The film *Sunrise: A Song of Two Humans* is a unique example of *kāma śṛṅgāra*. The story is set in a small village wherein a cruel woman incites the hero to fall in love with her. She asks him to sell-off his home and even tells him to drown his wife in the water. In a fit of madness and frenzy, the man decides to do exactly that, but he is unable to drown his wife. He then follows his scared wife to another town and spends a pleasant day with her, all the while

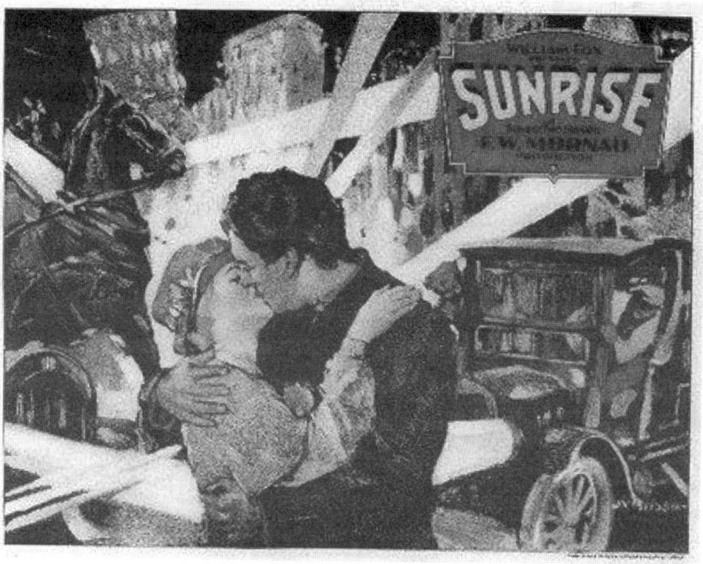

Sunrise: A Song of Two Humans (1927)

realizing his folly. The couple express their love by embracing each other in the middle of a street and cause a huge traffic jam. This is one of the most famous scenes of the film. The heroine's hairstyle (reminiscent of Da Vinci's heroines), first successful use of sound in the movies, the hero's barbarism all make this film a must watch.

A serious contemplation for polygamy has been raised in *Design for Living* (1933), a film directed by Ernst Lubitsch (1892–1947). Based on a play, the story revolves around a beautiful commercial cartoonist Gilda (played by Miriam Hopkins) who is unable to decide between two men who are good friends, played by Fredric March and Gary Cooper. In the end the trio agree to live together in a platonic relationship. It should be noted that almost all cultures have dealt with polygamy till the recent past except Catholic Christianity. It should be noted that *Design for Living* was a pre-code movie. Post-mid-1934 Motion Picture Production Code was enforced in America and now rest of the world typically have their censor boards and schemes.

His other film, *The Shop Around the Corner* (1940), is more of a romance than a comedy. It revolves around two employees of a general store who fall in love only through the letters they write to each other. Both are unaware of the other's real identity. The film has some good romantic scenes when the couple read the letters and some great scenes of comedy when they are at loggerheads at the shop. The film ends when the two realize who they are and embrace each other on Christmas eve.

Frank Capra (1897–1991), made a heart-warming famous film, *It Happened One Night* (1934). The film tells the story of the spoilt daughter of a rich man who runs away from home to marry her beau and gets stranded as she doesn't know anything. She is helped out by a fellow passenger in the bus, who has been kicked out of his job. The man falls in love with her, but even on realizing who she is promises to help her meet her lover. The end is happy as the girl too realizes that the hero truly loves her, as he is undeterred by the money offered to him by her father. Two Hindi remakes of this film; one in 1953 – *Chori-Chori*, starring Raj Kapoor and Nargis and the other in 1991 – *Dil Hai Ki Manta Nahi*, starring Aamir Khan, have made this film much loved and relished. The original film won many accolades and was a huge commercial success.

The personal excellence of two artists sometimes can be elevated to astounding heights when the two pair up and show unmatched chemistry onstage/screen. One such pair is of the dancing stars Fred Astaire (1899–1987) and Ginger Rogers (1911-95). The two acted in many musicals and showcased their unique style of dance. Some of the films which went on to win awards were *The Gay Divorcee* (1934), *Top Hat* (1935), *Swing Time* (1936), *Follow the Fleet* (1936) and *Shall We Dance* (1937). Fred Astaire famously once said: "Either the camera will dance or I will." In the films *Top Hat* and *Swing Time*, the hero and heroine are the determinants for each other's love, the plot of the film is just a reason to showcase their dancing talent. But this in no way troubles the viewer, just as we are aware that a drama is not related to real life, here too the mesmerizing duet dance and the swinging to perfect musical tunes brings the spectator to the ultimate experience of relishing the *rasa*. The role of the director is relegated to the background and the beautiful talent of both the artists help manifest the *rasa*.

Love Affair (1939) is a film to remember. Directed by Leo McCarey (1898–1969), the story revolves around a French painter and an American singer, who fall in love while on a cruise. But both are engaged to be married elsewhere. They give themselves six months to understand their position and decide a date and time to meet after that. Unexplainable circumstances don't allow them to meet on the scheduled date. They are of course reunited with each other and their love endures the time lapse. It is an unforgettable film of the *kāma śṛṅgāra*. The film has been remade as *An Affair to Remember* (1957) and in Bollywood as *Mann* (1999).

David Lean's (1908-91) all-time great romantic film, *Brief Encounter* (1945), tells a bitter–sweet love story between a married, middle-class housewife and a married doctor, who meet during a visit to the market. Their encounter turns into love, but due to marital constraints and societal norms they decide to remain separate. The film's universality and all-time appeal is due to its simple everyday story, the actor's voices, and the intensity of the eyes which tell the pain that the actors go through. The gist of the story lies in a dialogue said by the heroine – "I'm an ordinary woman. I didn't think such violent things could happen to ordinary people." The film epitomizes the *rasa-siddhānta* – wherein simpler the causes and determinants, greater the generalization of the *rasa*. If the manifestation of the *rasa* is easy, then the drama or film becomes all the more popular with the masses.

Director duo, Britishers, Michael Powell (1905-90) and Emeric Pressburger (1902-88) are famous for three films of the *kāma*

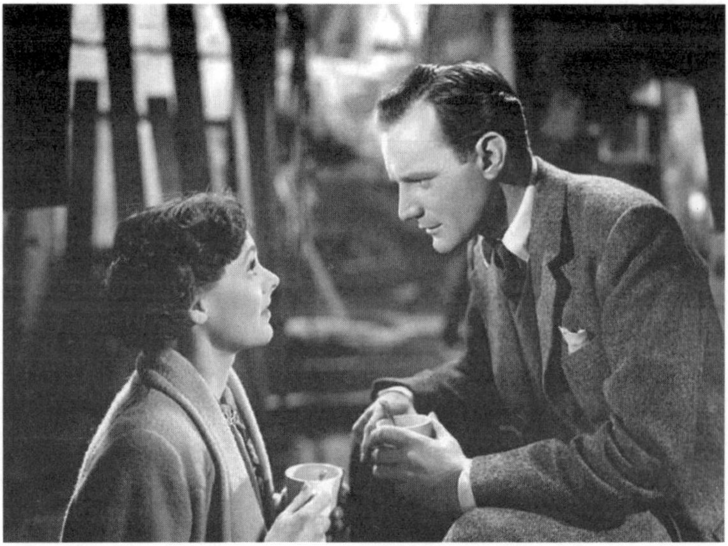

David Lean's *Brief Encounter* (1945)

śr̥ṅgāra: *I Know Where I'm Going* (1945), *A Matter of Life and Death* (1946) and *Red Shoes* (1948). In the film *I Know Where I'm Going*, a beautiful girl agrees to marry a rich old man, living on an uninhabited island. She is forced to seek shelter on a nearby island due to inclement weather, and there she falls in love with another man – a prince of that island. Bad weather makes her stay there and their love deepens. She is torn between her ambition and love. Love, however, overcomes all hurdles and the two unite. The film, *Red Shoes*, is inspired by Hans Christian Anderson's stories and based on the story of ballet. The use of beautiful colours, marvellous ballet, the tussle between love and duty form the backdrop for this unforgettable film.

The Chinese film *Spring in a Small Town* or *Xiaocheng Zhi Chun* (1948) was almost forgotten after the communist revolution in China. It was revived almost twenty years on and is now thought to be one of the greatest Chinese films. The story unfolds in a ruined family house after the Sino-Japanese war, the patriarch, a physically challenged man, lives with his self-centred wife and beautiful sixteen-year old sister. His friend and his wife's ex-flame comes to visit and a forgotten love revives in the house. The film details the love quadrangle between the hero, heroine, the friend and the teenaged sister. An old rambling house, music, small family games all help the love to blossom. Many modern Chinese directors have acknowledged the effect this film has had on Chinese films.

Most love stories gain credence due to the youth and popularity of the actors and actresses who play the central roles. One such hugely popular and exquisitely romantic film is *Roman Holiday* (1953). Directed by William Wyler (1902-81), it stars the breathtakingly beautiful, Audrey Hepburn and the tall, dark and handsome, Gregory Peck. The film tells the story of a bored princess who on a state visit to Rome, manages to escape from the hotel so that she can roam Rome as a commoner. She meets the hero, a reporter, who takes her for a tourist and mesmerized by her beauty offers to show her Rome. The film is filled with all the determinants (*vibhāvas*) which are necessary to call it a film of Śṛṅgāra Rasa; beautiful costumes, good music, games, tender love words, walks in the park and so on. Unmatched beauty and calmness always strengthen the backbone of the *rasa*. To quote, great Sanskrit poet Bhāravi from his *Kirātārjunīyam*, "it is so true that youth adds grace to the adornments and not vice versa".

विपत्रलेखा निरलक्तकाधरा निरञ्जनाक्षीरपि बिभ्रती: श्रियम्।
निरीक्ष्य रामा बुबुधे नभश्चरैरलंकृतं तद्वपुषैव मण्डनम् ॥

vipatralekā niralaktakādharā nirañjanākṣīrapi bibhratīḥ śriyam ।
nirīkṣya rāmā bubudhe nabhaścarairalaṁkṛtaṁ tadvapuṣaiva maṇḍanam ।।
– *Kirātārjunīyam* 8.40

The story of *The Crucified Lovers* or *Chikamatsu Monogatari* (1954), a film by Japanese director Kenji Mizoguchi (1898–1956), is the

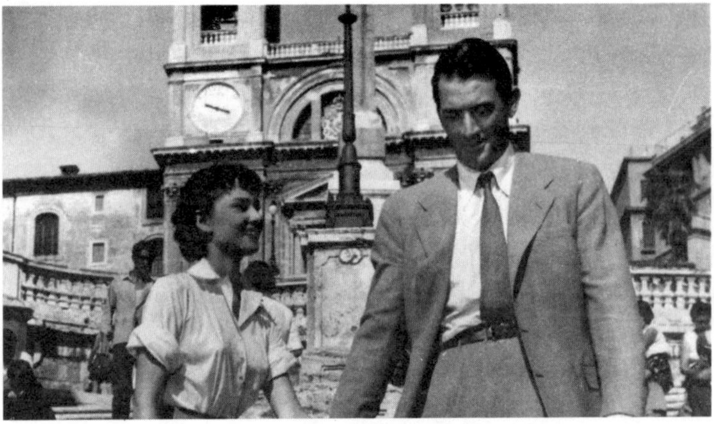

Roman Holiday (1953)

tragic tale of two runaway lovers. Then too, it is a story of sexual union in Śṛṅgāra Rasa. A miserly businessman buys a young wife, who is wrongly accused of having an affair with the accountant of the businessman. The punishment for the crime is death, therefore, both the accused run away. Their togetherness makes them fall in love with each other and they have a sexual relationship. With sex comes the worries of the future and love is tested many times. The couple are caught and sentenced to death. In the last scene of the film, the faces of the lovers depict utmost calm and inner glow.

क्षणे क्षणे यन्नवतामुपैति तदेव रूपं रमणीयतायाः ।

kṣaṇe kṣaṇe yannavatāmupaiti tadeva rūpaṁ ramaṇīyatāyāḥ ।

The gist of the above Sanskrit *śloka,* taken from Sanskrit poet Māgha's *Śiśupālavadham* 4.17, is that every moment which evolves into newer forms brings in more and more pleasantness. This is the rudimentary rule of the theory of aesthetics. That is also the reason why, French director, Jean-Luc Godard's films are an abridged, but special examples of the manifestation of Śṛṅgāra Rasa. In his films *Bande à Part* or *Band of Outsiders* (1964) and *Une Femme est Une Femme* or *A Woman Is a Woman* (1961), the common expectations of an onlooker seeking for moments of love and desire is broken. What one gets instead of seriousness is a fun-filled and boisterous camaraderie. Attractive costumes, elaborate hairdos, music and dance all point toward desire and the realization of Śṛṅgāra Rasa.

Woman in the Dunes (1964) is a Japanese film, based on a novel by writer Kobo Abe (1924-93). It was directed by Hiroshi Teshigahara (1927–2001). The story of the film says that love is necessary to bring some meaning to life. A school teacher is thrown into the sand dunes in a village, from where it is impossible to escape. A woman from the village is accursed to dig for sand in the same dune. Love happens between them even in this sandy prison, which seems to tell the viewer that accepting the present circumstances is the real and only name of love.

The aim of the film *Harold and Maude* (1971), which is a quirky love story between asymmetrically aged people, and *Ali: Fear Eats the Soul* (1974), directed by Rainer Werner Fassbinder (1945-82), is not to portray the exceptionality of love, but to help change the way life is seen and lived and to show the problems faced by immigrants. In the film *Harold and Maude*, an 18-year old young man, thirsting for love and prone to stage fake suicides, meets and falls in love with a 79-year old woman who teaches him to live life king-size. In the film *Ali: Fear Eats the Soul*, a 60-year old, single woman marries a 40-year old African-Muslim immigrant. It may seem quite incongruous to identify oneself with the characters of such films, but we must realize and remember that for a spectator to have a compassionate heart or to be one with the characters, his cultural upbringing, intelligence and individual likes and dislikes should be understood. This is important to understand the values and for the heart to understand its meaning.

The first of January calls for a celebration every year, as it did in the year 1976. The national television of the then Soviet Union, broadcast a telefilm, *The Irony of Fate: Enjoy Your Bath* or *Ironya Sudby Ili S Lyogkim Parom*. It was directed by Eldar

Ryazanov (1927–2015), based on his own famous drama. The film mesmerized the Russian people in such a way that even today, many of them watch this film on New Year's Day. The totally drunk hero catches a flight to Leningrad in place of his equally drunk friend and coincidentally gets to a house which bears the same number and is on a street with the same name. When the occupant of that house, an unmarried girl finds him asleep in her bed, she tries to get rid of him. Strange circumstances do not allow that to happen and they are forced to spent time in the same house, they fall in love. The film is graced with contemporary great Russian poets' poems and songs and is seen with great enthusiasm even today.

Being jilted in love, does not stop three young women from seeking and finding true love even at the age of forty. This is the story of the winner of the Academy award for Best Foreign film, director Vladimir Menshov's (b.1939), film *Moscow Does Not Believe in Tears* or *Moskva Slezam ne Verit* (1980). American President Ronald Reagan saw the film many times before meeting with President Mikhail Gorbachev. He said he wanted to understand the Russian psyche through the film.

Wings of Desire or *Der Himmel uber Berlin* (1987) and its sequel, *Faraway, So Close* (1993) is the story of two angels, who remain unseen and help human beings in every which way. One of the angels falls in love with a beautiful girl and takes human form and comes to earth. These are films of German director Wim Wenders (b.1945), whose another famous creation is, *Paris, Texas* (1984). It was remade in America as *City of Angels* (1998). The film, *Wings of Desire*, won many awards.

One remarkable film of Śṛṅgāra Rasa is the Vietnamese film, made in France, *The Scent of Green Papaya* or in Vietnamese, *Mui du du xanh* and in French, *L'Odeur de la papaye verte* (1992). The film tells the story of Mui, who works in a house as a maid and also grows up there itself. She is absorbed into the family on growing up. The eldest son of the house even marries her, leaving his fiancée, as he finds that Mui is very soft and kind hearted. The film has multiple stories running side by side, which makes it very interesting.

The trilogy by American director, Richard Linklater (b.1960) – *Before Sunrise* (1994), *Before Sunset* (2004) and *Before Midnight* (2013) – is quite remarkable and important for the *kāma śṛṅgāra.* All the three films have been made with an interval of nine years each in between them, starring the same set of actors. The actors meet, fall in love and separate and meet again after nine years – accept the other's love and marry. The faithfulness of love is amply displayed and accepted. This trilogy is very popular all over the world.

Śṛṅgāra in Separation

We have already discussed that sexual union and separation both together constitute Śṛṅgāra Rasa.

> एकस्मिञ्शयने पराङ्मुखतया वीतोत्तरं ताम्यतोरन्योन्यं हृदयस्थितेऽप्यनुनये संरक्षतोर्गौरवम् ।
> दम्पत्योः शनकैरपाङ्गवलनान्मिश्रीभवच्चक्षुषोर्भग्नो मानकलिः सहासरभव्यासक्तकण्ठग्रहम् ॥
>
> *ekasmiñ śayane parāṅmukhatayā vītottaraṁ tāmyato-ranyonyaṁ hṛdayasthite'pyanunaye saṁrakṣatorgauravam* ।
> *damptyoḥ śanakairapāṅgavalanānmiśrībhavaccakṣuṣor bhagno mānakaliḥ sahāsarabhavyāsaktakaṇṭhagraham* ॥
>
> – 21.33

The above *śloka* from the *Amarukaśataka*, a collection of poems dated to about seventh or eighth century, depicts the moods of a married couple who have just had an argument:

> Although both have the urge to persuade the other, but their ego does not permit them and both are lying on the bed not facing each other. Both are silent, but their eyes meet and immediately their ego disappear and both burst into laughter and finally embrace each other. – पारेख 1974: 78; द्विवेदी 1992: 134

It seems as though the film *L'Atalante* (1934) has been made just to justify the above *śloka*. Directed by highly talented, but short lived, Jean Vigo (1905-34), this film is an important film of the *kāma śṛṅgāra*. The emotional scene of union after separation from a beloved, makes this film a must-watch. The captain of a small barge marries and takes his newly-wedded wife to live on it, also doubling as their honeymoon. His crew accompanies him too. They visit many places, but his wife is enamoured of Paris and wants to spend more time there. The captain gets jealous of the attention his wife gets and in anger sets sail without her. His first mate helps to reunite the couple. The characters of the two crew members, the beautiful long shots of Paris skyline taken from the barge on the river, the romantic music played on the gramophone are enough to make this film poetic and pleasurable and worth seeing.

To understand the pain of separation, one must see the film, *Partie de Champagne* (1936). The film, directed by Jean Renoir (1894–1979) was based on a story by Guy de Maupassant. The forty-minute film tells the story of a small businessman who takes his wife, daughter and her fiancée on an excursion to a river-side resort. Some local men try to flirt with his wife and daughter and are successful in luring them away on a boat ride. His daughter, attracted to one man, has a sexual relation with him and all go their way. Years later, the now married girl and her past lover meet at the same spot and reminisce through actions only about their brief encounter and the painful parting thereafter. The film was released only about ten years after it was completed.

Jean Renoir's first colour film, *The River* (1951), was shot on locale in West Bengal. It was an inspirational film for many film-makers. Young and upcoming film-maker, Satyajit Ray, helped Renoir in searching for the shooting spots. The film shows how European girls growing up in Bengal are influenced by the Hindu culture and rituals, marriage and festival ceremonies, etc. The

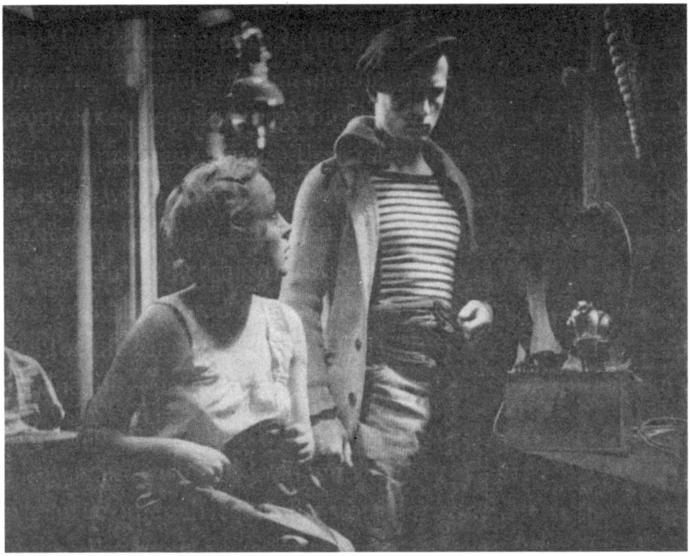

L' Atalante (1934)

young heroine falls in love with the handsome soldier, who has come home on leave and who is in love with another girl. The pain of young love and possible separation has been captured beautifully along with shots of the mighty River Gaṅgā.

The film *Algiers* (1938) is the American remake of a French film. It is also the reason why the film *Casablanca* was made. The heroine of *Algiers*, the very beautiful, Hedy Lamarr, was offered the role played by Ingrid Bergman, in *Casablanca*, but due to contractorial issues, she did not accept. In the film *Algiers*, a jewel thief, Pépé le Moko, hides out from the police in an area called "Casbah". The police cannot come into that area to arrest him fearing retaliation. Moko falls madly in love with a tourist and it is this passionate devotion toward her that becomes responsible for his arrest and death.

American director, Vincente Minnelli (1903-86) was quite famous for his musicals he worked with the famous actress Judy

Garland, and made the film *Meet Me in St. Louis* (1944). The film portrays the states of ambition and contemplation, very aptly. After the film was released, Minnelli married the heroine who was nineteen years younger to him. This film was well known for its beautiful music, dance and happy family scenes. It is a film which can be watched along with the entire family in a fun-filled and relaxed environment. The chief attraction of the film is the adolescent age love it portrays. Vincente Minnelli's another musical *An American in Paris* (1951) was full of dance numbers. Gene Kelly, hero of this movie, went on co-directing and choreographing his famous musical *Singin' in the Rain* (1952). Students of cinema studies should see these films for the varied themes, sets, colours and dance sequences. They can learn how Gene Kelly builds up the much-appreciated excellence in *Singin' in the Rain*, as a gradual enhancement from his earlier broadway musicals such as *On the Town* (1949) and *An American in Paris* (1951).

Judy Garland also acted in a George Cukor directed film, *A Star Is Born* (1954). It was a remake of a film made in 1937, having the same name. The film faced a number of problems during production, yet it was famous for its beautiful sets, stellar acting and great songs. It was the most expensive film of its time. The film tells the story of a famous actor who gives a break to an upcoming actress. The young actress goes on to achieve great success and the two marry each other. After marriage the success of the actress continues to rise, while that of the actor takes a tumble. Many scenes of this famous film have inspired scenes and remakes in Bollywood. Famous among them are *Sangam* (1964) and *Aashiqui-2* (2013).

German born director, Max Ophüls (1902-57), made many films while staying in Germany, France and America. One of his films, based on a novel *A Letter from an Unknown Woman* (1948), is the tragic story of an innocent, passionate young girl, who is madly in love with an older man, who is a musician. The man never notices her and she spends endless days hoping he will. They meet several times, but the man never recognizes her. After the girl grows older, they have a sexual relationship which leads to the girl bearing a child. She never tells him about it. Finally, as she is about to die of a grave illness, she writes him a letter telling her life story. He has no clue about her and questions his servant about her. The servant affirms the relationship and he feels a great remorse for all that he has done. In 2004, a Chinese remake of this tragic story was released.

Órfeu Negro or *Black Orpheu* (1959) is a Greek myth retold in the modern setting of the Rio de Janerio Carnival. The film by French director, Marcel Camus (1912-82), is in Portuguese and has been shot entirely in Brazil. It was awarded the Best Film at the Cannes Film Festival. The story is about a new actress, who falls in love with a trolley driver, who plays the guitar at sunrise. An unknown masked man wants to kill the actress and the hero starts talking to the soul of the actress through a medium. The story details the Greek mythical story of Orpheus and Eurydice. The atmosphere of the carnival, masked characters, sensational samba music, the talk of souls and after life all are the perfect ingredients to make this a film of Śṛṅgāra Rasa.

तदा रम्याण्यरम्याणि प्रियाः शल्यं तदासवः ।
तदैकाकी सबन्धुः सन्निष्टेन रहितो यदा ॥

tadā ramyāṇyaramyāṇi priyāḥ śalyaṁ tadāsavaḥ ।
tadaikākī sabandhuḥ sanniṣṭena rahito yadā ॥

– 11.28

The above *śloka* from Bhāravi's *Kirātārjunīyam* says that, when one's beloved is absent, even the most desirable things seem undesirable, what one likes, including one's own life becomes a pain, one feels lonely even in the midst of one's relatives. This is the import of separation.

The film *Shadows of Forgotten Ancestors* or *Tini Zabutykh Predkiv* (1964) is an Ukrainian film directed by Sergei Parajanov.

Ivan wants to marry his beloved, Marichka, who is also the daughter of his father's killer, but innocent Marichka dies untimely. Ivan cannot forget her even after his marriage to another woman. The film has scenes of beautiful mountains, lakes, beautiful foggy nights, folk music and picturization of various marriage rituals. The first scene shows that Ivan's brother is killed when a tree falls on him, for this scene Parajanov tied a camera to the tree's trunk, so that he could capture the perfect shot. The film, which has traditional costumes and is based on folklore, was blacklisted in the Soviet Union because the director did not toe the Marxist ideology. This film shows, very artistically, death due to separation.

The English Patient (1966) is a film about love and dejection. A cartographer recounts his tragic love affair with a friend's wife in the Saharan desert while he is on a survey there. He tells his story to a nurse, who calls him The English Patient as he cannot recall who he is but can speak English. The film is based on a novel and a few real-life characters. It was awarded nine Academy awards, five BAFTA awards and two Golden Globes.

People get married to somebody who is a total opposite to their nature and likes and dislikes. Here, we must remember that according to Vātsyāyana, lust is always opposite in nature. We are, of course, discussing the difference in the personality of the people. When Muni Vātsyāyana says opposite, he means the attraction toward the opposite gender. Love is always between people who have similar interests and values.

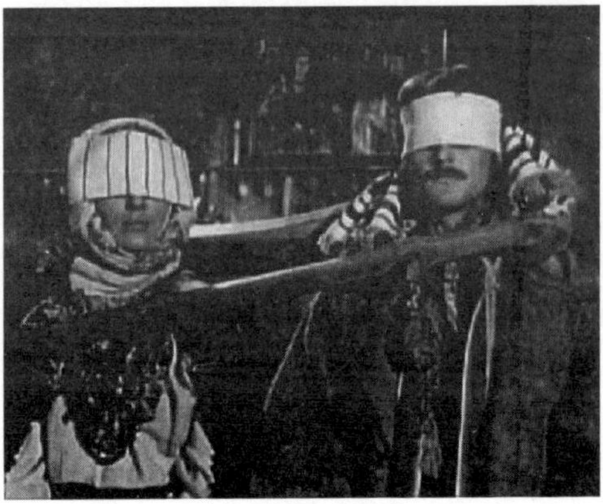

Shadows of Forgotten Ancestors (1964)

The last *śloka* of *Ṛgveda* says this in the context of marriage:

समानी व आकूति: समाना हृदयानि व: ।
समानमस्तु वो मनो यथा व: सुसहासति ॥

samānī va ākūtiḥ samānā hṛdayāni vaḥ ।
samānamastu vo mano yathā vaḥ susahāsati ॥
– X.191.4

> May all your commitments be the same, may your heart be the same, may your mind remain the same, so that all your mutual work gets fructified in totality.

The film, *In the Mood for Love* (2000), is very popular among the cine-lovers of the world. Love happens between two married people, but due to societal unacceptability, they do not give their relationship any concrete name. At the end of the film, the hero's helplessness is shown as he shouts out his misery into the hollow of a tree and covers it with mud. A caption says:

> He remembers those vanished years. As though looking through a dusty window pane, the past is something he could see, but not touch. And everything he sees is blurred and indistinct.

Many people are cursed to live in loveless and painful married

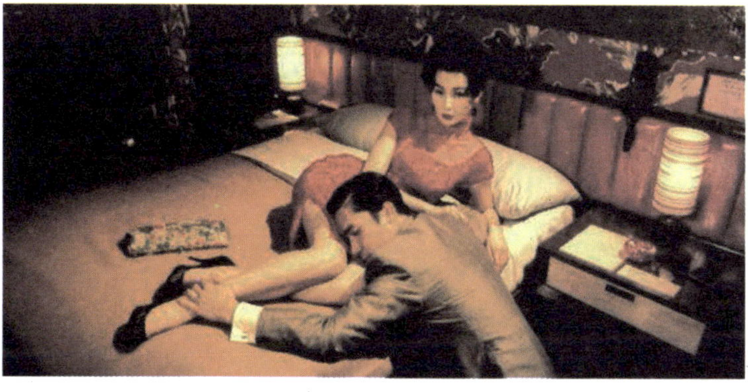

In the Mood for Love (2000)

lives. This film, though, is of one of them, is laced with old Chinese songs, saying love poems frame by frame, marvellously generalizes the manifestation of the *kāma* Śṛṅgāra Rasa.

11

Aesthetics of Cinema in Cinema

According to Śaiva Darśana and in the words of Govind Chandra Pande, the extensive explanation of aesthetics is as follows:

> The perception of the omnipresent Śaiva consciousness is seen in all forms and a quickening of the pulse is felt within, when a condensed perception is undertaken, which is not very different from recognizing the actual meaning (metaphysical reality) or the substantive miracle of the *rasa* realization. When one sees or hears of this beauty, the mind is greatly agitated as though remembering someone or something. The birth of the internal feelings is enough to transform the outer subject in such way that its direct perception forms an intense experience.
>
> – रस्तोगी 2012: 285

The *rasa-siddhānta*, which has been associated with the traditional Sanskrit dramas, has been subjected to a very harsh and limited explanation. This has been quite detrimental to the modern Indian aesthetics. Every Indian aesthete, begins his\her explanation of beauty with mentioning the *rasa* and its realization. It is important to understand that due to different thought processes and metaphysical viewpoints the meaning of *rasa* theory can substantially alter. Instead of laying down the rules for creation (as it has been done in the *Nāṭyaśāstra*), a master of aesthetics is required to answer the fundamental questions of aesthetics. Instead of focusing on the extensive explanation of the *Nāṭyaśāstra*, the rule book for guiding the actors, etc. we ended up mistaking the rules as a mandatory requirement for poetics creation. The world of art has become cumbersome, as it has been loaded with realization, intellectual exceptionality, miraculous logical deductions, history, poetry, archaeology and so many other subjects and their criticism. This has not created any new challenge for the *rasa-siddhānta*, but it has become necessary for us to expand our horizons to better understand the different aspects of aesthetics.

According to some scholars, the aim of art is two-pronged: (a) that which is directly perceived (*pratyakṣa*), and (b) that which is hidden or subtle (*parokṣa)*. The first aims immediate happiness and the second aims character building (पारेख 1974: 50, 52, 55). It is argued that Bharata Muni thought that the aim of drama is to preach. According to the tradition of Indian poetics, poetry has been called as *kānta sammita* (endearing persuasion), which is the advice given by a beloved (Paranjape and Visuvalingam 2006: 94).

Since we have glanced over multiple aspects of world cinema through Abhinavagupta's exegesis of *rasa-siddhānta*, let us re-look at its description in the light of Śaiva *darśana* with exact precision. In the words of Abhinavagupta as he comments in the *Abhinavabhāratī,* while giving an example of a frightful scene in the drama in his exegesis of *rasa* –

> ... the sensation of the fear, on the contrary, is the matter of cognition by a perception devoid of obstacles (*nirvighna*), and may be said to enter directly into our heart, to dance before our eyes: this is terrible *rasa*. In such a fear, one's own self is neither completely immersed nor in a state of particular emergence, and the same thing happens with other selves. As a result of this, the state of generality involved is not limited, but extended – as happens at the moment in which is formed the idea of invariable concomitance between smoke and fire or, in fact, between

trembling and fear. Therefore, this idea to be confronted, with a real experience is nourished by the combination of actors, etc. In this combination, indeed – in that the real limiting causes (*niyama hetu*), (time, space, the particularized cognizing subject, etc.) on one side, and those afforded by the poem of the other, neutralize each other and then completely disappear – the afore-mentioned state of generality is readily nourished; so that by virtue of the very uniformity (*ekaghanatā*) of the spectator's perception, it being so nourished, readily nourishes the *rasa* in all of them: and this occurs, because the latent impressions of their minds concord with each other, the minds being varied by beginningless latent impressions.

This (form of) consciousness without obstacles is called *camatkāra* (miracle); the physical effects of it, that is to say, trembling, horripilation, joyful motions of limbs, etc. are also *camatkāra*. Indeed, *camatkāra* may be likewise defined as an immersion in an enjoyment which can never satiate and is thus uninterrupted. The word *camatkāra*, indeed, properly means the action being done by a tasting subject (*camataḥ karaṇam*), in other words, by the enjoying subject, he who is immersed in the vibration (*spanda*) of a marvellous enjoyment (*adbhuta-bhoga*). It may be thought of either as a form of mental cognition (*manasādhyavasāya*) consisting of a direct experience, or of imagination (*saṅkalpa)* of or remembrance, which nevertheless, is manifested in a different manner to its ordinary nature.

– Gnoli 1968: 56-60

Mahākavi Kālidāsa said in his *Abhijñānaśākuntalam*:

रम्याणिवीक्ष्य मधुरांश्चनिशम्य शब्दान्पर्युत्सुकीभवति यत्सुखितोऽपिजन्तुः ।
तच्चेतसास्मरति नूनमबोधपूर्वं भावस्थिराणि जननान्तरसौहृदानि ॥

ramyāṇivīkṣya madhurāṁścaniśamya śabdān paryutsukī-
bhavati yatsukhito'pi jantuḥ ।
taccetasāsmarati nūnamabodhapūrvaṁ bhāvasthirāṇi
jananāntarasauhṛdāni ॥

– *Abhijñānaśākuntalam* 5.2

> Often a man, though happy, on seeing beautiful objects and hearing sweet music, becomes uneasy as he remembers in his soul, though vaguely, associations of former births and loves deeply ingrained in his memory.

The memory mentioned here is nothing but a perception, as we do not have a prior knowledge of it. It means what is described in the poem as a beautiful scene and sweet words are not the subject of a previous experience. But this memory is in the form of perception – a perception in which what appears as delight, consists of a tasting but which is not conditioned by any further specification or obstacles. Such a perception becomes an object of relish and does not form an ordinary cognition. It is neither erroneous nor ineffable. It is an intensification and a reproduction because it enhances the feelings and helps to repeat them. Therefore *rasa* is simply and solely a state of mind which recognizes the perception *sans* any obstacles (Gnoli 1968: 60-62; द्विवेदी 1992: 62; पारेख 1974).

The relishing of the *rasa* is in the form of a cognitive perception with a value comprehension. This value comprehension does not need to put any feasible effort to prove its knowability, rather it is easily discernible. In the above *śloka*, this value comprehension in the spectator comes from the memory of his past life. This is exactly the difference between aesthetic relishment and common entertainment. An aesthete will not sit peacefully on seeing a beautiful scene or hearing sweet words, a talented spectator, will after the perception through the senses, use his imagination, drown in the feelings, establish an identity with the supporting causes, become so engrossed in the feelings that he floats away from the objective knowledge, loses himself in the intensity of emotions and finds happiness as though he has found the supreme meaning, such a perception is never sorrowful. This perception with value comprehension is the fully blossomed manifestation of the *rasa*. We do relish the seeded form of the latent impressions present in our consciousness through this value comprehension but they have to be deeply rooted into culture. This is the very reason why many Indian films are not popular with and appreciated by the Western audiences. This saying is ample proof of that. Similarly, we too are sometimes not able to relish the films of other cultures as we are not aware of the nuances and values of that culture. Translation of poems and stories takes away their soul, but translation of a film's dialogue doesn't take us away from the scene, screenplay, acting or even the values of the film, and it can be better comprehended as compared to other art forms.

Simple entertainment doesn't need the sacrifice of ego or intellect for its value comprehension. We must ask ourselves whether we experience supreme happiness and self-repose when we see entertaining scenes. Do we get the satisfaction which leaves no room for doubt? Is art only the superficial emotion derived due to the perception of something good by the five senses? This is the difference between mere entertainment and *rasa* manifestation. This is the inherent difference between common cinema and good cinema.

People are not able to relish and savour the *rasa* due to many obstacles, they are:

1. *Implausible content* – The despondent feeling of something not possible at all.
2. *The over-absorption in temporal or spatial determination of personal or actor's happiness and sorrow* – The feeling a viewer gets that he/she is well versed with the happiness or sorrow of the actor/actress.
3. Totally compelled by his/her own happiness or sorrow.
4. *Defective state of the means of perception* – Feeling of a disconnection with the determinant causes, consequents and transient states.
5. The inability of *rasa* realization due to the seemingly ineffective the determinants.

6. Unable to perceive prominence in the stable state (and giving priority to lesser important subjects).
7. *Presence of Doubt* – the doubt which arises in the mind of the viewer about the capability of the transient and the consequent feelings (द्विवेदी 1992: 63; पारेख 1974).

Śānta Rasa is not found to be compatible with the Sanskrit dramas. It has more to do with the *mokṣa puruṣārtha*. The disregard for worldly objects (*śama*) is the instigator for Śānta Rasa. It has been written about Śānta Rasa in the *Abhinavabhāratī* that:

> wherever there is no happiness, or sorrow, nor is there malice or jealousy, and where an equal feeling is shown toward all beings, there Śānta Rasa is prevalent. When all the *rasas* reach their limits or attain their motives they get merged with the Śānta Rasa and even when their motive is not satisfied they merge with Śānta Rasa. Just as the waves of the ocean take birth in it and afterward merge into it so also is the case with Śānta Rasa. The real form of the word *śama* is metaphysical knowledge of the self. – द्विवेदी 1992: 206-36; पारेख 1974: 93-103

The enterprising thought of the basic *rasa* has been incorporated into the Indian thought or mediation from the Advaita (non-dual) philosophy. It has been the endeavour of many philosophers to prove that there is one ultimate reality. Abhinavagupta was associated with the Kashmiri non-dualism, Jagannātha and Bhoja were associated with Advaita Vedānta, where everything is the manifestation of one supreme reality.

We will stray from our subject if we criticize the metaphysical aspect of these thought systems. In the words of Govind Chandra Pande (2003: 132):

> The consciousness is the root substance, emotions are latent impressions (*bhāva saṁskāra*), when we stop or hesitate to do anything for the world, then, a consciousness *rasa* emerges. *Rasa* is constitutionally one, though it is varigated by emotions,

> it is differentiated by latent impressions and known by personal experience.

The basis of Govind Chandra Pande's argument is non-dualistic metaphysical stand where all emotions are essentially the manifestation of consciousness through a certain schema.

We have seen that there is a general consensus in the classical approach that establishes the relishment of *nāṭya* as a social endeavour. A social being may argue that *rasa* relishing is not intense in a particularly well-made, much appreciated movie. We must understand that relishing of the *rasa* is primarily dependent upon the talent of spectator as well as the oneness of his heart with the poet. If a viewer is not able to associate himself with storyline or the character, he will not be able to establish himself with the intent of the poet. As per Mammaṭa, a Kashmiri Sanskrit metorician of eleventh century, the poetic creation and its sensibility depends upon all three causes – (1) innate power, (2) derivate cause, and (3) practice (रस्तोगी 2012: 296). The innate power is related to natural talent an individual is born with. Derivative cause refers to society and surrounding environment which nurtures the talent. Practice refers to repeated effort to understand a subject. Therefore, the intensity of relishing, depends upon the nature of the spectator as well as the art object. For art objects, it can be argued that determinants, consequents and transitory feelings have not been properly arranged. Evaluation on such parameters can never be universal or objective due to cultural differences. *Rasa-siddhānta* does not aim for the critical review as typically desired by newspaper readers or TV viewers.

Many a time, viewers are left wondering if the scene pertains to the heroic *rasa* or disgust *rasa* or even the sorrowful *rasa*, what is the chief *rasa* here? Some may say that repeated occurrence and an intense relishing of *rasa* determines the chief *rasa*. But this view will not be correct. We must understand the concept of chief (*aṅgī*) *rasa*. In Indian philosophy, the soul is considered as the chief entity and the body is considered its part. Likewise, if one discards the notion of the soul, one may think that the body is chief and limbs, fingers, toes, etc. are parts of the body. The one that supports the existence of the rest is chief, whereas whatsoever is dependent should be considered a part. Frequent occurrence and intensity may be helpful in recognizing the chief *rasa*, but such a pursuit is merely directed toward identifying the name of the *rasa* than relishing it.

While discussing the best movies of twentieth century, we found that in modern art we discuss various facets of life more rigorously and with more specifications. The power of any theory can be judged by its concomitance. As per Indian tradition, all activities of life can be understood in the terms of "proclivity" and "retiring". Proclivity is the path to achieve the desired, while the retiring is the path of self-realization. Modern Kashmir Śaiva philosophers argue that art creation or even art apperception is the semi-circular path and the subsequent self-realization is like "retiring" which is the remaining semi-circular path. Therefore, the journey of *citta* (consciousness) starts from itself and returns to itself (पाण्डे 2003: 32).

Abhinavagupta proposes an important theory of the vibration of *citta* in the *rasa* theory. As per him, the consciousness of a person during art creation or art apperception turns toward the art object through determinants, consequents and transitory emotions, later on it communicates with heart when generalized and that is how it establishes its identity with the *sthāyī bhāva*. Thereafter, the consciousness forgets everything that is present and relishes its own beginningless impressions by contracting in its self-repose. This expansion and contraction of the consciousness is the entire process of relishing of *rasa*. This mental activity is a trans empirical savouring (रस्तोगी 2012: 304-06).

As per *rasa-siddhānta*, *rasa* can only be relished by someone eligible for its relishing without any obstacles. Such an eligible spectator should be pure, having a oneness of heart with the heart of the poet and endowed with talent. By pure, it means having a pure consciousness which can reflect like a clear mirror. Talent (*pratibhā*) means the ability to create without any external help and the ability for *rasa* apperception (रस्तोगी 2012: 278). Therefore, there are two kinds of talent: (1) Talent for creativity, and (2) talent for sensibility. For being a poet, one must have the talent for creativity and for being a good spectator one must have a talent for sensibility. Till now we have studied cinema through talent for sensibility. Just as in the *Rāmāyaṇa*, where Vālmīki is the creator as well as a character, every art discusses its creator as well as its creation process. Therefore, for the sake of completeness and to understand the miracle of creation, it is mandatory for us to study the aesthetics of cinema in cinema.

Federico Fellini (1920-93) was the first director who described the creation process of cinema in his artistic movie *Otto e Mezzo* or *8½* (1963). Adorned with Nina Rota's music, this film is about a film director who after completing eight movies is trying to make his new movie. Considered among all-time-great movies, this film shows the struggle of the film director while the scenes transcend from memories to dreams to reality. This movie must be watched by creative aspirants to understand the usual obstacles in the creation process.

French movie *Day for Night* or *La Nuit Américaine* (1973) directed by François Truffaut (1932-84) is about a movie shooting. The intent behind this movie is that the real life of participants in the moviemaking process is much more interesting, serious, complex and tough. It depicts the complexes carried over from childhood in the hero, the sensitive heart of lead actress and challenges encountered while making the movie. It further demonstrates trick shots, how to arrange the required material for shooting, how to arrange actors and extras along with essentials. It may seem that directing a movie is more of a managerial job than

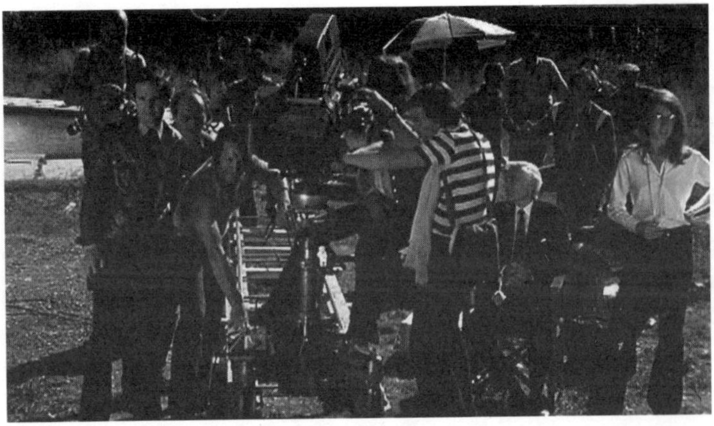

Day for Night (1973)

active participation in contemplating a scene or collaborating on cinematography or working on film editing.

Without a doubt, a director must be an efficient manager. That is why Iranian director Abbas Kiarostami (1940–2016) preferred smaller cast and crew. Demonstrating the multiple aspects of moviemaking, his movie *Close-Up* or *Nema-ye Nazdik* (1990) was based on a true story. A common man, Hussain starts acting like the famous Iranian director Mohsen Makhmalbaf when he is mistaken by a fellow bus traveller. Later on, when he was arrested for cheating, film director Abbas Kiarostami, a friend of Mohsen Makhmalbaf, tries to recreate the scene as it had happened. Hussain was pardoned by the other party after Mohsen Makhmalbaf personally intervened. His movie *Through the Olive Trees* (1994) also discusses the crucial aspects of moviemaking. A stonemason loves his beautiful, teenaged, orphan classmate and proposes marriage to her after a devastating earthquake hits the region. Interestingly a scene of the proposed movie was already a part of his earlier movie *Life, and Nothing More* (1991). This movie depicts the ordinary personal lives of participating actors. In the film, the stonemason says that if the rich should marry the poor, the literate should marry the illiterate, people having houses should marry the homeless, then, prosperity, knowledge and happiness can spread. This demonstrates the world-vision of the late director.

Fulfilling the role of a cine-master, Jean-Luc Godard (b.1930) made an eight-part video project *Histoire(s) du cinema* (1989-98) over a ten-year period. This was a perspective of the history of the concept of cinema and how it relates to the twentieth century over various upheavals. In these videos, Godard discusses film technique, aesthetics, history of cinema, social science and modern times and how it affects cinema. A student of cinema studies must watch this video project.

As the meaning of *nāṭya* is *rasa* in drama, the meaning of poetics is *rasa* in poetics, similarly the meaning of cinema which can be relished without any obstacle should be understood as *rasa* in cinema. Argentinean writer, Jorge Luis Borges remarked while comparing film and theatre:

> Films are even stranger, for what we are seeing are not disguised people but photographs of disguised people, and yet we believe them while the film is being shown.

Such additional disguise distinguishes cinema from drama and creates possibilities for newer dimensions in creativity. The journey from disguise to truth is the subject matter of aesthetics.

As per Bharata Muni, and written in *rasa-siddhānta*, acting becomes the paramount means for the genesis of *rasa*. The utility of an actor lies in his being a means to *rasa* relishing, therefore, he is called *pātra* (vessel in English). The simile can be understood as a vessel is only used for drinking similarly, actors are a means for relishing the *rasa* (रस्तोगी 2012: 267). Bharata Muni enumerates eleven parts of *nāṭya*: *rasa, bhāva, abhinaya, dharmī, vr̥tti, pravr̥tti, siddhi, svara, ātodya, gāna* and *raṅga*. As we have already discussed, that *rasa* is the chief amongst all (द्विवेदी 1992: 11-12; पारेख 1974). While analysing cinema, apart from the four types of acting, perspective of camera, its dynamic focus and editing become important. Whereas actors are most important for relishing of the *rasa* in drama, in cinema they are pushed behind the stunning visuals and exceptional music which are difficult to match in a drama. Cinema offers complicated situations of narrative such as animated movies and storyline without actors. Similar to drama, there are infinite determinants in movies. Technological advances are paramount in movies such as natural beauty captured by camera, computer-generated imagery, possibility of repeating scenes through editing, background scores, etc. These techniques further intensify the consequents and determinants in ever new ways. It can be hoped that *rasa-siddhānta* and its analysis will be instrumental in self-realization.

It is a request to students and teachers alike, that we should strive to translate subtitles into the regional languages and make it available for ready usage. The aim of this book is directly opposite to that of the movie business, i.e. viewing movies by paying for them. While modern cinema business is promoting consumerism, and various kinds of promotions waste our precious time in bad TV shows and ill-made films prevalent in theatre, we should strive to watch excellent movies for our own benefit. At the same time, we should accept that there are thinking minds in cinema which are against rampant exploitation and thought imperialism. It can be safely imagined that by viewing excellent cinemas, readers will have a self-realization that may help them and mankind at large. And we should witness the beauty which is trans-worldly and witness moments of happiness or grief which is not personal and yet belong to all of us. May we witness ourselves in the ever-flowing stream of transcendental bliss:

प्रतिफलित हुई सब आँखें
उस प्रेम-ज्योति-विमला से,
सब पहचाने से लगते

अपनी ही एक कला से।

समरस थे जड़ या चेतन
सुन्दर साकार बना था,
चेतनता एक विलसती
आनंद अखंड घना था। – जयशंकर प्रसाद, आनन्दसर्ग, कामायनी

All the eyes regarded
That loving pure light;
Everything looked as familiar
In their innate, integral unity

Harmonious was matter or spirit
In that exquisite form
Consciousness alone was blossoming
Transcendental, indivisible, bliss. – Jaishankar Prasad,
Ānandasarga, *Kāmāyanī*

Glossary

Words and meanings often take centre stage in the Indian philosophical discourse. When the task of explaining the infinite with a limited set of words is taken up, it is seen that different schools of thoughts and opposing ideas are often expressed through the same word. Due to this incidental similarity, the exact meaning often remains elusive to young readers. Therefore, the definitions of key terms and a brief explanation with its context is not only complementary but mandatory as well.

In the logical discourse, every word can be understood by two meanings: 1. Connotative (the wide array of positive and negative associations that most words carry with them). 2. Denotative (is the precise and literal meaning of the word that might be found in the dictionary). In the context of this book, connotative meaning has been used.

Abhinavabhāratī – It is a treatise written by Abhinavagupta, a tenth-century Kashmiri Śaiva philosopher. Apparently, this book strongly affected the Indian culture and tradition. It is believed to have been lost in the sixteenth century, and around 1910, a copy was found in Kerala, India. It has immensely helped understand the *Nāṭyaśāstra*. It is also called the *Nāṭyavedavṛtti*.

Abhinaya – The intent of *abhinaya* (acting) is to convey the meaning attached to any word or phrase to the heart of viewers/audience. Acting can be of four types:

i. *Āhārya* – This type of acting is not pure acting but pertains to background works like decoration of stage and specific costumes for characters.

ii. *Āṅgika* – The acting done using gestures of the body, face, hands and feet is called *āṅgika abhinaya*. It has been divided into *aṅga*, *pratyaṅga* and *upāṅga*.

iii. *Vācika* – All that the actor says with his mouth is classified as *vācika abhinaya*.

iv. *Sāttvika* – The depiction of the involuntary/physio-psychological emotions through acting is called *sāttvika abhinaya*. The following are the *sāttvika* emotions:

1. *stambha* (paralysis),
2. *sveda* (sweating),
3. *romāñca* (horripilation),
4. *svarabheda* (feebleness or change in voice),
5. *vepathu* (trembling),
6. *vaivarṇya* (change of colour of face),
7. *aśru* (shedding tears), and
8. *pralaya* (loss of senses or fainting).

Āgama – They are texts similar to the Veda. They are a collection of scriptures which literally mean "which helps to correctly comprehend the meaning surpassing all possible biases". The Buddhists, Jainas and Śaivites each follow different Āgama.

Anubhāva – In a drama, the actors depict the intrinsic sentiments through wordplay, bodily actions and physio-psychological gestures, these are called as *anubhāvas* (effects or consequents) of the drama. The actions which help depict the inner feelings or sentiments are called *anubhāvas*. The consequents are shown outside the body through facial expressions or body expressions, although they deal with the feelings pertaining to the mind. *Anubhāvas* (effect of the manifestation) of the *rasa* don't happen after the sentiments are felt or are registered in the mind, they happen along with the feelings felt, i.e. the sentiment and the action/effect of the sentiment go hand in hand.

Ātmā/Puruṣa – The *ātmā* is a concept of our spiritual entity. It is the established inner consciousness which is immortal. It is believed that the *ātmā* drives or conducts the activities pertaining to our five external senses (sight, hearing, touch, smell and taste) and also the internal senses of mind, intelligence and ego. The Indian philosophy advocates that the *ātmā* is reborn in another body. It is also called as *puruṣa* or *jīva*. According to Ādi Śaṅkarācārya, *ātmā* means that which pervades all; which is the subject and which knows, experiences and illuminates the objects and which remains immortal and always the same. Buddhists do not believe in the *ātmā* being immortal although they believe in the afterlife. It is imperative here to elucidate two important and ancient theories.

> To believe that pleasure, grief and immortal *ātmā* are an absolute truth is called Śāśvatavāda. According to Ajit Keśakambalī, to believe that it is only the physical body which is true and after death everything is turned to dust is called Ucchedavāda.

Ātodya – Musical instruments used on the stage come under this category. They are *tantu-vādya* (chordophones) or string instruments (*vīṇā*), *avanaddha vādya* (membranophones) or percussion instruments (*tablā*, drums), *ghana-vādya* (idiophones) or solid instruments (bells, *jala-taraṅga*) and the *suśira-vādya* (aerophones) or wind instruments (flute, *śehanāī*).

Bhāva – The heart (taken as contemplative, aware consciousness) of every individual is suffused with certain basic emotions which are recognized by the actions done by the person or the mood of the person. According to Bharata Muni, these emotions (or mental dispositions) which pervade the heart are called *bhāvas*. There are three kinds of *bhāvas*:

i. *Sthāyī bhāvas* – The emotions, which are present in the seed form in our consciousness, are called *sthāyī bhāvas*. They are eight in number: *rati* (love), *hāsa* (laughter), *śoka* (sorrow), *krodha* (anger), *utsāha* (heroism), *bhaya* (fear), *jugupsā* (disgust) and *vismaya* (wonder).

ii. *Vyabhicārī bhāvas*– The emotions which come and go in an irregular way and are able to fortify and support the *sthāyī bhāvas* are called *sañcārī/vyabhicārī bhāvas*.

iii. *Sāttvika bhāvas* – They are the involuntary physio-psychological sentiments which arise out of our sensitive heart and mind, they are the physical expression of the concentrated feelings of our mind. For example, tears, and romantic feelings. Therefore, the feelings which are born in the involved mind but are manifested physically are called *sāttvika bhāvas*.

Buddhism, various schools of – Approximately a hundred years after the death of Buddha, a discord arose among his followers at the second Buddhist conference. The elders among the disciples gathered there, threw out those disciples who were causing dissent. The outcast followers called themselves as the Mahāyāna while the rest were the Hīnayāna.

i. *Hīnayāna* – The followers of the Buddha who don't believe in God, but in action (*karma*). They believe that it is through individual effort and action that a person attains *nirvāṇa*.

   a. *Metaphysical aspect* – Momentariness is the main concept of this doctrine. The conscious self and the unconscious matter both are momentary, everything is conditional, dependent and relative. The soul is a bundle of five *skandhas*: the *rūpa* (matter), *vedanā* (feelings), *sañjā* (perception), *saṁskāra* (disposition) and *vijñāna* (consciousness). The physical *rūpa* is made up of atoms of earth, water, fire and air.

   b. *Main subsystems* – There are three main viewpoints of Hīnayāna:

- *Thervāda* – It is the original form of Hīnayāna. It is still prevalent in Sri Lanka.
- *Sarvāstivāda* (*Vaibhāṣika*) – This believes that external objects are directly perceived. This is Hīnayāna's main group.
- *Sautrāntika*– According to this, external objects are not perceived directly, they are only inferred.

ii. *Mahāyāna* – According to Mahāyāna, *nirvāṇa* is not a negative cessation of misery but a positive state of bliss. It says *nirvāṇa* can't be attained alone and needs the help of a *bodhisattva* (an ideal saint) who by deferring his own salvation, helps others in their liberation. The *bodhisattva* guides the misery-stricken people toward salvation. The Mahāyāna reveres such *bodhisattvas* and treat them like gods.

   a. *Metaphysical aspect* – The Mahāyāna followers have corrected the Hīnayāna doctrine and said that truth can't be approached through intellect but through self-experience. Therefore, the goal of life should be to realize the non-relative non-dual truth through spiritual pursuits.

   b. *Epistemological aspect* – The Buddhists rely on perception and inference for proving their doctrines.

   c. *Main subsystems* – There are three main theories. They are:

      - *Śūnyavāda* – Nāgārjuna is the first systematic expounder of this theory. Śūnyavādins call themselves Mādhyamikas (those following the middle path). *Śūnya* according to Mādhyamikas is not "nothing" or an "empty void", it is indescribable – it is reality which ultimately transcends existence, non-existence, both and neither. It is neither affirmation nor negation, nor both nor neither. Nāgārjuna has used the word *tattva* for *śūnya* and says that it can only be realized when it is felt by the five senses. *Śūnya*, therefore, does not mean "void" but "devoid" as far as appearances are concerned of ultimate reality and as far as reality is concerned of plurality. Everything is *śūnya*, appearances are *svabhāva śūnya* and reality is *prapañca śūnya*.

- *Yogācāra* (*Vijñānavāda*) – Ārya Maitreyanātha, Ārya Asaṅga, Ārya Vasubandhu and Ārya Sthiramati are the propounders of Vijñānavāda. According to this school, whatever we see is Vijñāna. Vijñāna is the one and only truth. The followers are called Yogācāras because they emphasize the importance of *yoga* for the realization of pure knowledge.
- *Sautrāntika Yogācāra or Svatantra Vijñānavāda* – Ācārya Diṅnāga was the propagator of this school. Ācārya Dharmakīrti was also one of the main teachers. It accepts the metaphysical truth of Vijñānavāda that reality is pure consciousness and wants to support it with logical arguments. It wants to combine the metaphysical idealism of Vijñānavāda with the logical and epistemological critical realism of the Sautrāntika school. We may call it the logical school of Buddhism.

Cārvāka (Lokāyata) Darśana – This is a materialistic philosophy. It was propounded by Acharya Bṛhaspati. According to him the main aim of life should be to amass wealth and happiness. Most of the Indian philosophies have criticized this school.

i. *Metaphysical Aspect* – The unconscious object is given precedence over conscious self. Earth, water, fire, and air are the only truth and it is from the grouping of these that our body, the five senses and matter are made.

ii. *Epistemological Aspect* – Perception is given weightage and it has been postulated that inference and verbal testimony are based on perception.

Cinema – or motion picture is the art of moving images; a commercial visual medium where captured images and sound are displayed with the aid of technology similar to a traditional dramatic experience. It was created in the dusk of the nineteenth century and the beginning of the twentieth century, it is the world's most recent art form which commercially entertains people. The direction, production, distribution and other related activities can be defined under the head of cinema itself. Due to the non-availability of sound technology, cinema was at first silent and in black and white. With the advent of sound in 1927, talkies become popular. After 1950s majority of motion pictures were made in colour. Cinema can be considered as first-hand drama because it has both speech and sight together, along with acting.

Citta – According to Śaiva philosophy, it denotes our consciousness, i.e. mind, intellect and ego.

Dharmī – The theory about the transformation which takes place on the stage is called *dharmī*. It may be simple or embellished. There are two types of *dharmī*s: (i) *Lokadharmī* is when the transformation on the stage takes place within the worldly terms, and (ii) *nāṭyadharmī* is when the transformation takes place leading to embellishment or intense significance.

Early Buddhist Thoughts – The sermons that Siddhārtha Gautama or Gautama Buddha gave after he attained enlightenment are called as the doctrines of Buddhism. The ancient epic *Tripiṭaka* contains the teachings of the Buddha. Unlike other philosophies, Buddhism concentrates on the widespread suffering and the cessation of suffering of the human beings. Buddhism says that truth is momentary and non-routine.

i. *Noble Truths* – Suffering, cause of suffering, cessation of suffering and the path leading to cessation of suffering are the four noble truths. The first truth says that the world is full of suffering. The second says that suffering has a definite cause. *Avidyā* (incomplete knowledge) is the cause for suffering. The third truth says that if the cause for suffering is finished or taken away then suffering ceases. The fourth truth says that there is an ethical and spiritual path which, if followed, can lead to the removal of suffering and misery. The Noble Eightfold Path is the way to cease misery and pain.

ii. *Pratītyasamutpāda* – The doctrine of *pratītyasamutpāda* (dependent origination) is contained in the second noble truth which gives us the cause of suffering and in the third noble truth which shows the cessation of suffering. It is relative as well as impersonal. Relatively it is the world full of suffering and impersonally it is *nirvāṇa*. This doctrine works on the formula – "Depending on the cause, the effect arises".

Gāna – The songs sung on stage are of five types:

Praveśaka – the song sung on entry of the actors.

Ākṣepaka – the song sung when a scene or act changes.

Niṣkrāmaka – the song sung when the actor leaves the stage.

Prāsādika – the song which conveys a special meaning to the audience.

Āntarā – the songs which are sung to denote tempo and motion.

Indian Poetics, Schools of – To appreciate poetry, in literary criticism apart from *rasa* other important aspects are considered. They are:

i. *Dhvani* – The "sound theory" is related mainly to word power and semantics. The word power is the subject of language philosophy and semantics is important for language as well as for aesthetics and poetics. Ānandavardhana has discussed this in his text *Dhvanyāloka*. According to him, poetry is sound. Poetry does not reveal as much as it sounds to our ears, but it also has the capability to reach even the most profound meaning to our heart. This beautiful panoramic meaning is manifested by word power which is an amalgamation of literal meaning (*abhidhā*), figurative or contextual meaning (*lakṣaṇā*) and poetic suggestion or euphemism (*vyañjanā*).

ii. *Alaṅkāra* – Anything which can adorn another is called *alaṅkāra* (a figure of speech). Just as ornaments enhance the beauty of a woman, *alaṅkāra* enhances the beauty of a poem. *Alaṁ karoti iti alaṅkāraḥ* (whatever adorns is the adornment itself). There are nine types of *alaṅkāra* in Hindi literature: Anuprāsa (Alliteration), Upamā (Simile), Rūpaka (Metaphor), Ananvaya (Conclusion), Yamaka (Rhyming), Śleṣa (Pun), Utprekṣā (Fanciful Affirmation), Sandeha (Doubt), Atiśayokti (Exaggeration).

iii. *Aucitya* – Abhinavagupta's disciple, Kṣemendra, says that any poetry can only become full of life when poetic propriety or poetic justification is understood. In his book *Aucitya Vicāra Carcā*, he declared a new theory by saying that the living or self-justification element of *rasasiddha* poetry is known as *aucitya* (justification). According to Ānandavardhana, the main cause of *rasa doṣa* is lack of justification. Therefore, the poet must always keep in mind the justification of poetry. Unless the ornamentation and attributes are appropriate, poetry will not be miraculous. Kṣemendra also said that poetry cannot be justified if the ornamentation and the attributes cannot invoke an interest. Poetic justification or propriety has been called the soul of poetry.

iv. *Rīti* – It has been described as the "style" of writing. Just as every living being adapts to different styles as per his/her liking, in the same way the poet too creates his poems based on different styles of writing and languages. *Rīti* has been defined as the creative ways in which a language can be used. In the text *Kāvyālaṁkārasūtravṛtti*, *rīti* too has been designated as the soul of poetry. Ācārya Vāmana is the propounder of this theory.

v. *Vakrokti* – The language used to bring out the hidden meanings or innuendos of the poem or drama is called *vakrokti*. Ācārya Bhāmaha is the founder of this theory, he says that *vakrokti* is also a poetic embellishment and is the union of two words: *vkṛ* and *ukti*, where *ukti* means anything which is apart from the normal. It has been formulated as a total theory in which all the parts of poetry have been included to give it a whole meaning.

vi. *Guṇa/Doṣa* – They are the attributes and the faults in a poem. Poetry should always be full of attributes and devoid of faults.

Jaina Darśana – The Jaina philosophy is an extremely ancient school of thought. The time span of the first sage (*tīrthaṅkara*) who advocated this system cannot be ascertained. But modern Jainism believes that Mahāvīr, the twenty-fourth *tīrthaṅkara*, was able to explain all the postulates in an absorbable form. According to Jainism, the Inner Self and the actions of a human being are interlinked and inseparable – like water from milk. Jainism postulates that when the Inner Self is able to liberate itself from the bondage of actions (*karma*), only then it will become one with God. For this it has to follow the right path, with the right knowledge and with the right conduct, so as to attain the life goals. The word "Jainism" is derived from *jina* which means conqueror or one who has conquered his passions and desires and has attained emancipation from the mortal world. Śvetāmbara and Digambara are the two sects of Jainism.

i. *Metaphysical Aspect* – The Jaina metaphysics is a realistic and relativistic pluralism. It is called Anekāntavāda or the doctrine of the many-sidedness in reality. According to this doctrine, the world is full of things and all things have their own character. Matter (*pudgala*) and the conscious self are regarded as separate and independent realities. There are innumerable material atoms and innumerable souls which are all separate and independently real. The word *pudgala* in other philosophies has been used for the conscious self.

ii. *Epistemological Aspect* – Since all materials have many characters, knowledge about them is relative. We can know about anything by its substance, form, location and time. Knowledge in Jaina system is of two types:

   a. *Aparokṣa* – The knowledge for which the soul does not need the five senses or the mind, and what can be perceived immediately is *aparokṣa*. It is divided into *avadhi* (clairvoyance), *manaḥparyāya* (telepathy) and *kevala* (omniscience).

   b. *Parokṣa* – The knowledge for which the soul requires the help of the five senses or the mind or both is called *parokṣa*. *Mati* (external senses, internal senses such as mind and inference) and *śruta* (testimony of Jaināgama) are types of *parokṣa*.

Jñāna-Mīmāṁsā or Epistemology – The word *mīmāṁsā* in Sanskrit means reflection or critical investigation, and the word *jñāna* means knowledge. So, Jñāna-Mīmāṁsā is a branch of philosophy dealing with knower, object of knowledge and knowledge. Although the various philosophical systems differ in enumerating the meaning of knowledge, nevertheless there are three means of assessing knowledge which are typically accepted or rejected or debated in various Indian philosophical systems: *pratyakṣa* (perception), *anumāna* (inference) and *śabda* (verbal testimony).

i. *Perception* (*pratyakṣa*) – To know or understand anything by the interaction of the five external senses with other worldly objects and with the internal senses like intellect and mind is called as perception. Memory aids in the comprehension of the knowledge gained through perception. Two states of perception are:

a. *Nirvikalpa* – When the perception has not been validated by the knower it is said to be in a *nirvikalpa* (not admitting an alternative) state. This type of perception cannot be remembered.

b. *Savikalpa* – When the perception is validated and we can understand the colour, form, properties and attributes of the object before us, the perception is said to be in a *savikalpa* (alternative or conceptualizing) state. This perception can be remembered.

ii. *Inference* (*anumāna*) – Knowledge which can be understood through the cause and effect relationship constraints. Observing smoke and inferring fire is an example of *anumāna*, but it is based on its universal applicability of relationship between smoke and fire.

iii. *Testimony* (*śabda*) – Gaining a true knowledge through a testimony from a source is called as *śabda*, e.g. formulae in a science textbook, dates mentioned in a history book for some historic events, whether a fruit is edible or not, etc.

Kalā – The ability to express oneself in different forms is called *kalā*. It is one of the categories of the Śaiva philosophy. The Śaivāgamas say that *kalā* is the manifestation of *māyā*, where the Lord's limitless power gets restricted and should be understood as limited agency. In the same vein *kalā* is something that gives pleasure and it is created by the imagination of the consciousness and the inner-self of the creator/author/poet/painter/sculptor, etc. This has also been the subject matter of many philosophic viewpoints. It is imperative to note here that *kāvya* has been denoted to mean literature, epic poems or narrated sagas and it is nearly impossible to represent *kāvya* without *kalā*.

Kāla – Śaiva philosophy says that *kāla* is the eternity of *Parameśvara* which has been limited power to experience succession at first in what one identifies himself with. It can also be understood in the specific sense of time, as form of sensibility, where it denotes the past, present and future.

Kashmir Non-Dualism, various schools of – There are four schools followed by the Kashmiri Śaivites: (1) Spanda, (2) Kula, (3) Krama, and (4) Pratyabhijnā. Accordingly, the whole world is a reflection of Parama-Śiva.

i. *Metaphysical aspect* – Kashmir Śaivism admits thirty-six *tattvas* (principles) of cosmic manifestations. It has three divisions: *śiva-tattva*, *vidyā-tattva* and *ātma-tattva*. *Ātma-tattva* (illusory aspect) accepts all the principles of the Sāṁkhya philosophy. Here *tattva* is a categorical classification of reality, where the smaller classes get merged into the bigger.

   a. *Śiva-tattva* – *Śiva-tattva* and *Śakti-tattva* are the balancing factors of this division. Śiva is the first manifestation and the power of being (*citta*) predominates it. It is pure subjective and has no predicative or objective reference. The experience of this state is pure "I" (*aham*), if the use of such a word is permissible. Śakti is the second category and follows Śiva in manifestation which is marked by addition of element of "am" to the "I" as "I am" (*aham asmi*). In this state of manifestation of the *ānanda*, *śakti* predominates. Śiva is the light and Śakti is recognition or knowledge of this light. The whole world of matter and souls exists potentially in Śakti who is the inseparable power of Śiva.

   b. *Vidya-tattva* – consists of Sadāśiva, *Īśvara*, *śuddha-vidyā*. Sadāśiva is the third category and the power of will predominates in it. This state of experience may be conveyed as "I am this" (*aham idam*). In *Īśvara*, power of knowledge predominates. In this state, "this" element in the Sadāśiva finds predominance. This state is represented by the expression "This I am". *Śuddha-vidyā* or *sad-vidyā* is the fifth category which is marked by the predominance of action. In this, the objective is not so obscure as in the Sadāśiva state, nor so prominent as in the *Īśvara* state but in the state of perfect equality with the subjective. The experience in the state is "I am this".

c. *Ātma-tattva* – *Māyā* segregates *aham* and *idam*. The difference in their nature starts here. *Aham* is classified as *Puruṣa*, *idam* as *Prakṛti*. *Māyā*, which is the sixth aspect of Śakti, through which the infinite appear as finite, gives rise to five conditions: *kalā* (limited power of action), *vidyā* (limited knowledge), *rāga* (passionate objective propensity), *kāla* (succession) and *niyati* (causal necessity). These are called *kañcuka*s (coverings) because they cover the character of a being. It is because of this that the powers of a human being get constricted. In Śāṅkara Vedānta and Trika *darśana*, *māyā* (the power of obscuration) is not one, many a time, *māyā* is the harbinger, in this philosophy, *māyā* is the blossomed form of Śiva's independent power through which he manifests his glory. The following are the thirty attributes described for *ātma-tattva*:

- *Māyā*.
- *Kañcuka*s (or veils) of *māyā* – *kalā, vidyā, rāga, kāla* and *niyati*.
- *Puruṣa*.
- *Prakṛti*, intelligence, ego, mind.
- *Five external sense organs* (*jñānendriyas*) – Nose (smelling or olfaction), eyes (seeing), ears (hearing),

skin (somatosensorial or touch) and tongue (tasting or gustation).

- *Five motor organs* – Feet, hands, speech, organs of excretion and organs of reproduction.
- *Five tanmātra* – Smell, taste, form, touch and sound.
- *Five gross categories of the universe* – earth, water, fire, air and space.

ii. *Epistemological aspect* – In the Pratyabhijñā philosophical system, knowledge is understood in four ways: awareness or consciousness, power (*śakti*) (power of knowledge, power of differentiation by exclusion and power of remembrance), realization (*bodha)* and experience (*anubhava*).

- *Pramā,* which means delusion free and indisputable knowledge, works toward the systematic arrangement of the real meaning. *Pramāṇa* (validity) of knowledge is the vehicle of *pramā*. There are three ways to validate knowledge:
  - *Pratyakṣa (perception)* – It includes sensory perception, perception through the mind and perception through *yoga*.
  - *Āgama* – Validity through testimony.
  - *Anumana* (*inference*) – Determination of knowledge through alternate conception or reasoning.

Kashmir Non-dualistic Śaivism – Śaiva philosophy believes in the Advaita system just as Śaṅkara's Advaita philosophy does. The sacred literature of the Śaivites is the Śaivāgama. Śaivism is divided into Southern Śaivism or Śaiva Siddhānta and Northern Śaivism or Kashmir Śaivism. The Śaivites believe that Śiva is the only reality. He is Infinite consciousness and absolute independence. He makes the world appear in Himself as if it were distinct from Him, though not really so: just as objects appear in the mirror, image and mirror-image. Recognition (*pratyabhijnā*) of this reality is essential to liberation. Just as a pearl of the ocean gives out light but it does not recognize that the source of light is itself, so also it is necessary to recognize that Śiva is the Knowledge and Existence and the only Reality. Recognition at once overcomes bondage. The liberated soul becomes one with Śiva. This philosophy says that it is in *Parameśvara* that the world is perceived as a reflection.

Kāvya – The fount of creative knowledge created and endowed with the quality of pleasing as well as being meritorious can be understood as *kāvya*. It is a knowledge which gives happiness, but has no relation to analysis, alternatives or science. Noted poet, Jaishankar Prasad says that it is the special experience of the soul.

Mīmāṁsā – The word *mīmāṁsā* literally means "revered thought" and was originally applied to the interpretation of the Vedic rituals which commanded the highest reverence. The main *gurus* who propounded this school are Maharṣi Jaimini, Prabhākara Miśra and Kumārila Bhaṭṭa. The school is based on pluralistic realism. Mīmāṁsā and Vedānta are treated as allied systems as both try to interpret and revere the Vedas. It is also called as Pūrva-Mīmāṁsā, Karma-Mīmāṁsā or Dharma-Mīmāṁsā. According to this system, the unconscious categories and the soul – all are the truth. The world has neither been created nor destroyed by a catastrophe.

i. *Metaphysical Aspect* – According to Prabhākara Miśra, there are eight categories, i.e. *dravya* (substance), *guṇa* (quality), *karma* (action), *sāmānya* (generality), *paratantratā* (inherence), *śakti* (force), *sādṛśya* (similarity) and *saṁkhyā* (statistics). Kumārila Bhaṭṭa postulates five categories: substance, quality, action, generality and non-Being (*abhāva*).

ii. *Epistemological Aspect* – Sage Jaimini puts forward three aspects: perception, inference and verbal testimony. Prabhākara Miśra says that there are five validities; they are perception, inference, verbal testimony, comparison and postulation/implication. Kumārila Bhaṭṭa talks about six validities: perception, inference, verbal testimony, comparison, implication and negative cognition.

Nāṭya – According to Bharata Muni, the pleasures and displeasures of this world, which have been enacted using gestures, words and songs, have been termed as *nāṭya*. According to Ācārya Abhinavagupta, the meaning of poetry when shown through aural–visual medium via enactment on stage and in theatres by dedicated actors and which is relished by mesmerized spectators is called *nāṭya*. The "meaning" in the drama and poetry when expressed by actors and perceived as direct perception and has been grasped by a keen and contemplative mind is called as *nāṭya*.

The root of the word *nāṭya* is *naṭ* which means to dance (*nartana/nṛtya*). These words have their root in *nṛt* which means movement of limbs. Some dance forms don't need the meaning of the song to be understood, just music is enough to perform the body movements. The dance forms which require the meaning and expression to be emoted are called as *nṛtya*, *nṛtta* and *nṛtya* are the first two stages of *nartana*. According to Bharata Muni, *nāṭya* is the third stage where words are enacted and shown on stage thereby manifesting the *rasa* in a compassionate heart. According to Abhinavagupta, *nāṭya* is not an imitated form on stage but it is recreation of *bhāva*s. In the *Nāṭyaśāstra*, eleven divisions of dramatics have been enumerated. They are *rasa, bhāva, abhinaya, dharmī, vṛtti, pravṛtti, siddhi, svara, ātodya, gāna* and *raṅga*.

Nāṭyaśāstra – It is an ancient Sanskrit text on the performing arts. It is believed to have been written and improvised between 500 BCE to 500 CE by many sages and wise men. Bharata Muni is said to be its author. It contains thirty-six chapters, consisting of 6,000 *śloka*s. The subjects covered by the treatise include dramatic composition, structure of a play and the construction of a stage to host it, genres of acting, body movements, make up and costumes, the musical scales, musical instruments and the integration of music for wholesome dramatic performance. It is also notable for its aesthetic *rasa* theory, which asserts that entertainment is a desired effect of performance arts but not the primary goal, and that the primary goal is to transport the individual in the audience into another parallel reality, full of wonder, where he experiences the essence of his own consciousness and reflects on spiritual and moral questions.

Niyati – It is that power which limits causal efficiency of everything. It may be termed as mechanical cause–effect relationship in certain field. This is also one of the limiting conditions of an individual, because he is controlled in his activities by this power.

Nyāya Darśana – Sage Akṣapāda Gautama is the founder of this school. The *Nyāyasūtra* is the ancient text which elucidates this philosophy. It came into existence in the fourth century BCE. Nyāya means argumentation and suggests that the system is predominantly intellectual, analytical, logical and epistemological. It is also called Tarkaśāstra (science of reasoning). The Vaiśeṣika system and the Nyāya system are correlated and hence are *samāna-tantra*. Both agree that bondage is due to ignorance and liberation is due to right knowledge.

i. *Metaphysical Aspect* – Nyāya recognizes sixteen categories along with the seven categories of Vaiśeṣika.

ii. *Epistemological Aspect* – Nyāya recognizes perception, inference, comparison and verbal testimony.

Parā – All sounds in the universe are manifestations of *parā*. All kinds of sound ranging from delicate to subtle to rough or even thoughts are contained in it. *Parā* can be further understood in three different ways – *paśyantī, madhyamā* and *vaikharī*. These are further recognized by three more divisions: *Parā* (pure conscious form), subtle (desirous form) and rough (action form). Abhinavagupta, in his book *Tantrāloka*, says that in songs and music the rough sounds have been described as:

a. *Paśyantī* – The base notes or tunes which are yodelled, in which the pronunciation of individual vowels are not segregated is in this category.

b. *Madhyamā* – The sounds of the percussion instruments, where there is no pure segregation of the base notes comes in this category.

c. *Vaikharī* – The segregated vowels which clearly tell the meaning and usage of the words is called *vaikharī.*

Paramātmā/Brahman/Śiva – Many Indian philosophies believe that *Paramātmā*/*Brahman*/Śiva is the creator of the entire universe and the very reason for its existence. In the Vedānta, the *ātmā* and *Paramātmā* have been likened to the waves of the ocean and the vast, endless ocean itself. According to Śaiva non-dualistic philosophy, Parama-Śiva himself got shrivelled by some illusory aspect of phenomenal world that leads into a small manifestation, which can be traced to the emergence of *puruṣa* or *ātmā.*

Philosophical Systems (Thought Systems) – In the Western tradition, philosophy literally means "love of wisdom". It is the study of general and fundamental problems concerning matters such as existence, knowledge, values, reason, mind and language. Philosophical methods include questioning, critical discussion, rational argument and systematic presentation. Classic philosophical questions include: Is it possible to know anything and to prove it? What is real? In the Indian context, *darśana* which is loosely translated as philosophy, means "through which it is seen" or "in which it is seen". By *darśana*, we can understand it as the meaning obtained after rigorous analysis. The more modern meaning of philosophy is reality and quest for knowledge. In the Indian thought processes, there are four main dimensions which can be ascertained: 1. Sat-Mīmāṁsā (ontology), 2. Jñāna-Mīmāṁsā (epistemology), 3. Paramārtha-Mīmāṁsā (metaphysics), and 4. Mūlya-Mīmāṁsā (ethical discourse). For our purpose, we should familiarize ourselves with the metaphysical aspect (Tattva-Mīmāṁsā) and the epistemological aspect (Jñāna-Mīmāṁsā) of any philosophical system. The main philosophies in the Indian context are understood in the following two categories:

i. *Āstika darśana* – The philosophies which believe in the teachings of the Vedas. They usually occur in pairs like "Sāṁkhya-Yoga", "Nyāya–Vaiśeṣika" and "Mīmāṁsā–Vedānta". Śaiva philosophy is not against the Vedas, but it is based on Śaivāgama.

ii. *Nāstika darśana* – The philosophies which do not believe in the teachings of the Vedas. The Jainas, Buddhists and the Cārvākas are some of them.

Pratibhā – In the realm of understanding poetics, *pratibhā* essentially means, without external support, the ability to create poetics (poem, drama, song, etc.) and having the sensibility to relish the *rasa*.

Pravr̥tti – The input of the various regional styles of production, costumes, local dialects, food habits and culture is called *pravr̥tti*. It can be subdivided into five types: *āvantī, dākṣiṇātya, pāñcālī, madhyamā* and *auḍramāgadhī*.

Preyas – The meaning of *preyas* is something which is liked or is pleasing or someone who is dear to oneself. The meaning should be taken in the worldly context.

Puruṣārtha – The word *puruṣārtha* is made up of two words: *puruṣa* which means human being or soul and *artha* which means purpose or object. Together they mean what a social being ought to do. *Puruṣārtha* is a logical, cultural concept, which is unlike irrevocable commands based on faith, but a value disposition which aims to encapsulate and fulfil worldly and non-worldly goals together. A human being's consciousness is much more than body and sensory pleasures, but a self-aware consciousness. When the human consciousness becomes self-aware, it wants to acquire meaning in life and in the world. The *puruṣārtha* theory can be comprehended as the formal balance of the four goals which help man lead a fulfilling life. The four life pursuits are:

i. *Dharma* – It should be understood as a set of activities related to self-preservation, reactive measures to external exceedingly affecting activities, activities related to knowledge, will and endeavour, mutually dependent set of business activities, beneficial activities for self and others and to the community at large. To decide righteous actions in a complex set of situations, one should consider four sources: Śruti texts, Śmr̥ti texts, action history of socially laudable personalities and what is suitable to one own's nature. Any action (*karma*) based on such contemplation can be called *dharma*.

ii. *Artha* – Signifies the means to achieve the fulfilment of *dharma* or any other desire.

iii. *Kāma* – Signifies the desire where object is specific in nature.

iv. *Mokṣa* – Signifies emancipation, liberation or release. Though *mokṣa* connotes freedom from *saṁsāra*, the cycle of death and birth, *mokṣa* also connotes freedom, self-knowledge, self-realization and liberation in this life, it should be understood as liberation from any constraint in the context of *puruṣārtha* theory.

Puruṣārtha theory – It claims that *dharma* can never be without *nīti*. *Nīti* can never be with impractical set of actions (improper *vyavahāra*). *Vyavahāra* can never be without *karma*. *Karma* can never be caused without any external factor's affection to a being (*prabhāva*). External factor's affection (*prabhāva*) can never be realized without being aided by original *svabhāva* (innate nature) of a being. The following five aspects of *puruṣārtha* theory are further elaborated as:

i. *Svabhāva* – The specific nature of existence of a being is called *svabhāva* by which a being is identified. The attributes and properties of a being are the innate activities caused by its *svabhāva*.

ii. *Prabhāva* – It should be understood as affections caused by external factors, bringing forth attributes different to the current state of a being.

iii. *Karma* – The actions which are done by a being due to his/her knowledge, will and endeavour are called *karma*. The endeavour in action is often linked with ethics, the knowledge due to economic purport and the desire to achieve certain means and the satisfaction/dissatisfaction is for means.

iv. *Vyavahāra* – It should be understood as a set of behavioural actions in different contexts. *Vyavahāra* is a set of *karma* done for others where others are in the accusative case, instrumental case, dative case, locative case of *karma*.

v. *Nīti* – Although loosely translated as policy which puts forth a set of actions to be done, it should be understood as a set of characterized patterns of prohibited behavioural actions. It encompasses prohibition of any *vyavahāra* in front of others or the community that is against oneself or community at large.

Rāga – The meaning of the word *rāga* should be understood as passionate propensity to an objective reference, in other words to get attached to something. The Kashmiri Śaivites say that *rāga* is something that satisfies oneself. It is through *māyā* that the infinite Parama-Śiva gets attached to something finite. It is responsible for an individual's choice of a particular activity, to the exclusion of all else that he knows. It may be called a desire of having an objective reference but without reference to any particular object.

Raṅga – The stage which is used to depict the drama is called *raṅgamaṇḍapa* or *raṅgamañca*.

Rasa – In the course of watching a drama, a compassionate spectator feels drawn to the meaning that is being acted out on stage, such meaning and its joyous enjoyment are called *rasa*. In other words, when the meaning of the drama is directly communicated to the heart, *rasa* is said to be manifested. *Rasa* is the object of aesthetic relishing as well as process of such joyous relishing. According to Abhinavagupta, *ṇātya* itself is *rasa* and *rasa* is *ṇātya*.

i. The description of *rasa* according to the *Abhinavabhāratī* is that the meaning expressed in a drama, by the use of worldly songs, musical instruments, depicting good virtues and using flowery rhetoric one can show intense beauty which increases the glory of the poem or drama and generalizes it for social viewing, where the spectator who understands the emotions felt in the heart of the poet or is the *sahr̥daya*, identifies himself with the protagonist and relishes uninhibited self-reflective repose which can be called *rasa*. Such an unbiased knowledge of identification is transcendental in nature and is not same as other means of knowledge such as inference, testimony, or even personal life. The *rasa* theory asserts that entertainment is a desired effect of performance arts but is not the primary goal, and that the primary goal is to transport the individual in the audience into another parallel reality, full of wonder, where he experiences the essence of his own consciousness, and reflects on spiritual and moral questions.

ii. The *Nāṭyaśāstra* notifies eight *rasas* – Śr̥ṅgāra, Hāsya, Karuṇa, Raudra, Vīra, Bhayānaka, Vībhatsa and Adbhuta.

Sahr̥daya – If the perceiver has a similar heart (as a synonym for reflective aware consciousness) to the poet, i.e. he experiences the same emotions or sentiments as the poet, he is said to be a *sahr̥daya* (a oneness with the poet).

Śaivāgama – The Śaiva philosophy is based on ancient texts called as Āgama. This philosophy deals with systematic processes through which one can achieve the supreme reality through worldly experiences. Śaiva philosophy has five main branches: Pāśupata, Vīraśaiva, Trika Darśana, Śaiva Siddhānta and Kāpālika. Philosophically there are three types of Śaiva sects: Dvaita, Viśiṣṭādvaita and Advaita. The established texts of the Śaiva Siddhānta are twenty-eight for Śaivāgama and sixty-four for Bhairavāgama. The Śaivāgama texts are the recorded conversations between Lord Śiva and his consort Pārvatī, they are written as ten Śaivāgamas and eighteen Rudrāgamas.

i. *Śaivāgama* – The ten Śaivāgamas are: 1. Kāmika, 2. Yogaja, 3. Cintya, 4. Kāraṇa, 5. Ajita, 6. Sudīptaka, 7. Sūkṣma, 8. Sahastra, 9. Suprabheda, and 10. Anśumāna.

ii. *Rudrāgama* – The eighteen Rudrāgamas are: 1. Vijaya, 2. Niśvāsa, 3. Parameśvara, 4. Prodgnīt, 5. Mukhabimba, 6. Siddha, 7. Santāna, 8. Narasiṁha, 9. Candrāṅśu, 10. Vīrabhadra, 11. Svayambhū, 12. Virakta, 13. Kauravya, 14. Mukuṭa, 15. Kiraṇa, 16. Lalita, 17. Āgneya, and 18. Vātula.

Sāṁkhya Darśana – It is an old philosophical system of India. Sage Kapila is credited to be the founder of this system. Sāṁkhya Darśana maintains a clear-cut dualism between *Puruṣa* and *Prakṛti*. The system is predominantly intellectual and theoretical. Right knowledge is the knowledge of the separation of the *Puruṣa* from the *Prakṛti*. Sāṁkhya recognizes the unconscious principle *Prakṛti* as well as the conscious principle *Puruṣa*. The original Sāṁkhya was monistic and theistic. But the classical Sāṁkhya *darśana* perhaps under the influence of materialism, Jainism and early Buddhism became atheistic. According to Ādi Śaṅkarācārya, Sāṁkhya Darśana is the principal opponent of the Vedas. He also highlights that Sāṁkhya Darśana is not a Vedic philosophy although it believes in the Vedas.

i. *Metaphysical Aspect* – It is a philosophy of numbers. The twenty-four divisions of *Prakṛti* are:

   a. *Prakṛti* (Nature), mind (*manas*), intellect (*buddhi*) and ego-sense (*ahaṁkāra*).

   b. Five external sense organs (*jñānendriyas*): Nose (smelling or olfaction), eyes (seeing), ears (hearing), skin (somatosensorial or touch) and tongue (tasting or gustation).

   c. Five motor sense organs (feet, hands, organs of excretion, organs of reproduction and speech).

   d. Five *tanmātras* (subtle elements) forming the object of *jñānendriyas* (smell, taste, form, touch and sound).

   e. Five elements (earth, water, fire, air and space).

   f. These twenty-four divisions, along with the conscious *Puruṣa,* make up the twenty-five elements of Sāṁkhya *darśana.*

ii. *Epistemological Aspect* – In the Sāṁkhya philosophy perception, inference and verbal testimony have been considered as valid means of knowledge.

Śāstra – *śāsu anuśiṣṭau.* Its etymological root is *śās.* It is typically understood as "precept, rules, manual, compendium, book or treatise". The word is generally used as a suffix in the Indian literary context for technical or specialized knowledge in a defined area of practice.

Saundarya – The meaning of the word *saundarya* (synonymous with beauty) is anything which makes the mind happy or anything which soaks the psyche. It is said that a thing of beauty can be blissful but anything which makes one happy may not necessarily be beautiful. Many philosophers claim that beauty depends on subjective approach and imagination. In the metaphysical, grammarian and epistemological context *saundarya* is the subject matter of philosophy.

Siddhi – It means the success of the drama in the eyes of both God and men.

Smṛti – It means that "which is remembered". It refers to a body of ancient Indian texts usually attributed to an author, traditionally written down but constantly revised. Smṛti is a derivative secondary work. It is less authoritative compared to Vedic literature, e.g. the epics the *Rāmāyaṇa* and *Mahābhārata*, Purāṇas, etc.

Śreyas – The meaning of *śreyas* is one who is meritorious or preferable. The meaning should be understood in the spiritual and other-worldly context.

Śruti – The meaning of the word is "knowledge that has been heard". Vedic literature is considered authorless and has been transmitted through generations and is thought to be eternal. They are the most authoritative, ancient religious texts comprising the central canon of ancient Indian knowledge, e.g. the four Vedas, Upaniṣadas, Āraṇyakas, etc.

Svara – The voice of the actors, be it dialogues or songs or sounds of the string instruments like the *vīṇā*,is called *svara*. It is of seven types: *ṣaḍja* (षड्ज), *ṛṣabha* (ऋषभ), *gāndhāra* (गान्धार), *madhyama* (मध्यम), *pañcama* (पञ्चम), *dhaivata* (धैवत) and *niṣāda* (निषाद). They are *sā*, *re*, *gā*, *mā*, *pā*, *dhā*, *nī*.

Tattva-Mīmāṁsā or Metaphysics – The meaning of the word *tattva* should be understood as reality or truth or "That which is, so that". Any study or thought which involves reality and truth is called Tattva-Mīmāṁsā. In philosophical studies, there has always been a tussle between the sentient and the insentient. It is said that the body becomes inanimate after death, then, how come consciousness is there in our body. Every Indian philosophical system has explained this in a very detailed way. The Vedānta system believes only in the consciousness and says that unconsciousness is only perceived and it has no independent realities. The Sāṁkhya system accepts both the sentient and the insentient as independent realities. Western philosophies term Tattva-Mīmāṁsā as metaphysics, it is therefore the study of laws which in turn govern physics.

Upadeśa – The term *upadeśa* means to give guidance through a *guru* or teacher. In the Indian cultural context, *upadeśa* can be of three types:

i. *Prabhu sammita*: The teachings or advice given directly by God, e.g. Śruti.

ii. *Suhṛt sammita*: The advice which is taken from societal norms or what societal behaviour teaches each other, e.g. what has been said in Smṛti.

iii. *Kānta sammita*: Advice given by a lover/beloved. In the Indian tradition, drama is usually accepted as similar to *kānta sammita upadeśa* (endearing persuation).

Vaiśeṣika Darśana – The Vaiśeṣika system is next to Sāṁkhya in origin and is of a greater antiquity than the Nyāya. It is prior to Buddhism and Jainism. It was propounded by Sage Kaṇāda. The Vaiśeṣika philosophy, therefore, is pluralistic realism which emphasizes that diversity is the soul of the universe. Nyāya has accepted the metaphysical elements of Vaiśeṣika. There is no separate epistemology discernible in this system.

Metaphysical Aspect – The Vaiśeṣika system establishes the study of categories and the concept of atomistic pluralism. A category is called *padhārtha* and the entire universe is reduced to two *padārthas*. A category (*padārtha*) can be named and studied. They are: *bhāvātmaka* (being) and *abhāvātmaka* (non-being).

a. *Bhāvātmaka* – *Dravya* (substance), *guṇa* (quality), *karma* (action), *sāmānya* (generality), *viśeṣa* (particularity) and *samavāya* (inherence).

b. *Abhāvātmaka* – Kaṇāda didn't give importance to non-being as a category but later philosophers divided it into four parts: *Prāgabhāva* (antecedent non-existence), *pradhvaṁsābhāva* (subsequent non-existence), *anyonyābhāva* (mutual non-existence) and atyantābhāva (absolute non-existence). These categories are negative in nature.

Vāṇī – According to the *Bṛhadāraṇyaka Upaniṣad*, *vāṇī* is the form of anything which can be experienced. *Vāṇī* takes on the character of that knowledge and protects it.

> चत्वारि वाक्परिमिता पदानि तानि विदुर्ब्राह्मणा ये मनीषिणः।
> गुहा त्रीणि निहिता नेङ्गयन्ति तुरीयं वाचो मनुष्या वदन्ति ॥
>
> *catvāri vāk parimitā padāni tāni vidurbrāhmaṇā ye manīṣiṇaḥ* ।
> *guhā trīṇi nihitā neṅgayanti turīyaṁ vāco manuṣyā vadanti* ॥
>
> – *Ṛgveda* I.164.45

This means that speech has been measured out in four divisions, known only to the wise brāhmaṇas. Three of them are kept in concealment within the body and only the fourth is used by man in his daily life. These are *parā, paśyantī, madhyamā* and *vaikharī*. *Parā* is the spiritual sound of *Brahman*, it is the finest level of language. *Paśyantī* is "that which witnesses", it is the finest level of speech where there is no distinction between word and meaning; it is the seed of all thought, speech and action. *Madhyamā* represents the thinking level of the mind prior to audible speech. *Vaikharī* is the most external and differentiated level of language. The following *ślokas* taken from Bhartṛhari's *Vākyapadīya* elucidate them.

> स्थानेषु विवृते वायौ कृतवर्णपरिग्रहा।
> वैखरी वाक्प्रयोक्तॄणां प्राणवृत्तिनिबन्धना ॥
>
> *sthāneṣu vivṛte vāyau kṛtavarṇaparigrahā* ।
> *vaikharī vākprayoktṝṇā prāṇavṛttinibandhanā* ॥
>
> – *Vākyapadīya* 1.165

The audible speech, *vaikharī* is possible because air strikes the articulation point and every syllable is singularly produced. It is based on the activity of speaker's breath:

> केवलं बुद्ध्युपादान-क्रमरूपानुपातिनी ।
> प्राणवृत्तिं अतिक्रम्य मध्यमा वाक्प्रवर्तते ॥
>
> *kevalaṁ buddhyupādāna-kramarūpānupātinī* ।
> *prāṇavṛttim atīkramya madhyamā vākpravartate* ॥
>
> – Ibid. 1.166

Madhyamā represents the thinking level of the mind residing in intellect prior to audible speech, where internal sounds are in the successive form. It infringes on the breathing of person:

> अविभागा तु पश्यन्ती सर्वतः संहृतक्रमा ।
> स्वरूपज्योतिरेवान्तः सूक्ष्मा वागनपायिनी ॥
>
> *avibhāgā tu paśyantī sarvataḥ saṁhṛtakramā* ।
> *svarūpajyotirevāntaḥ sūkṣmā vāganapāyinī* ॥
>
> – Ibid. 1.167

There is no prescribed order in the sounds or phrases of *paśyantī*. Therefore, it can't be divided or described. This delicate form of language is imperishable and subtle, which is equivalent to light in its essence. Through this stage of language, a man understands the internal enlightenment he attains.

According to Kashmiri Śaiva philosophy, there are two ways in which word formation can be understood: the way a word is read/pronounced by the reader or speaker and the way its meaning is understood by the listener. The word which is read can be deliberated upon and the meaning of the word shines through itself when it is spoken. The unity between the speech and speaker is Parama-Śiva himself. The entire process of expression of words, even songs and music, is based on this principle.

Vedānta Darśana – The major texts of the Vedānta system are the Upaniṣadas, *Brahmasūtra* and *Bhagavadgītā*. Upaniṣadas are the end of the Vedic literature, hence the name Vedānta. The founders of this school are Gauḍapādācārya, Ādi Śaṅkarācārya,

Rāmānujācārya, Madhvācārya, Nimbārkācārya and Vallabhācārya. Vedānta recognizes the conscious truth, because this alone urges a person on to the path of gaining knowledge. This school recognizes that *Brahman* is the pivot and our self and the world are separate from it. It considers that truth can neither be created nor destroyed.

i. *Metaphysical aspect* – according to the Vedānta school the universal conscious self is the one and only truth. The unconscious things are felt through illusion, which have a practical reality. The world which is illusory has a dream-like reality to it.

ii. *Epistemological aspect* – According to Vedānta, the knower, the knowable and the knowledge are one and the same. Knowledge is *Brahman* personified and it is the calming effect for our inner consciousness.

Vedānta, various schools of– The different schools of Vedānta are:

i. *Advaita* – The founders of this school are Gauḍapādācārya and Ādi Śaṅkarācārya. Advaita Vedānta considers the inner self and *Brahman* as one and the same.

ii. *Dvaita* – The proposer of this school was the thirteenth-century Sage Madhvācārya. This school advocates that the inner self and *Brahman* are separate entities.

iii. *Bhedābheda* – In this school the thought propagated is that the characteristic position of all the different Bhedābheda Vedānta schools is that the individual self is both different and not different from the ultimate reality known as *Brahman*. Bhedābheda reconciles the positions of two other major schools of Vedānta.

   a. *Viśiṣṭādvaita* – This school was founded by eleventh-century Sage Rāmānujācārya.

   b. *Dvaitādvaita* – This was founded by thirteenth-century Sage Nimbārkācārya.

c. *Śuddhādvaita* – This was founded by fifteenth-century Sage Vallabhācārya.

d. *Acintyabhedābheda* – This was advocated by fifteenth-century Sage Caitanya Mahāprabhu.

Vedas – They are the most ancient of the religious texts of the Indian culture. They are derived from the Sanskrit root *vid*. It literally means "treatise of knowledge". In tradition, these are believed to be the words of God. They are authorless and are called texts of knowledge (Śruti). The Vedas have been subclassified into four major text types – the Saṁhitās (*mantra*s and benedictions), the Āraṇyakas (text on rituals, ceremonies, sacrifices and symbolic-sacrifices), the Brāhmaṇas (commentaries on rituals, ceremonies and sacrifices) and the Upaniṣads (texts discussing meditation, philosophy and spiritual knowledge. There are four Veda Saṁhitās: the *R̥gveda*, *Sāmaveda*, *Yajurveda* and *Atharvaveda*.

i. *R̥gveda* – It is the most ancient Veda and contains the description of the virtues of the deities and hymns for their praise.

ii. *Sāmaveda* – It contains melodious hymns for worship of gods.

iii. *Yajurveda* – It is a compilation of prose *mantra*s, recited by a priest during the rituals or offerings.

iv. *Atharvaveda* – Consists of poems to describe virtues, ethics, health and sacrificial rituals.

Vibhāva – The inherent reasons by which we enjoy the manifestation of *rasa* are called *vibhāva*s. These *vibhāva*s are also called as signifiers or determinants. They are of two types – (a) *ālambana* (supporting reasons), they bring the viewer nearer to the meaning, and (b) *uddīpana* (inciting reasons), they increase the effect of the expression.

Vidyā – According to Kashmiri Śaiva philosophy, *vidyā* is nothing but the finite knowledge of the all-knowing, infinite *Parameśvara*. The *vidyā-tattva* associated with the limited self partly restores the power of knowledge. The function of *vidyā* is to know the various objects of reflection in *buddhi* (intellect) as distinct from one another.

Vṛtti – They are the divisions of dramatic enactments. They are of four types:

i. *Bhāratī* – The argumentative enactment.

ii. *Ārbhaṭī* – The robust and actionable enactment.

iii. *Sātvatī* – The heroic enactment.

iv. *Kaiśikī* – the erotic enactment. Just as the hair on the head is just an embellishment, so also any such adornments are called *kaiśikī*. The use of *apsarās* in Sanskrit drama is a form of *kaiśikī*.

Yoga Darśana – Sage Patañjali is the founder of the Yoga system. The main objective of this philosophical system is to show man the road to attain his ultimate goal which is *mokṣa*. According to Sage Patañjali, Yoga does not mean only union, but a spiritual effort to attain perfection through the control of the body, senses and mind and through right discrimination between *Puruṣa* and *Prakṛti*. Yoga is intimately allied to Sāṁkhya. According to the *Bhagavadgītā*, Yoga is spiritual action, while Sāṁkhya is knowledge. Sāṁkhya is theory and Yoga is practice. Yoga accepts the metaphysical and epistemological elements of Sāṁkhya. Yoga believes in God as the highest self, distinct from other selves, hence it is called Śeśvara Sāṁkhya, while classical Sāṁkhya is called Nirīśvara Sāṁkhya. To cleanse and purify the body, five senses and mind, Yoga describes an eightfold path (*aṣṭāṅga yoga*).

Filmography

Sl. No	English Name	Original Title	Director	Release Year	Language	Country
1.	12 *Angry Men*	12 *Angry Men*	Sidney Lumet	1957	English	USA
2.	2001: *A Space Odyssey*	2001: *A Space Odyssey*	Stanley Kubrick	1968	English	USA
3.	8½	*Otto e mezzo*	Federico Fellini	1963	Italian	Italy, France
4.	*A Clockwork Orange*	*A Clockwork Orange*	Stanley Kubrick	1971	English	USA
5.	*A Day at the Races*	*A Day at the Races*	Sam Wood	1937	English	USA
6.	*A Day in the Country*	*Partie de champagne*	Jean Renoir	1936	French	France
7.	*A Generation*	*Pokolenie*	Andrzej Wajda	1954	Polish	Poland
8.	*A King in New York*	*A King in New York*	Charles Chaplin	1957	English	UK
9.	*A Man for All Seasons*	*A Man for All Seasons*	Fred Zinnemann	1966	English	UK
10.	*A Matter of Life and Death*	*A Matter of Life and Death*	Michael Powell and Emeric Pressburger	1946	English	UK
11.	*A Night at the Opera*	*A Night at the Opera*	Sam Wood	1935	English	USA
12.	*A Short Story about Love*	*Krótki film o miłości*	Krzysztof Kieślowski	1988	Polish	Poland
13.	*A Star Is Born*	*A Star Is Born*	George Cukor	1954	English	USA
14.	*A Street Car Named Desire*	*A Street Car Named Desire*	Elia Kazan	1951	English	USA
15.	*A Trip to the Moon*	*Le Voyage dans la Lune*	Georges Méliès	1902	Silent	France
16.	*A Woman Is a Woman*	*Une Femme est Une Femme*	Jean-Luc Godard	1961	French	France

cont.

Sl. No	English Name	Original Title	Director	Release Year	Language	Country
17.	*A Woman under the Influence*	*A Woman under the Influence*	John Cassavetes	1974	English	USA
18.	*Aashirwad*	आशीर्वाद	Hrishikesh Mukherjee	1968	Hindi	India
19.	*After the Fox*	*Caccia alla volpe*	Vittorio De Sica	1966	Italian	Italy, UK
20.	*After the Thin Man*	*After the Thin Man*	W.S. Van Dyke	1936	English	USA
21.	*Agurrie, the Wrath of God*	*Aguirre, der Zorn Gottes*	Werner Herzog	1972	German	West Germany
22.	*Algiers*	*Algiers*	John Cromwell	1938	English	USA
23.	*Ali: Fear Eats the Soul*	*Angst essen Seele auf*	Rainer Werner Fassbinder	1974	German	West Germany
24.	*Alien*	*Alien*	Ridley Scott	1979	English	USA
25.	*Aliens*	*Aliens*	James Cameron	1986	English	USA
26.	*All about Eve*	*All about Eve*	Joseph L. Mankiewicz	1950	English	USA
27.	*All about My Mother*	*Todo sobre mi madre*	Pedro Almodóvar	1999	Spanish	Spain
28.	*All Quiet on the Western Front*	*All Quiet on the Western Front*	Lewis Milestone	1930	English	USA
29.	*Amadeus*	*Amadeus*	Miloš Forman	1984	English	USA
30.	*Amarcord*	*Amarcord*	Federico Fellini	1973	Italian	Italy, France

31.	*Amélie*	*Le Fabuleux Destin d'Amélie Poulain*	Jean-Pierre Jeunet	2001	French	France
32.	*An Affair to Remember*	*An Affair to Remember*	Leo McCarey	1957	English	USA
33.	*An American in Paris*	*An American in Paris*	Vincente Minnelli	1951	English	USA
34.	*An Andalusian Dog*	*Un Chien Andalou*	Luis Buñuel	1929	Silent	France
35.	*Anand*	आनंद	Hrishikesh Mukherjee	1971	Hindi	India
36.	*Andrei Rublev*	*Andrey Rublyov*	Andrei Tarkovsky	1966	Russian	USSR
37.	*Annie Hall*	*Annie Hall*	Woody Allen	1977	English	USA
38.	*Another Thin Man*	*Another Thin Man*	W.S. Van Dyke	1939	English	USA
39.	*Antichrist*	*Antichrist*	Lars von Trier	2009	English	Denmark
40.	*Anupama*	अनुपमा	Hrishikesh Mukherjee	1966	Hindi	India
41.	*Aparajito*	अपराजितो	Satyajit Ray	1956	Bengali	India
42.	*Arabian Nights*	*Il fiore delle mille e una notte*	Pier Paolo Pasolini	1974	Italian	Italy
43.	*Aranyer Din Ratri*	অরণ্যের দিনরাত্রি	Satyajit Ray	1969	Bengali	India
44.	*Ashani Sanket*	অশনসিংকতে	Satyajit Ray	1973	Bengali	India
45.	*Ashes and Diamonds*	*Popiół i diament*	Andrzej Wajda	1958	Polish	Poland
46.	*Ashik Kerib*	*Ashug-Karibi*	Sergei Parajanov	1988	Georgian	USSR
47.	*Au hasard Balthazar*	*Au hasard Balthazar*	Robert Bresson	1966	French	France, Sweden
48.	*Aurat*	औरत	Mehboob Khan	1940	Hindi	India

cont.

Sl. No	English Name	Original Title	Director	Release Year	Language	Country
49.	*Avatar*	*Avatar*	James Cameron	2009	English	USA
50.	*Babette's Feast*	*Babettes gæstebud*	Gabriel Axel	1987	Danish	Denmark
51.	*Band of Outsiders*	*Bande à Part*	Jean-Luc Godard	1964	French	France
52.	*Bandini*	बंदिनी	Bimal Roy	1963	Hindi	India
53.	*Barton Fink*	*Barton Fink*	Joel Coen and Ethan Coen	1991	English	USA
54.	*Batman Begins*	*Batman Begins*	Christopher Nolan	2005	English	USA
55.	*Battleship Potemkin*	*Bronenosets Potemkin*	Sergei Eisenstein	1925	Silent	USSR
56.	*Bawarchi*	बावर्ची	Hrishikesh Mukherjee	1972	Hindi	India
57.	*Beauty of the Day*	*Belle De Jour*	Luis Buñuel	1967	French, Spanish	France, Spain
58.	*Before Midnight*	*Before Midnight*	Richard Linklater	2013	English	USA
59.	*Before Sunrise*	*Before Sunrise*	Richard Linklater	1995	English	USA, Austria, Switzerland
60.	*Before Sunset*	*Before Sunset*	Richard Linklater	2004	English	USA
61.	*Ben-Hur*	*Ben-Hur*	William Wyler	1959	English	USA
62.	*Bicycle Thieves*	*Ladri di Biciclette*	Vittorio De Sica	1948	Italian	Italy
63.	*Big Business*	*Big Business*	Leo McCarey	1929	Silent	USA
64.	*Black Orpheus*	*Orfeu Negro*	Marcel Camus	1959	Portuguese	Brazil

65.	*Black Sunday*	*La maschera del demonio*	Mario Bava	1960	Italian	Italy
66.	*Blade Runner*	*Blade Runner*	Ridley Scott	1982	English	USA
67.	*Blue Jasmine*	*Blue Jasmine*	Woody Allen	2013	English	USA
68.	*Blue Velvet*	*Blue Velvet*	David Lynch	1986	English	USA
69.	*Bonnie and Clyde*	*Bonnie and Clyde*	Arthur Penn	1967	English	USA
70.	*Braveheart*	*Braveheart*	Mel Gibson	1955	English	USA
71.	*Brazil*	*Brazil*	Terry Gillaim	1985	English	UK, USA
72.	*Breaking Away*	*Breaking Away*	Peter Yates	1979	English	USA
73.	*Breathless*	*À bout de souffle*	Jean-Luc Godard	1960	French	France
74.	*Bride of Frankenstein*	*Bride of Frankenstein*	James Whale	1935	English	USA
75.	*Brief Encounter*	*Brief Encounter*	David Lean	1945	English	UK, USA
76.	*Brightness*	*Yeelen*	Souleymane Cissé	1987	Bambara, Fula	Mali
77.	*Bringing Up Baby*	*Bringing Up Baby*	Howard Hawks	1938	English	USA
78.	*Broken Blossoms*	*Broken Blossoms or The Yellow Man and the Girl*	D.W. Griffith	1919	Silent	USA
79.	*Burn After Reading*	*Burn After Reading*	Joel Coen and Ethan Coen	2008	English	USA
80.	*Cannibal Holocaust*	*Cannibal Holocaust*	Ruggero Deodato	1980	English	USA
81.	*Casablanca*	*Casablanca*	Michael Curtiz	1942	English	USA

cont.

Sl. No	English Name	Original Title	Director	Release Year	Language	Country
82.	*Cat People*	*Cat People*	Jacques Tourneur	1942	English	USA
83.	*Chariots of Fire*	*Chariots of Fire*	Hugh Hudson	1981	English	UK
84.	*Children of Heaven*	*Bacheha-Ye Aseman*	Majid Majidi	1997	Persian	Iran
85.	*Children of Paradise*	*Les Enfants du Paradis*	Marcel Carné	1945	French	France
86.	*Chimes at Midnight*	*Falstaff*	Orson Welles	1965	English	Spain, Switzerland
87.	*Chinatown*	*Chinatown*	Roman Polanski	1974	English	USA
88.	*Chitralekha*	चित्रलेखा	Kidar Sharma	1941	Hindi	India
89.	*Chupke Chupke*	चुपके-चुपके	Hrishikesh Mukherjee	1975	Hindi	India
90.	*Cinema Paradiso*	*Nuovo Cinema Paradiso*	Giuseppe Tornatore	1988	Italian	Italy
91.	*Citizen Kane*	*Citizen Kane*	Orson Welles	1941	English	USA
92.	*City Lights*	*City Lights*	Charles Chaplin	1931,	English, Silent	USA
93.	*City of Angels*	*City of Angels*	Brad Silberling	1998	English	USA
94.	*Cleopatra*	*Cleopatra*	Joseph L. Mankiewicz	1963	English	USA
95.	*Close Up*	*Nemā-ye nazdīk*	Abbas Kiarostami	1990	Persian	Iran
96.	*Closely Watched Trains*	*Ostře sledované vlaky*	Jiri Menzel	1966	Czech	Czechoslovakia
97.	*Come and See*	*Idi i smotri*	Elem Klimov	1985	Belarusian	USSR
98.	*Cries and Whispers*	*Viskningar och rop*	Ingmar Bergman	1972	Swedish	Sweden

99.	*Cross of Iron*	*Cross of Iron*	Sam Peckinpah	1977	English	UK
100.	*Crouching Tiger, Hidden Dragon*	*Wo hu cang long*	Ang Lee	2000	Mandarin	China, USA
101.	*Daera*	दायरा	Kamaal Amrohi	1953	Hindi	India
102.	*Damnation*	*Kárhozat*	Béla Tarr	1988	Hungarian	Hungary
103.	*Dancer in the Dark*	*Danser i mørket*	Lars von Trier	2000	English	Denmark
104.	*Day for Night*	*La Nuit Américaine*	François Truffaut	1973	French	France
105.	*Dersu Uzala*	*Dersu Uzala*	Akira Kurosawa	1975	Russian	USSR, Japan
106.	*Design for Living*	*Design for Living*	Ernst Lubitsch	1933	English	USA
107.	*Detour*	*Detour*	Edgar G. Ulmer	1945	English	USA
108.	*Diabolique*	*Les Diaboliques*	Henri-Georges Clouzot	1955	French	France
109.	*Dial M for Murder*	*Dial M for Murder*	Alfred Hitchcock	1954	English	USA
110.	*Diary of a Country Priest*	*Journal d'un curé de campagne-*	Robert Bresson	1951	French	France
111.	*Divorce Italian Style*	*Divorzio all'italiana*	Pietro Germi	1961	Italian	Italy
112.	*Django Unchained*	*Django Unchained*	Quentin Tarantino	2012	English	USA
113.	*Do Ankhen Barah Haath*	दो आँखे बारह हाथ	V. Shantaram	1957	Hindi	India
114.	*Do Bigha Zamin*	दो बीघा जमीन	Bimal Roy	1953	Hindi	India
115.	*Doctor Zhivago*	*Doctor Zhivago*	David Lean	1965	English	UK, USA
116.	*Don't Look Now*	*Don't Look Now*	Nicolas Roeg	1973	English	UK

cont.

Sl. No	English Name	Original Title	Director	Release Year	Language	Country
117.	*Dosti*	दोस्ती	Satyen Bose	1964	Hindi	India
118.	*Double Indemnity*	*Double Indemnity*	Billy Wilder	1944	English	USA
119.	*Dr. Jekyll & Mr Hyde*	*Dr. Jekyll & Mr Hyde*	Rouben Mamoulian	1931	English	USA
120.	*Dr. Strangelove*	*Dr. Strangelove or: How I Learned to Stop Worrying and Love the Bomb*	Stanley Kubrick	1964	English	USA
121.	*Dr. Mabuse the Gambler*	*Dr. Mabuse, der Spieler – Ein Bild der Zeit*	Fritz Lang	1922	Silent	Germany
122.	*Dracula*	*Dracula*	Tod Browning	1931	English	USA
123.	*Dreams*	*Yume*	Akira Kurosawa	1990	Japanese	Japan
124.	*Duck Soup*	*Duck Soup*	Leo McCarey	1933	English	USA
125.	*E.T. the Extra-Terrestrial*	*E.T. the Extra-Terrestrial*	Steven Spielberg	1982	English	USA
126.	*Early Summer*	*Bakushū*	Yasujirō Ozu	1951	Japanese	Japan
127.	*Earth*	*Zemlya*	Alexander Dovzhenko	1930	Silent	USSR
128.	*Él - This Strange Passion*	*Él - This Strange Passion*	Luis Buñuel	1953	Spanish	Mexico
129.	*Enter the Dragon*	*Enter the Dragon*	Robert Clouse, Bruce Lee	1973	English	Hong Kong, USA
130.	*Equinox Flower*	*Higanbana*	Yasujirō Ozu	1958	Japanese	Japan
131.	*Eraserhead*	*Eraserhead*	David Lynch	1977	English	USA

132.	*Eternity and a Day*	*Mia aioniotita kai mia mera*	Theo Angelopoulos	1998	Greek	Greece
133.	*Faces*	*Faces*	John Cassavetes	1968	English	USA
134.	*Fanny and Alexander*	*Fanny och Alexander*	Ingmar Bergman	1982	Swedish	Sweden, France, West Germany
135.	*Faraway, So Close!*	*In weiter Ferne, so nah!*	Wim Wenders	1993	German	West Germany
136.	*Farewell My Concubine*	*Farewell My Concubine*	Chen Kaige	1993	Mandarin	China
137.	*Fargo*	*Fargo*	Joel Coen and Ethan Coen	1996	English	USA
138.	*Film*	*Film*	Alan Schneider	1965	Silent	USA
139.	*Floating Weeds*	*Ukikusa Monogatari*	Yasujirō Ozu	1959	Japanese	Japan
140.	*Follow the Fleet*	*Follow the Fleet*	Mark Sandrich	1936	English	USA
141.	*For a Few Dollars More*	*Per qualche dollaro in più*	Sergio Leone	1965	Italian, English	Italy, West Germany, Spain
142.	*Fort Apache*	*Fort Apache*	John Ford	1948	English	USA
143.	*Frankenstein*	*Frankenstein*	James Whale	1931	English	USA
144.	*From Here to Eternity*	*From Here to Eternity*	Fred Zinnemann	1953	English	USA
145.	*Fury*	*Fury*	Fritz Lang	1936	English	USA
146.	*Gangs of New York*	*Gangs of New York*	Martin Scorsese	2002	English	USA, Italy
147.	*Geet Gaaya Pattharon Ne*	गीत गाया पत्थरों ने	V. Shantaram	1963	Hindi	India

cont.

Sl. No	*English Name*	*Original Title*	*Director*	*Release Year*	*Language*	*Country*
148.	*Gertrud*	*Gertrud*	Carl Dreyer	1964	Danish	Denmark
149.	*Gladiator*	*Gladiator*	Ridley Scott	2000	English	UK, USA
150.	*Gloria*	*Gloria*	John Cassavetes	1980	English	USA
151.	*Going My Way*	*Going My Way*	Leo McCarey	1944	English	USA
152.	*Gone with the Wind*	*Gone with the Wind*	Victor Flemming	1939	English	USA
153.	*Goodfellas*	*Goodfellas*	Martin Scorsese	1990	English	USA
154.	*Goopy Gyne Bagha Byne*	গুপী গাইন বাঘা বাইন	Satyajit Ray	1969	Bengali	India
155.	*Grave of Fireflies*	*Hotaru no Haka*	Isao Takahata	1988	Japanese	Japan
156.	*Great Expectations*	*Great Expectations*	David Lean	1946	English	UK
157.	*Guess Who's Coming to Dinner*	*Guess Who's Coming to Dinner*	Stanley Kramer	1967	English	USA
158.	*Hannibal*	*Hannibal*	Ridley Scott	2001	English	USA
159.	*Harold and Maude*	*Harold and Maude*	Hal Ashby	1971	English	USA
160.	*Heaven Can Wait*	*Heaven Can Wait*	Ernst Lubitsch	1943	English	USA
161.	*Heer Raanjha*	हीर राँझा	Chetan Anand	1970	Hindi	India
162.	*Hero*	*Ying xiong*	Zhang Yimou	2002	Mandarin	China, Hong Kong
163.	*High and Low*	*Tengoku to jigoku*	Akira Kurosawa	1963	Japanese	Japan

164.	*High Noon*	*High Noon*	Fred Zinnemann	1952	English	USA
165.	*His Girl Friday*	*His Girl Friday*	Howard Hawks	1940	English	USA
166.	*Histoire(s) du cinéma*	*Histoire(s) du cinéma: Toutes les histoires*	Jean-Luc Godard	1988	French	France
167.	*Hour of the Wolf*	*Vargtimmen*	Ingmar Bergman	1968	Swedish	Sweden
168.	*House of Flying Daggers*	*Shi mian mai fu*	Zhang Yimou	2004	Mandarin	China, Hong Kong
169.	*How Green Was My Valley*	*How Green Was My Valley*	John Ford	1941	English	USA
170.	*Hugo*	*Hugo*	Martin Scorsese	2011	English	USA
171.	*I Am a Fugitive from a Chain Gang*	*I Am a Fugitive from a Chain Gang*	Mervyn LeRoy	1932	English	USA
172.	*I Confess*	*I Confess*	Alfred Hitchcock	1952	English	USA
173.	*IKnow Where I'm Going*	*I Know Where I'm Going*	Michael Powell and Emeric Pressburger	1945	English	UK
174.	*I Vitelloni*	*I vitelloni*	Federico Fellini	1953	Italian	Italy
175.	*Ikiru*	*Ikiru*	Akira Kurosawa	1951	Japanese	Japan
176.	*In the Mood for Love*	*Fa yeung nin wa*	Wong Kar-wai	2000	Cantonese, Mandarin	Hong Kong
177.	*Inception*	*Inception*	Christopher Nolan	2010	English	USA
178.	*Inglourious Basterds*	*Inglourious Basterds*	Quentin Tarantino	2009	English, German, French	USA, Germany

cont.

Sl. No	English Name	Original Title	Director	Release Year	Language	Country
179.	*Inland Empire*	*Inland Empire*	David Lynch	2006	English	USA
180.	*Intolerance*	*Intolerance: Love's Struggle Throughout the Ages*	D.W. Griffith	1916	Silent	USA
181.	*Irma La Douce*	*Irma La Douce*	Billy Wilder	1963	English	USA
182.	*It Happened One Night*	*It Happened One Night*	Frank Capra	1934	English	USA
183.	*It's a Mad, Mad, Mad, Mad World*	*It's a Mad, Mad, Mad, Mad World*	Stanley Kramer	1963	English	USA
184.	*It's a Wonderful Life*	*It's a Wonderful Life*	Frank Capra	1946	English	USA
185.	*Ivan the Terrible – Part 1*	*Ivan Groznyy*	Sergei Eisenstein	1944	Russian	USSR
186.	*Ivan the Terrible – Part 2*	*Ivan Groznyy. Skaz vtoroy: Boyarskiy zagovor*	Sergei Eisenstein	1958	Russian	USSR
187.	*Ivan's Childhood*	*Ivanovo detstvo*	Andrei Tarkovsky	1962	Russian	USSR
188.	*Jaldeep*	जलदीप	Kidar Sharma	1956	Hindi	India
189.	*Jewel Thief*	ज्वैल थीफ	Vijay Anand	1967	Hindi	India
190.	*Jezebel*	*Jezebel*	William Wyler	1938	English	USA
191.	*Jhanak Jhanak Payal Baaje*	झनक-झनक पायल बाजे	V. Shantaram	1955	Hindi	India
192.	*Jogan*	जोगन	Kidar Sharma	1950	Hindi	India
193.	*Joi Baba Felunath*	জয় বাবা ফেলুনাথ	Satyajit Ray	1979	Bengali	India
194.	*Jurassic Park*	*Jurassic Park*	Steven Spielberg	1993	English	USA

195.	*Kanal*	*Kanał*	Andrzej Wajda	1956	Polish	Poland
196.	*Kill Bill :Vol. 1*	*Kill Bill: Vol. 1*	Quentin Tarantino	2003	English	USA
197.	*Kill Bill :Vol.2*	*Kill Bill: Vol. 2*	Quentin Tarantino	2004	English	USA
198.	*Kind Hearts and Coronets*	*Kind Hearts and Coronets*	Robert Hamer	1949	English	UK
199.	*King Kong*	*King Kong*	Merian C. Cooper	1933	English	USA
200.	*Kiss Me Deadly*	*Kiss Me Deadly*	Robert Aldrich	1955	English	USA
201.	*Knife in the Water*	*Nóż w wodzie*	Roman Polanski	1962	Polish	Poland
202.	*Komal Gandhar*	কোমল গান্ধার	Ritwik Ghatak	1961	Bengali	India
203.	*La Dolce Vita*	*La Dolce Vita*	Federico Fellini	1960	Italian	Italy, France
204.	*La Jetée*	*La Jetée*	Chris Marker	1962	French	France
205.	*La Notte*	*La Notte*	Michelangelo Antonioni	1961	Italian	Italy, France
206.	*La Strada*	*La strada*	Federico Fellini	1954	Italian	Italy
207.	*Larks on a String*	*Skřivánci na niti*	Jiri Menzel	1969	Czech	Czechoslovakia
208.	*Last Tango in Paris*	*Ultimo tango a Parigi*	Bernardo Bertolucci	1972	English, French	France, Italy
209.	*L'Atalante*	*L'Atalante*	Jean Vigo	1934	French	France
210.	*Late Spring*	*Banshun*	Yasujirō Ozu	1949	Japanese	Japan
211.	*Laura*	*Laura*	Otto Preminger	1944	English	USA
212.	*L'Avventura*	*L'avventura*	Michelangelo Antonioni	1960	Italian	Italy

cont.

Sl. No	English Name	Original Title	Director	Release Year	Language	Country
213.	*Lawrence of Arabia*	*Lawrence of Arabia*	David Lean	1962	English	UK
214.	*Let the Right One In*	*Låt den rätte komma in*	Tomas Alfredson	2008	Swedish	Sweden
215.	*Letter from an Unknown Woman*	*Letter from an Unknown Woman*	Max Ophüls	1948	English	USA
216.	*Life Is Beautiful*	*La vita è bella*	Roberto Benigni	1997	Italian	Italy
217.	*Life, and Nothing More …*	*Zendegi va digar hich*	Abbas Kiarostami	1991	Persian	Iran
218.	*Little Caesar*	*Little Caesar*	Mervyn LeRoy	1931	English	USA
219.	*Los Olvidados*	*Los Olvidados*	Luis Buñuel	1950	Spanish	Mexico
220.	*Lost Highway*	*Lost Highway*	David Lynch	1997	English	USA
221.	*Love Affair*	*Love Affair*	Leo McCarey	1939	English	USA
222.	*Loves of a Blonde*	*Lásky jedné plavovlásky*	Milos Forman	1965	Czech	Czechoslovakia
223.	*M*	*M*	Fritz Lang	1931	Silent	Germany
224.	*Macbeth*	*Macbeth*	Orson Welles	1948	English	USA
225.	*Madhumati*	मधुमती	Bimal Roy	1958	Hindi	India
226.	*Mahal*	महल	Kamaal Amrohi	1949	Hindi	India
227.	*Mahapurush*	মহাপুরুষ	Satyajit Ray	1965	Bengali	India
228.	*Manhattan*	*Manhattan*	Woody Allen	1979	English	USA
229.	*Marnie*	*Marnie*	Alfred Hitchcock	1964	English	USA
230.	*Mary Poppins*	*Mary Poppins*	Robert Stevenson	1964	English	USA

231.	*MASH*	*MASH*	Robert Altman	1970	English	USA
232.	*McCabe & Mrs. Miller*	*McCabe & Mrs. Miller*	Robert Altman	1971	English	USA
233.	*Meet John Doe*	*Meet John Doe*	Frank Capra	1941	English	USA
234.	*Meet Me in St. Louis*	*Meet Me in St. Louis*	Vincente Minnelli	1944	English	USA
235.	*Meghe Dhaka Tara*	মেঘে ঢাকা তারা	Ritwik Ghatak	1960	Bengali	India
236.	*Metropolis*	*Metropolis*	Fritz Lang	1927	Silent	Germany
237.	*Mildred Pierce*	*Mildred Pierce*	Michael Curtiz	1945	English	USA
238.	*Million Dollar Baby*	*Million Dollar Baby*	Clint Eastwood	2004	English	USA
239.	*Modern Times*	*Modern Times*	Charles Chaplin	1936	English	USA
240.	*Money*	*L'argent*	Robert Bresson	1983	French	France, Switzerland
241.	*Monkey Business*	*Monkey Business*	Norman Z. McLeod	1931	English	USA
242.	*Monsieur Hulot's Holiday*	*Les Vacances de M. Hulot*	Jacques Tati	1953	French	France
243.	*Monsieur Verdoux*	*Monsieur Verdoux*	Charles Chaplin	1947	English	USA
244.	*Moscow Does Not Believe in Tears*	*Moskva slezam ne verit*	Vladimir Menshov	1980	Russian	USSR
245.	*Mother India*	मदर इंडिया	Mehboob Khan	1957	Hindi	India
246.	*Mouchette*	*Mouchette*	Robert Bresson	1967	French	France
247.	*Mr. and Mrs. Smith*	*Mr. and Mrs. Smith*	Alfred Hitchcock	1941	English	USA

cont.

Sl. No	English Name	Original Title	Director	Release Year	Language	Country
248.	*Mr. Smith Goes to Washington*	*Mr. Smith Goes to Washington*	Frank Capra	1939	English	USA
249.	*Mulholland Drive*	*Mulholland Drive*	David Lynch	2001	English	USA
250.	*Murder My Sweet*	*Murder My Sweet*	Edward Dmytryk	1944	English	USA
251.	*My Darling Clementine*	*My Darling Clementine*	John Ford	1946	English	USA
252.	*My Fair Lady*	*My Fair Lady*	George Cukor	1964	English	USA
253.	*My Neighbor Totoro*	*Tonari no Totoro*	Hayao Miyazaki	1988	Japanese	Japan
254.	*My Sweet Little Village*	*Vesničko má středisková*	Jiri Menzel	1986	Czech	Czechoslovakia
255.	*My Uncle*	*Mon Oncle*	Jacques Tati	1958	French	France
256.	*Nashville*	*Nashville*	Robert Altman	1975	English	USA
257.	*Navrang*	नवरंग	V. Shantaram	1959	Hindi	India
258.	*Neecha Nagar*	नीचा नगर	Chetan Anand	1946	Hindi	India
259.	*Night and the City*	*Night and the City*	Jules Dassin	1950	English	USA
260.	*Night of the Demon*	*Night of the Demon*	Jacques Tourneur	1957	English	UK
261.	*Nights of Cabiria*	*Le notti di Cabiria*	Federico Fellini	1957	Italian	Italy, France
262.	*Ninotchka*	*Ninotchka*	Ernst Lubitsch	1939	English	USA
263.	*No Country for Old Men*	*No Country for Old Men*	Joel Coen & Ethan Coen	2007	English	USA

264.	*Nosferatu*	*Nosferatu, eine Symphonie des Grauens*	F.W. Murnau	1922	Silent	Germany
265.	*Nosferatu The Vampyre*	*Nosferatu: Phantom der Nacht*	Werner Herzog	1979	German	Germany
266.	*Nostalagia*	*Nostalaghia*	Andrei Tarkovsky	1983	Italian, Russian	USSR, Italy
267.	*Nostalgia*	*Nostalghia*	Andrei Tarkovsky	1983	Italian	Italy
268.	*O Brother, Where Art Thou?*	*O Brother, Where Art Thou?*	Joel Coen & Ethan Coen	2000	English	USA
269.	*Ocean's 11*	*Ocean's 11*	Lewis Milestone	1960	English	USA
270.	*Oedipus Rex*	*Edipo re*	Pier Paolo Pasolini	1967	Italian	Italy
271.	*Oliver Twist*	*Oliver Twist*	David Lean	1948	English	UK
272.	*On the Town*	*On the Town*	Stanley Donen	1949	English	USA
273.	*On the Waterfront*	*On the Waterfront*	Elia Kazan	1954	English	USA
274.	*Once Upon a Time in the West*	*C'era una volta il West*	Sergio Leone	1968	English	Italy, USA, Spain
275.	*One Flew Over the Cuckoo's Nest*	*One Flew Over the Cuckoo's Nest*	Miloš Forman	1975	English	USA
276.	*One Song a Day Takes Mischief Away*	*Tko pjeva zlo ne misli*	Krešo Golik	1970	Croatian	Yugoslavia
277.	*Our Hospitality*	*Our Hospitality*	Buster Keaton	1923	Silent	USA

cont.

Sl. No	English Name	Original Title	Director	Release Year	Language	Country
278.	*Out of The Past*	*Out of the Past*	Jacques Tourneur	1947	English	USA
279.	*Pakeezah*	पाकीज़ा	Kamaal Amrohi	1972	Hindi	India
280.	*Pan's Labyrinth*	*El laberinto del fauno*	Guillermo del Toro	2006	Spanish	Mexico
281.	*Paras Patthar*	পরশ পাথর	Satyajit Ray	1958	Bengali	India
282.	*Parineeta*	परिणीता	Bimal Roy	1953	Hindi	India
283.	*Paris, Texas*	*Paris, Texas*	Wim Wenders	1984	English	West Germany, France, UK, USA
284.	*Pather Panchali*	পথের পাঁচালী	Satyajit Ray	1955	Bengali	India
285.	*Peeping Tom*	*Peeping Tom*	Michael Powell	1960	English	UK
286.	*Perfume – The Story of a Murderer*	*Perfume – The Story of a Murderer*	Tom Tykwer	2006	English	Germany
287.	*Persona*	*Persona*	Ingmar Bergman	1966	Swedish	Sweden
288.	*Pickpocket*	*Pickpocket*	Robert Bresson	1959	French	France
289.	*Pierrot le Fou*	*Pierrot le Fou*	Jean-Luc Godard	1965	French	France
290.	*Playtime*	*Playtime*	Jacques Tati	1967	French	France
291.	*Port of Shadows*	*Le Quai des brumes*	Marcel Carné	1937	French	France
292.	*Princess Mononoke*	*Mononoke-hime*	Hayao Miyazaki	1997	Japanese	Japan

293.	*Psycho*	*Psycho*	Alfred Hitchcock	1960	English	USA
294.	*Pulp Fiction*	*Pulp Fiction*	Quentin Tarantino	1994	English	USA
295.	*Raging Bull*	*Raging Bull*	Martin Scorsese	1980	English	USA
296.	*Raise the Red Lantern*	*Dà Hóng Dēnglong Gāogāo Guà*	Zhang Yimou	1991	Mandarin	China, Hong Kong, Taiwan
297.	*Ran*	*Ran*	Akira Kurosawa	1985	Japanese	Japan
298.	*Rancho Notorious*	*Rancho Notorious*	Fritz Lang	1952	English	USA
299.	*Rashomon*	*Rashômon*	Akira Kurosawa	1950	Japanese	Japan
300.	*Razia Sultan*	रज़िया सुल्तान	Kamaal Amrohi	1983	Hindi	India
301.	*Rear Window*	*Rear Window*	Alfred Hitchcock	1954	English	USA
302.	*Rebecca*	*Rebecca*	Alfred Hitchcock	1940	English	USA
303.	*Rebel Without a Cause*	*Rebel Without a Cause*	Nicholas Ray	1955	English	USA
304.	*Red Beard*	*Akahige*	Akira Kurosawa	1965	Japanese	Japan
305.	*Red Desert*	*Il deserto rosso*	Michelangelo Antonioni	1964	Italian	Italy/France
306.	*Red River*	*Red River*	Howard Hawks	1948	English	USA
307.	*Repulsion*	*Repulsion*	Roman Polanski	1965	English	UK
308.	*Reservoir Dogs*	*Reservoir Dogs*	Quentin Tarantino	1992	English	USA
309.	*Ring*	*Ringu*	Hideo Nakata	1998	Japanese	Japan
310.	*Rio Bravo*	*Rio Bravo*	George Stevens	1959	English	USA
311.	*Roman Holiday*	*Roman Holiday*	William Wyler	1953	English	USA

cont.

Sl. No	English Name	Original Title	Director	Release Year	Language	Country
312.	*Roman, Open City*	*Roma città aperta*	Roberto Rossellini	1945	Italian	Italy
313.	*Rosemary's Baby*	*Rosemary's Baby*	Roman Polanski	1968	English	USA
314.	*Safety Last!*	*Safety Last!*	Fred C. Newmeyer	1923	Silent	USA
315.	*Salo, or the 120 Days of Sodom*	*Salò o le 120 giornate di Sodoma*	Pier Paolo Pasolini	1975	Italian	Italy
316.	*Satantango*	*Sátántangó*	Béla Tarr	1994	Hungarian	Hungary
317.	*Satyakam*	सत्यकाम	Hrishikesh Mukherjee	1969	Hindi	India
318.	*Satyricon*	*Fellini – Satyricon*	Federico Fellini	1969	Italian	Italy
319.	*Saw*	*Saw*	James Wan	2004	English	USA
320.	*Scarface*	*Scarface*	Howard Hawks	1932	English	USA
321.	*Scarlet Street*	*Scarlet Street*	Fritz Lang	1945	Silent	Germany
322.	*Seduced and Abandoned*	*Sedotta e abbandonata*	Pietro Germi	1964	Italian	Italy
323.	*Sergeant York*	*Sergeant York*	Howard Hawks	1941	English	USA
324.	*Seven Brides for Seven Brothers*	*Seven Brides for Seven Brothers*	Stanley Donen	1954	English	USA
325.	*Seven Samurai*	*Shichinin no samurai*	Akira Kurosawa	1954	Japanese	Japan
326.	*Seven Year Itch*	*Seven Year Itch*	Billy Wilder	1955	English	USA
327.	*Seven Years Bad Luck*	*Seven Years Bad Luck*	Max Linder	1921	Silent	USA

328.	*Shadow of a Doubt*	*Shadow of a Doubt*	Alfred Hitchcock	1943	English	USA
329.	*Shadows*	*Shadows*	John Cassavetes	1959	English	USA
330.	*Shadows of Forgotten Ancestors*	*Tini zabutykh predkiv*	Sergei Parajanov	1965	Ukrainian	USSR
331.	*Shall We Dance*	*Shall We Dance*	Mark Sandrich	1937	English	USA
332.	*Shane*	*Shane*	Howard Hawks	1953	English	USA
333.	*She Wore a Yellow Ribbon*	*She Wore a Yellow Ribbon*	John Ford	1949	English	USA
334.	*Sherlock Jr.*	*Sherlock Jr.*	Buster Keaton	1924	Silent	USA
335.	*Shoeshine*	*Sciuscià*	Vittorio De Sica	1946	Italian	Italy
336.	*Singin' in the Rain*	*Singin' in the Rain*	Stanley Donen	1952	English	USA
337.	*Slumdog Millionaire*	*Slumdog Millionaire*	Danny Boyle	2008	English	USA
338.	*Smiles of a Summer Night*	*Sommarnattens leende*	Ingmar Bergman	1955	Swedish	Sweden
339.	*Some Like It Hot*	*Some Like It Hot*	Billy Wilder	1959	English	USA
340.	*Sonar Kella*	সোনার কেল্লা	Satyajit Ray	1974	Bengali	India
341.	*Sons of the Desert*	*Sons of the Desert*	William A. Seiter	1932	English	USA
342.	*Spartacus*	*Spartacus*	Stanley Kubrick	1960	English	USA
343.	*Spiderman*	*Spiderman*	Sam Raimi	2002	English	USA
344.	*Spirited Away*	*Sen to Chihiro no Kamikakushi*	Hayao Miyazaki	2001	Japanese	Japan
345.	*Spring in a Small Town*	*Xiǎochéng zhī chun*	Fei Mu	1948	Mandarin	China

cont.

Sl. No	English Name	Original Title	Director	Release Year	Language	Country
346.	*Stage Coach*	*Stage Coach*	John Ford	1939	English	USA
347.	*Star Wars Episode IV: A New Hope*	*Star Wars*	George Lucas	1977	English	USA
348.	*Strangers on a Train*	*Strangers on a Train*	Alfred Hitchcock	1951	English	USA
349.	*Subarnrekha*	সুবর্ণরেখা	Ritwik Ghatak	1963	Bengali	India
350.	*Sujata*	सुजाता	Bimal Roy	1960	Hindi	India
351.	*Sullivan's Travels*	*Sullivan's Travels*	Preston Sturges	1941	English	USA
352.	*Sunrise: A Song of Two Humans*	*Sunrise: A Song of Two Humans*	F. W. Murnau	1929	Silent	USA
353.	*Sunset Boulevard*	*Sunset Boulevard*	Billy Wilder	1950	English	USA
354.	*Superman*	*Superman*	Richard Donner	1978	English	USA
355.	*Swing Time*	*Swing Time*	George Stevens	1936	English	USA
356.	*Talk to Her*	*Hable con ella*	Pedro Almodóvar	2002	Spanish	Spain
357.	*Taxi Driver*	*Taxi Driver*	Martin Scorsese	1976	English	USA
358.	*Teen Kanya*	তিন কন্যা	Satyajit Ray	1961	Bengali	India
359.	*Teorema*	*Teorema*	Pier Paolo Pasolini	1968	Italian	Italy
360.	*That Obscure Object of Desire*	*Cet obscur objet du désir*	Luis Buñuel	1977	French, Spanish	France, Spain

361.	*The Double Life of Véronique*	*La double vie de Véronique*	Krzysztof Kieślowski	1991	Polish	Poland
362.	*The 400 Blows*	*Les Quatre Cents Coups*	François Truffaut	1959	French	France
363.	*The Adventures of Tintin*	*The Adventures of Tintin*	Steven Spielberg	2011	English	USA
364.	*The Apartment*	*The Apartment*	Billy Wilder	1960	English	USA
365.	*The Battle of Algiers*	*La battaglia di Algeri*	Gillo Pontecorvo	1966	Italian	Italy, Algeria
366.	*The Bells at St. Mary's*	*The Bells at St. Mary's*	Leo McCarey	1945	English	USA
367.	*The Big Lebowski*	*The Big Lebowski*	Joel Coen and Ethan Coen	1998	English	USA
368.	*The Big Sleep*	*The Big Sleep*	Howard Hawks	1946	English	USA
369.	*The Birds*	*The Birds*	Alfred Hitchcock	1963	English	USA
370.	*The Birds, the Bees and the Italians*	*Signore & signori*	Pietro Germi	1966	Italian	Italy
371.	*The Birth of a Nation*	*The Birth of a Nation*	D.W. Griffith	1915	Silent	USA
372.	*The Black Cat*	*The Black Cat*	Edgar G. Ulmer	1934	English	USA
373.	*The Body Snatcher*	*The Body Snatcher*	Robert Wise	1945	English	USA
374.	*The Burmese Harp*	*Biruma no tategoto*	Kon Ichikawa	1956	Japanese	Japan
375.	*The Butch Cassidy and Sundance Kid*	*The Butch Cassidy and Sundance Kid*	George Roy Hill	1969	English	USA
376.	*The Cabinet of Dr. Caligari*	*Das Cabinet des Dr. Caligari*	Robert Wiene	1920	Silent	Germany

cont.

Sl. No	English Name	Original Title	Director	Release Year	Language	Country
377.	*The Canterbury Tales*	*I racconti di Canterbury*	Pier Paolo Pasolini	1972	Italian	Italy
378.	*The Chase*	*The Chase*	Arthur Penn	1966	English	USA
379.	*The Circus*	*The Circus*	Charles Chaplin	1928	Silent	USA
380.	*The City of Lost Children*	*La cité des enfants perdus*	Jean-Pierre Jeunet	1995	French	France
381.	*The Color of Pomegranates*	*Sayat Nova*	Sergei Parajanov	1969	Armenian, Georgian	USSR
382.	*The Conformist*	*Il conformista*	Bernardo Bertolucci	1970	Italian, French	Italy, France, West Germany
383.	*The Crucified Lovers*	*Chikamatsu Monogatari*	Kenji Mizoguchi	1954	Japanese	Japan
384.	*The Dark Knight*	*The Dark Knight*	Christopher Nolan	2008	English	USA
385.	*The Dark Knight Rises*	*The Dark Knight Rises*	Christopher Nolan	2012	English	USA
386.	*The Day of the Jackal*	*The Day of the Jackal*	Fred Zinnemann	1973	English	UK, France
387.	*The Decalogue*	*Dekalog*	Krzysztof Kieślowski	1989	Polish, French	France, Poland, Norway
388.	*The Decameron*	*Il Decameron*	Pier Paolo Pasolini	1971	Italian	Italy
389.	*The Devil Probably*	*Le diable probablement*	Robert Bresson	1977	French	France
390.	*The Discreet Charm of the Bourgeoisie*	*Le charme discret de la bourgeoisie*	Luis Buñuel	1972	French	Spain, France, Italy

391.	*The Element of Crime*	*Forbrydelsens element*	Lars von Trier	1984	English	Denmark
392.	*The Elephant Man*	*The Elephant Man*	David Lynch	1980	English	USA
393.	*The English Patient*	*The English Patient*	Anthony Minghella	1996	English	USA
394.	*The Exorcist*	*The Exorcist*	William Friedkin	1973	English	USA
395.	*The Fifth Seal*	*Az ötödik pecsét*	Zoltán Fábri	1976	Hungarian	Hungary
396.	*The Fireman's Ball*	*Hoří, má panenko*	Milos Forman	1967	Czech	Czechoslovakia
397.	*The Flavor of Green Tea over Rice*	*Ochazuke no aji*	Yasujirō Ozu	1952	Japanese	Japan
398.	*The French Connection*	*The French Connection*	William Friedkin	1971	English	USA
399.	*The Gay Divorce*	*The Gay Divorcee*	Mark Sandrich	1934	English	USA
400.	*The General*	*The General*	Buster Keaton	1926	Silent	USA
401.	*The Godfather*	*The Godfather*	Francis Ford Coppola	1972	English	USA
402.	*The Godfather: Part II*	*The Godfather: Part II*	Francis Ford Coppola	1974	English	USA
403.	*The Gold Rush*	*The Gold Rush*	Charles Chaplin	1925	Silent	USA
404.	*The Good, the Bad and the Ugly*	*Il buono, il brutto, il cattivo*	Sergio Leone	1966	Italian, English	Italy, West Germany, Spain
405.	*The Gospel According to St. Matthew*	*Il vangelo secondo Matteo*	Pier Paolo Pasolini	1964	Italian	Italy

cont.

Sl. No	*English Name*	*Original Title*	*Director*	*Release Year*	*Language*	*Country*
406.	*The Grand Illusion*	*La Grande Illusion*	Jean Renoir	1937	French	France
407.	*The Grapes of Wrath*	*The Grapes of Wrath*	John Ford	1940	English	USA
408.	*The Great Dictator*	*The Great Dictator*	Charles Chaplin	1940	English	USA
409.	*The Great Madcap*	*El Gran Calavera*	Luis Buñuel	1949	Spanish	Mexico
410.	*The Great Train Robbery*	*The Great Train Robbery*	Edwin S. Porter	1903	Silent	USA
411.	*The Haunting*	*The Haunting*	Robert Wise	1963	English	UK
412.	*The Hidden Fortress*	*Kakushi-toride no san-akunin*	Akira Kurosawa	1958	Japanese	Japan
413.	*The Informer*	*The Informer*	John Ford	1935	English	USA
414.	*The Innocents*	*The Innocents*	Jack Clayton	1961	English	UK
415.	*The Invisible Man*	*The Invisible Man*	James Whale	1933	English	USA
416.	*The Irony of Fate, or Enjoy Your Bath!*	*Ironiya sudby, ili S legkim parom!*	Eldar Ryazanov	1976	Russian	USSR
417.	*The Italian Job*	*The Italian Job*	Peter Collinson	1967	English	UK
418.	*The Kid*	*The Kid*	Charles Chaplin	1921	English, Silent	USA
419.	*The Lady Eve*	*The Lady Eve*	Preston Sturges	1941	English	USA
420.	*The Lady from Shanghai*	*The Lady from Shanghai*	Orson Welles	1947	English	USA

421.	*The Ladykillers*	*The Ladykillers*	Alexander Mackendrick	1955	English	UK
422.	*The Last Emperor*	*The Last Emperor*	Bernardo Bertolucci	1987	English	China, United Kingdom, Italy
423.	*The Legend of Suram Fortress*	*The Legend of Suram Fortress*	Sergei Parajanov	1985	Georgian	USSR
424.	*The Lord of the Rings*	*The Lord of the Rings: The Return of the King*	Peter Jackson	2003	English	USA
425.	*The Magic Flute*	*Trollflöjten*	Ingmar Bergman	1975	Swedish	Sweden
426.	*The Magnificent Ambersons*	*The Magnificent Ambersons*	Orson Welles	1942	English	USA
427.	*The Magnificent Seven*	*The Magnificent Seven*	John Sturges	1960	English	USA
428.	*The Maltese Falcon*	*The Maltese Falcon*	John Houston	1941	English	USA
429.	*The Man Who Loved Women*	*L'Homme qui aimait les femmes*	François Truffaut	1977	French	France
430.	*The Man Who Shot Liberty Valance*	*The Man Who Shot Liberty Valance*	John Ford	1962	English	USA
431.	*The Merry Widow*	*The Merry Widow*	Ernst Lubitsch	1934	English	USA
432.	*The Mill and the Cross*	*Mlyn i krzyz*	Lech Majewski	2011	English, Spanish	Poland, Sweden
433.	*The Miracle Worker*	*The Miracle Worker*	Arthur Penn	1962	English	USA
434.	*The Mirror*	*Zerkalo*	Andrei Tarkovsky	1975	Russian	USSR
435.	*The Mummy*	*The Mummy*	Karl Freund	1932	English	USA

cont.

Sl. No	*English Name*	*Original Title*	*Director*	*Release Year*	*Language*	*Country*
436.	*The Music Box*	*The Music Box*	James Parrott	1932	English	USA
437.	*The Night of the Hunter*	*The Night of the Hunter*	Charles Laughton	1955	English	USA
438.	*The Old Dark House*	*The Old Dark House*	James Whale	1932	English	USA
439.	*The Passion of Joan of Arc*	*La passion de Jeanne d'Arc*	Carl Dreyer	1928	Silent	France
440.	*The Phantom Carriage*	*Körkarlen*	Victor Sjöström	1921	Silent	Sweden
441.	*The Phantom of Liberty*	*Le fantôme de la liberté*	Luis Buñuel	1974	French	France/Italy
442.	*The Phantom of the Opera*	*The Phantom of the Opera*	Rupert Julian	1925	Silent	USA
443.	*The Philadelphia Story*	*The Philadelphia Story*	George Cukor	1940	English	USA
444.	*The Pianist*	*The Pianist*	Roman Polanski	2002	Multi Lingual	France, UK, Germany, Poland
445.	*The Pride of the Yankees*	*The Pride of the Yankees*	Sam Wood	1942	English	USA
446.	*The Public Enemy*	*The Public Enemy*	William A. Wellman	1931	English	USA
447.	*The Red Shoes*	*The Red Shoes*	Michael Powell and Emeric Pressburger	1948	English	UK
448.	*The River*	*Le Fleuve*	Jean Renoir	1951	English, Bengali	France, India, USA
449.	*The Rules of the Game*	*La Règle du jeu*	Jean Renoir	1939	French	France

450.	*The Russians are coming, the Russians are coming*	*The Russians are coming, the Russians are coming*	Norman Jewison	1966	English	USA
451.	*The Sacrifice*	*Offret*	Andrei Tarkovsky	1986	Swedish, French	Sweden, UK, France
452.	*The Scent of Green Papaya*	*Mùi đu đủ xanh*	Tran Anh Hung	1992	Vietnamese	France
453.	*The Searchers*	*The Searchers*	John Ford	1956	English	USA
454.	*The Seventh Continent*	*Der siebente Kontinent*	Michael Haneke	1989	German	Austria
455.	*The Seventh Seal*	*Det sjunde inseglet*	Ingmar Bergman	1957	Swedish	Sweden
456.	*The Shining*	*The Shining*	Stanley Kubrick	1980	English	USA
457.	*The Shop Around the Corner*	*The Shop Around the Corner*	Ernst Lubitsch	1940	English	USA
458.	*The Silences of the Lambs*	*The Silences of the Lambs*	Jonathan Demme	1991	English	USA
459.	*The Sound of Music*	*The Sound of Music*	Robert Wise	1965	English	USA
460.	*The Ten Commandments*	*The Ten Commandments*	Cecil B. DeMille	1956	English	USA
461.	*The Tenant*	*Le locataire*	Roman Polanski	1976	French	France
462.	*The Testament of Dr. Mabuse*	*Das Testament des Dr. Mabuse*	Fritz Lang	1933	German, French	Germany
463.	*The Thin Man*	*The Thin Man*	W.S. Van Dyke	1934	English	USA
464.	*The Thing*	*The Thing*	John Carpenter	1982	English	USA
465.	*The Third Man*	*The Third Man*	Carol Reed	1949	English	UK, USA

cont.

Sl. No	*English Name*	*Original Title*	*Director*	*Release Year*	*Language*	*Country*
466.	*The Treasure of Sierre Madre*	*The Treasure of Sierre Madre*	John Houston	1948	English	USA
467.	*The Trial of Joan of Arc*	*Procès de Jeanne d'Arc*	Robert Bresson	1962	French	France
468.	*The Trouble with Harry*	*The Trouble with Harry*	Alfred Hitchcock	1955	English	USA
469.	*The Wages of Fear*	*Le salaire de la peur*	Henri-Georges Clouzot	1953	French	France, Italy
470.	*The Weiry Death: Destiny*	*Der müde Tod*	Fritz Lang	1921	Silent	Germany
471.	*The White Sheik*	*Lo sceicco bianco*	Federico Fellini	1952	Italian	Italy
472.	*The Wild Bunch*	*The Wild Bunch*	Sam Peckinpah	1969	English	USA
473.	*The Wind Rises*	*Kaze Tachinu*	Hayao Miyazaki	2013	Japanese	Japan
474.	*The Wizard of Oz*	*The Wizard of Oz*	Victor Flemming	1939	English	USA
475.	*The Woman in the Window*	*The Woman in the Window*	Fritz Lang	1944	Silent	Germany
476.	*The World of Apu*	অপুর সংসার	Satyajit Ray	1959	Bengali	India
477.	*The Wrong Man*	*The Wrong Man*	Alfred Hitchcock	1956	English	USA
478.	*There Will Be Blood*	*There Will Be Blood*	Paul Thomas Anderson	2007	English	USA
479.	*Three Colors: Blue*	*Trois couleurs: Bleu*	Krzysztof Kieślowski	1993	French, Romanian, Polish	France, Poland, Switzerland

480.	*Three Colors: Red*	*Trois couleurs: Rouge*	Krzysztof Kieślowski	1994	French	France, Poland, Switzerland
481.	*Three Colors: White*	*Trois couleurs: Blanc*	Krzysztof Kieślowski	1994	French, Polish, English, Russian	France, Poland, Switzerland
482.	*Throne of Blood*	*Kumonosu-jô*	Akira Kurosawa	1957	Japanese	Japan
483.	*Through the Eyes of a Painter*	*Through the Eyes of a Painter*	M.F. Husain	1967	Silent	India
484.	*Through the Olive Trees*	*Zire darakhatan zeyton*	Abbas Kiarostami	1994	Persian	Iran
485.	*Titanic*	*Titanic*	James Cameron	1997	English	USA
486.	*To Be or Not to Be*	*To Be or Not to Be*	Ernst Lubitsch	1942	English	USA
487.	*To Kill a Mocking Bird*	*To Kill a Mocking Bird*	Robert Mulligan	1962	English	USA
488.	*To Live*	*Huózhe*	Zhang Yimou	1991	Mandarin	China
489.	*To Rome with Love*	*To Rome with Love*	Woody Allen	2012	English	USA, Italy
490.	*Tokyo Story*	*Tōkyō Monogatari*	Yasujirō Ozu	1953	Japanese	Japan
491.	*Too Much Johnson*	*Too Much Johnson*	Orson Welles	1938	English	USA
492.	*Top Hat*	*Top Hat*	Mark Sandrich	1935	English	USA

cont.

Sl. No	English Name	Original Title	Director	Release Year	Language	Country
493.	*Touch of Evil*	*Touch of Evil*	Orson Welles	1958	English	USA
494.	*Tristana*	*Tristana*	Luis Buñuel	1970	Spanish	Spain, France, Italy
495.	*Triumph of the Will*	*Triumph des Willens*	Leni Riefenstahl	1935	German	Germany
496.	*Trouble in Paradise*	*Trouble in Paradise*	Ernst Lubitsch	1932	English	USA
497.	*Twenty Hours*	*Húsz óra*	Zoltán Fábri	1965	Hungarian	Hungary
498.	*Twin Peaks: Fire Walk with Me*	*Twin Peaks: Fire Walk with Me*	David Lynch	1992	English	USA
499.	*Typhoon*	*Polizeiakte 909*	Robert Wiene	1933	German	Germany
500.	*Ugetsu*	*Ugetsu Monogatari*	Kenji Mizoguchi	1953	Japanese	Japan
501.	*Ulysses' Gaze*	*To vlemma tou Odyssea*	Theo Angelopoulos	1995	Greek	Greece
502.	*Umberto D*	*Umberto D*	Vittorio De Sica	1951	Italian	Italy
503.	*Unforgiven*	*Unforgiven*	Clint Eastwood	1992	English	USA
504.	*Vampyr*	*Vampyr*	Carl Dreyer	1932	German	Germany
505.	*Vertigo*	*Vertigo*	Alfred Hitchcock	1958	English	USA
506.	*Viridiana*	*Viridiana*	Luis Buñuel	1961	Spanish	Spain
507.	*Waltz with Bashir*	*Vals Im Bashir*	Ari Folman	2008	Hebrew	Israel
508.	*War and Peace*	*Voyna i mir*	Sergey Bondarchuk	1966	Russian	USSR
509.	*War and Peace*	*War and Peace*	King Wallis Vidor	1956	English	USA

510.	*War and Peace: Part II*	*Voyna i mir II: Natasha Rostova*	Sergey Bondarchuk	1966	Russian	USSR
511.	*War and Peace: Part III*	*Voyna i mir III: 1812 god*	Sergey Bondarchuk	1967	Russian	USSR
512.	*War and Peace: Part IV*	*Voyna i mir IV: Pierre Bezukhov*	Sergey Bondarchuk	1967	Russian	USSR
513.	*Way Down East*	*Way Down East*	D.W. Griffith	1920	Silent	USA
514.	*Werckmeister Harmonies*	*Werckmeister harmóniák*	Béla Tarr	2000	Hungarian	Hungary
515.	*West Side Story*	*West Side Story*	Robert Wise	1961	English	USA
516.	*Western Union*	*Western Union*	Fritz Lang	1941	English	USA
517.	*Where Is the Friend's Home*	*Khane-ye doust kodjast?*	Abbas Kiarostami	1987	Persian	Iran
518.	*White Heat*	*White Heat*	Raoul Walsh	1949	English	USA
519.	*Wild Strawberries*	*Smultronstället*	Ingmar Bergman	1957	Swedish	Sweden
520.	*Wings of Desire*	*Der Himmel über Berlin*	Wim Wenders	1987	German, English, French	West Germany, France
521.	*Woman in the Dunes*	*Suna no Onna*	Hiroshi Teshigahara	1964	Japanese	Japan
522.	*Woman in the Moon*	*Frau im Mond*	Fritz Lang	1929	Silent	Germany
523.	*Women on the Verge of a Nervous Breakdown*	*Mujeres al borde de un ataque de nervios*	Pedro Almodóvar	1988	Spanish	Spain
524.	*Wuthering Heights*	*Wuthering Heights*	William Wyler	1939	English	USA
525.	*Yojimbo*	*Yôjinbô*	Akira Kurosawa	1961	Japanese	Japan

Bibliography

अग्रवाल, वासुदेव शरण, 1988, *कादम्बरी – एक सांस्कृतिक अध्ययन*, वाराणसी : चौखम्बा विद्याभवन, तृतीय संस्करण।

गुप्ता, गणपति चंद्र, 1972, *भारतीय साहित्य में श्रृंगार रस*, नई दिल्ली : नेशनल पब्लिशिंग हाउस ।

गोस्वामी, श्याम मनोहर, 2011, *पुरुषार्थ व्यवस्था*, मुम्बई : स्वस्तिक सोसायटी।

पाण्डे, गोविन्द चन्द्र, 2003, *सौन्दर्य-दर्शन-विमर्श*, अनुवादक, जगन्नाथ पाठक, इलाहाबाद : राका प्रकाशन।

पारेख, नगीनदास, 1974, *अभिनव का रस विवेचन*, वाराणसी : विश्वविद्यालय प्रकाशन।

प्रसाद, जयशंकर, 1939, *काव्य और कला तथा अन्य निबन्ध*, लोकभारती प्रकाशन (पुनर्मुद्रण 2007)।

द्विवेदी, पारसनाथ, 1992, *भरतमुनिप्रणीतं नाट्यशास्त्रम्* (द्वितीय भाग), वाराणसी : संपूर्णानंद संस्कृत विश्वविद्यालय।

द्विवेदी, हज़ारी प्रसाद और पृथ्वीनाथ द्विवेदी, 1963, *नाट्यशास्त्र की भारतीय परम्परा और दशरूपक*, नई दिल्ली : राजकमल प्रकाशन।

नगेन्द्र, 1969, *रस सिद्धांत*, दिल्ली : नेशनल पब्लिशिंग हाउस।

रस्तोगी, नवजीवन, 2012, *अभिनवगुप्त का तंत्रागमीय दर्शन : इतिहास-संस्कृति-सौंदर्य और तत्त्व-चिन्तन*, सागर : विश्वविद्यालय प्रकाशन (द्वितीय संशोधित संस्करण, नई दिल्ली : डी०के० प्रिण्टवर्ल्ड, 2018)।

शर्मा, अम्बिका दत्त, 2015, *भारतीयता के सामासिक अर्थ-सन्दर्भ*, नई दिल्ली : भारतीय ज्ञानपीठ।

शर्मा, चन्द्रधर, 1995, *भारतीय दर्शन – आलोचन और अनुशीलन*, दिल्ली : मोतीलाल बनारसीदास।

Bergson, Henri, 1901, *Laughter: An Essay on the Meaning of Comic.*

Chakrabarti, Arindam, 2002, "Disgust and the Ugly in Indian Aesthetics", in *La Pluralità: Lasciti e irradiazioni oltre il Novecento, Associazionne Italiana Studi di Estetica*, Turin: Trauben.

Deshpande, G.T., 1989, *Abhinavagupta*, New Delhi: Sahitya Akademi.

Ghosh, Manomohan, 1950, *The Natyashastra: A Treatise on Hindu Dramaturgy and Histronics – Ascribed to Bharata Muni* (vol. 1), Calcutta: The Royal Asiatic Society of Bengal.

Gnoli, R., 1968, *The Aesthetics Experience of According to Abhinavagupta*, Varanasi: The Chowkhambha Sanskrit Series Office.

Gupt, Bharat, 1994, *Dramatic Concepts: Greek and Indian – A Study of Poetics and Nāṭyaśāstra*, New Delhi: D.K. Printworld

Hiriyanna, M., 1993, *Outlines of Indian Philosophy*, Delhi: Motilal Banarsidass.

Morris, Gary (ed.), 2009, *Action!: Interviews with Directors from Classical Hollywood to Contemporary Iran (New Perspectives on World Cinema)*, New York: Anthem Press.

Paranjape, Makarand and Sunthar Visuvalingam (eds), 2006, *Evam: Forum on Indian Representations: Abhinavagupta: Reconsiderations*, Delhi: Samvad India Foundation.

Shah, 2007, *Approaches to Bharat's Natyashastra*, Delhi: Sangeet Natak Akademi.

The Internet Movie Database – www.imdb.com

Visuvalingam, Sunthar, 1983, *Abhinavagupta's Conception of Humor*, Varanasi: Banaras Hindu University.

General Index

Film Index